Industry, Labour and Society

Industry, Labour and Society

Sharit K. Bhowmik

Orient BlackSwan

INDUSTRY, LABOUR AND SOCIETY

ORIENT BLACKSWAN PRIVATE LIMITED

Registered Office
3-6-752 Himayatnagar, Hyderabad 500 029, Telangana, India
Email: centraloffice@orientblackswan.com

Other Offices
Bengaluru, Chennai, Guwahati, Hyderabad, Kolkata, Mumbai, New Delhi, Noida, Patna

First Published 2012
Reprinted 2024

041766

ISBN 978 81 250 4762 9

Typeset in Adobe Garamond 11/13 by
Jojy Philip, New Delhi 110 015

Printed at
Kensington Printing & Packaging, Noida 201 301

Published by
Orient Blackswan Private Limited
3-6-752, Himayatnagar, Hyderabad 500 029, Telangana, India
Email: info@orientblackswan.com

Contents

Tables

Abbreviations

AFL-CIO	American Federation of Labor-Congress of Industrial Organizations
AGIL	Adaptation, Goal Gratification, Integration, Latent Pattern Maintenance (sub-systems for stability in management, according to Parsons)
AIADMK	All-India Anna Dravida Munnetra Kazhagam
AITUC	All India Trade Union Congress
AR	Assistant Registrar (in universities)
BDLB	Bombay Dock Labour Board
BHEL	Bharat Heavy Electricals Limited
BJP	Bharatiya Janata Party
BKS	Bharatiya Kamgar Sena
BMS	Bharatiya Mazdur Sangh
BPO	Business Process Outsourcing
CAD	Computer Aided Design
CITU	Centre of Indian Trade Unions
CNC	Computerised Numerically Controlled (machines)
CPM	Communist Party of India (Marxist)
DA	Dearness Allowance
DGB	Confederation of German Unions
DMK	Dravida Munnetra Kazhagam
DR	Deputy Registrar (of university)
ESI	Employees' State Insurance Corporation
GATT	General Agreement on Trade and Tariffs
GCT	General Confederation of Workers

HEC	Heavy Engineering Corporation
HHI	Household industry
HMP	Hind Mazdur Panchayat
HMS	Hind Mazdur Sabha
HR	Human Relations
ID (ACT)	Industrial Disputes (ACT)
IFTU	Indian Federation of Trade Unions
ILC	Indian Labour Conference
ILO	International Labour Organization
ILS	International Labour Standards
IMF	International Monetary Fund
INTUC	Indian National Trade Union Congress
IR	Industrial Relations
ITUC	International Trade Union Confederation
JMC	Joint management councils
LPG	Liberalisation, Privatisation, Globalisation (abbreviation used ironically)
MGNREGS	Mahatma Gandhi National Rural Employment Guarantee Scheme
MRTP	Monopolies and Restrictive Trade Practices Act
NASVI	National Association of Street Vendors of India
NCEUS	National Commission for Enterprises in the Unorganised Sector
NDA	National Democratic Alliance
NDP	New Democratic Party
PPE	Personal protective equipment
PSP	Praja Socialist Party
RAY	Rajeev Awas Yojana
RMMS	Rashtriya Mill Mazdur Sangh
RSP	Revolutionary Socialist Party
RSS	Rashtriya Swayamsevak Sangh
SEWA	Self-employed Women's Association

SSP	Samyukta Socialist Party
TISS	Tata Institute of Social Sciences
TLA	Textile Labour Association
TU (ACT)	Trade Union (ACT)
TUC	Trades Union Congress (in UK)
UN-HABITAT	United Nations Human Settlements Programme
UTUC	United Trade Union Congress
UTUC (BB)	UTUC (Bow Bazaar)
UTUC (LS)	UTUC (Lenin Sarani)
VRS	Voluntary Retirement Scheme
VSNL	Videsh Sanchar Nigam Limited
WC	Works Committee
WB	World Bank
WCL	World Confederation of Labour
WD	Worker Director
WPM	Workers' Participation in Management
WTO	World Trade Organization
WWI	World War I (First World War)
WWII	World War II (Second World War)

INTRODUCTION

Industrial sociology is taught in many universities and colleges in the country. Management institutes also teach this subject as a part of their regular curriculum. In these institutes, the subject is taught as a part of industrial relations (IR). In most management institutes, IR or human resources (HR) management is not very popular as most students prefer to take up finance or marketing as they offer careers with better salaries (the students refer to these as 'packages'). This is true of the IIMs and other well-known institutions. However, of late, IR and HR are gaining ground as subjects in the curriculum. Firms, too, are increasingly becoming aware that their success lies in not merely paying their employees well but also in ensuring their commitment to work.

In such cases, psychology is preferred because it lays stress on human behaviour and the workings of the human mind. It sounds more interesting if not more mysterious. Hence, organisational behaviour which analyses interpersonal relations among employees in a firm or in a department of the firm is something more remote than sociology of organisations; the latter deals mainly with power relations within the organisation and issues concerning hierarchy and compliance. It also takes into account the influence of wider social processes while analysing the functioning of organisations. Sociology, by and large, deals with the human activities. It does not explore the inner issues that the actor faces. In order to analyse external actions, the social system needs to be considered.

WHY INDUSTRIAL SOCIOLOGY?

Industrial sociology is the best option for analysing interpersonal relations in the workplace, and it also tries to investigate how these relations originate, the social processes that shape the relations and the impact they have on society.

The American sociologist, Talcott Parsons (1902–79), had stated that when two or more individuals interact with each other in a controlled situation and their actions have a bearing on each other, it is a social system. The important point is that the actions of individuals have an impact on their behaviour. Parsons explains that actions of individuals are determined by the values (shared beliefs) and norms (rules of behaviour) prevalent in society. Hence we can find that people (actors) facing the same situation may behave differently because of different situations. For example, people in an organisation in India may behave differently with their superiors from people in the same situation in an American organisation. In India, because of the cultural factors (values) at work, subordinates may show greater respect to their superiors than in the US. Similarly, one will find that student-teacher relations differ depending upon social settings. In the US or Britain, students may address their teachers by their first names. In India, a majority of students would never think of doing this.

Analysing society through the lens of functionalism may appear logical as following norms based on values helps in maintaining stability. However, there would be people like conflict theorists and Marxists who may argue that progress cannot be achieved through stability but by redefining social norms and values. The shared beliefs that values are supposed to represent are those of the ruling class that have been spread to all parts of society through social institutions. Hence norms and values should not be taken as self-evident for they arise out of human interactions, especially of people belonging to the ruling class who benefit from social inequality perpetuated by these institutions. These contradictions became clear after the industrial revolution which marked a radical departure from the earlier feudal relations. I have discussed these changes in the first chapter.

PITFALLS OF MANAGEMENT-ORIENTED STUDIES

Industrial sociology as a sub-discipline selects industrial society as the analytical focal point due to the new features of such a society. One has to differentiate between industrial and non-industrial or pre-industrial societies. One of the important concerns of industrial sociology is to examine the impact industry has on social structures and institutions (see Chapter 1). However, these grand ideas were not the focus of industrial sociology when it developed as a sub-discipline of sociology. The earlier sociologists, like F. W. Taylor, and Elton Mayo and his team, among others, were more interested in studying the behaviour of humans (meaning the labour force/workers) and their interaction in industry. Their researches were mainly directed towards ways and means of increasing labour productivity. This narrow view had its pitfalls because studying industry without relating it to society reveals only a small part of the picture. Changes in society due to the process of industrialisation were equally, if not more, important in understanding industrial behaviour. The earlier industrial sociologists did not take this into account and it is no wonder that most of their recommendations were not successful when replicated. We have dealt with this in further detail in Chapter 2.

One of the ways to incorporate industrial sociology into the wider sphere was the study of social and industrial organisations. Sociologists like Amitai Etzioni and William Foote Whyte were among the pioneers in the study of organisations. However, in these cases too, more emphasis was placed on the work groups in large factories. In most cases they ignored the conflict in the very nature of industrial relations. The role of the community in creating or diverting conflicts was also overlooked. One of the reasons could be that most of these studies were studied within a functionalist framework.

FROM INDUSTRY TO WORK: THE CLASH OF VIEWS

By the 1940s, industrial sociology started looking more towards the nature of work. This gave rise to the sociology of work that looked at occupations as a whole and not merely as behaviour at the workplace. Sociologists now studied the meaning of work, its consequences, and the effect of work on attitudes and relationships. It also included the study of work and alienation. In addition, theorists developed the sociology of organisations different from the studies of organisations discussed earlier. Industrial sociology had been reduced to plant-level sociology; sociology of organisations looked at extra-plant concerns. There was a growing interest in community studies and political parties. These streams of new research drew sociology into new fields. Hence what started as plant sociology grew into a discipline that was concerned with industrial behaviour, and harmonious relations between labour and management. In the late 1950s, John Thomas

Dunlop and others were attempting to study trade unions from the functionalist perspective. This annoyed the radicals interested in studying the relationship between industry and society, and the effect of industrialisation on society and social institutions. In the following chapters, we will deal with some of these issues.

The radicals who challenged the functionalist view were of two kinds. The first were the pluralists who stressed more on the role of conflict in industrial relations. Ralf Dahrendorf was one of the founders of this school. In his book, *Class and Class Conflict in Industrial Society*, Dahrendorf argues that conflicts, rather than cooperation, were responsible for changes in industrial relations. Other conflict theorists argued that opposition by labour to management was responsible for bringing dynamism in industrial behaviour.

At the same time, the conflict theorists were keen to show that conflicts in fact strengthened the existing relations. Georg Simmel wrote about how conflict could be seen as a form of cooperation. This could be done if conflicts were institutionalised. For example, trade unions expressed the views of workers. Different workers have different views. If an employer wants to take into account the views of each worker it will lead to chaos as there will be divergent views. Instead, if workers form a trade union their views will be channelled through the union as a single view. This will help the management in tackling problems relating to workers and management will recognise the trade union as an integral part of industrial relations. In this way, the trade union will be co-opted by management, and conflicts will be institutionalised, which is what conflict theorists lay stress on.

The conflict theorists have a lot in common with the functionalists as both believe that the existing system is ideal and does not need change, thereby supporting the status quo. The means of this support may differ but the final goal is the same. Another important but controversial assumption is that labour and capital (workers and management) are evenly balanced. We can see that this is not true for management seems always to have the upper hand. The section on pluralist theorists in Chapter 4 will explore this aspect in more detail.

The Marxists have another way of looking at conflict. They believe that the differences between labour and capital are irreconcilable. Industrial conflicts are due to class conflicts, and classes are groups that stand opposed to each other. Labour and management form opposing groups as they represent different class interests. Trade unions may to some extent solve the problems of labour in their workplace which may help workers to get better jobs and fair working hours. However, because of the basic contradiction between labour and capital, there cannot be a final solution within the existing framework.

This is where the Marxists differ substantially with functionalists and conflict theorists. Marxists contend that the solution to the problems of labour lies only in its dominance over capital. There cannot be institutionalisation of conflict as it mainly centres on control over the means of production. Both sides try to exert control over the labour process and this leads to constant friction between them. For example, workers and their unions may want fewer working hours and more leisure while management may want longer working hours.

On 1 May 1886, a group of workers assembled at the Hay Market in Chicago to demand for an eight-hour working day. The police attacked the meeting to beat up the protesters. Some of them were shot dead. Later, the workers removed the blood-soaked shirts of the slain workers and used them as flags to symbolise the working-class revolt. This is why most of the flags of the trade unions are red in colour. The May Day (International Workers' Day on 1 May, commemorating the Chicago protests, formally recognised as an annual event in 1891) could be taken as a watershed in the struggle for control over the labour process. This has also been discussed in Chapter 1.

In those days (late nineteenth century) workers had to work long hours in factories. All too often, men, women and children worked for more than twelve hours a day under gruelling conditions. By making a demand for an eight-hour day, the workers challenged management's control over the labour process. In due course of time, the working class movement ensured that factories enforced an eight-hour day. This was also accepted by other organisations. These issues and others will be dealt in more detail in Chapter 4 that deals with trade unions.

This book also contains discussions on other important issues relating to labour such as workers participation in management (Chapter 3). This was a very important issue in the pre-liberalisation era. We have discussed the different ways in which workers can participate and the success or failures of these methods. This chapter also discusses the success and failures of worker co-operatives as organisations of workers' control.

Chapter 5 deals with the labour movement in India. We have traced the growth of trade unions and the subsequent laws that were passed for regulation of work. The role of the state in solving industrial disputes is also critically evaluated.

Informal employment or, the unorganised sector as it is called in India, occupies a very important place in the employment scenario. An overwhelming majority of the working population are engaged in this sector. In Chapter 6 we have tried to explore the working and living conditions in informal employment besides discussing the theories relating to this sector. An issue that is linked with growing informalisation is globalisation. This phenomenon, in its present form, has led to far reaching changes in our society. The industrial policy statement of 1991 marked the intensification of liberalisation, privatisation and globalisation (LPG). Chapter 7 discusses the repercussion of globalisation on the working class. We have attempted to show the different types of outsourcing that have resulted in making developing countries as suppliers of components to the global production process.

We have touched on the issue of decent work and international labour standards as espoused by the International Labour Organisation (ILO) in the last chapter. We thought of including this aspect, because in this era where it is believed that efficiency in manufacturing can be achieved only by cutting down on labour costs, decent work helps us understand that providing labour rights is a more effective way of increasing efficiency and productivity. Apart from examining the implications of decent work, there has been an attempt to see how it can transform relations at the shop-floor.

SCOPE OF THE BOOK

This book is a compilation of my lectures and notes for the master's courses on different aspects of industrial sociology in the several universities that I have taught. These include North Bengal University, Universities of Delhi and Mumbai, Maharashtra Institute of Labour Studies and Tata Institute of Social Sciences (TISS). Hence I feel that it has direct relevance as a textbook to the courses relating to industry, work and society.

This is meant to be a textbook for students of industrial sociology, labour studies and studies in informal economy and economics. This should also be of interest to students of gender studies and social exclusion because these courses normally overlook issues concerning labour, while concentrating on other aspects such as discrimination, cultural deprivation, etc. However, it is necessary for any course on social sciences to understand that work and livelihood form the basis of human development and in fact are the core of social activities. We have tried to explain this in the first chapter which deals with changes in society due to industrialisation.

This is not a common textbook which can be used for any elementary course in sociology. It is primarily meant to be a textbook for postgraduate students because it does not merely explain phenomena but also critically evaluates them. This is necessary for the discerning student of a postgraduate course. It may not be very useful for, let us say, a student in higher secondary or in the earlier stages of graduation.

The issues dealt with in the book will be of interest to practitioners of human resource management and labour relations, which include managers as well as trade unionists. This textbook is not restricted to the subject of industrial relations but also covers the social aspects of industry and business organisations. It covers two important aspects of work and employment in contemporary society, namely, informal employment and work in a globalising economy.

Finally, I wish to thank my innumerable students who have given me valuable feedback on how the subject should be taught. This encouraged me to write this textbook. I thank Ms Indira Gartenberg who collaborated with me in writing this book. Her crucial inputs in the manuscript have been invaluable.

1

Industrialisation and Social Change

Chapter Highlights

- » Factory production
- » Urbanisation
- » Trade and market
- » New class structure
- » Gender and caste
- » Changing role of the family

The Industrial Revolution which began in the mid-eighteenth century had far-reaching implications for the lives of people around the globe. Firstly, there were massive changes in methods of production of manufactured goods. Industrialisation basically meant the change from animate to inanimate power. Till the time of the industrial revolution, all forms of production and manufacture were done through the use of animate power. This meant that it was power drawn from animals, such as horses, cows, bullocks, etc., or through human energy, as in the case of weaving, pottery and other types of manual activities. Industrialisation initially introduced steam as a form of power and later electricity. The difference between the two systems, namely pre-industrial and industrial, was vast because inanimate power (such as steam and electricity) can be used without restriction for manufacture, whereas animate power has its limits.

INCREASED DEMAND FOR HUMAN LABOUR

Mere changes in production were not what industrialisation achieved. There was far greater impact on the social lives of the people. Factory production which is essentially the bulwark of industrialisation implies concentration of manufacture in smaller areas for it needs smaller space for producing goods than the traditional means of production. For example, one textile mill can produce cloth that thousands of weavers can produce. These handloom weavers would be spread in different villages occupying large areas. The factory on the other hand requires a smaller space, maybe ten or fifteen acres, for producing the same amount of goods. This also implies that factories come up in areas that are not necessarily near the villages where manual production was undertaken. A factory not only produces large quantities of goods but it also engages a large number of people working at different levels, from management to menial. Such a large concentration of population within a few acres would imply that industrialisation leads to migration from rural areas to the industrial sectors. This is known as spatial juxtaposition, i.e., a large number of people from different regions being placed close together in a comparatively small area.

Concentration of people around the factory would imply that other services would have to develop including housing, roads and infrastructure, shops and supply of provisions. Hence industrialisation is coterminous with urbanisation. It is true that urban centres had existed long before the industrial revolution. In fact, the ancient civilisations of Rome, Greece and Egypt were all centred around cities. In India, too, Harappa and Mohenjo-daro were urban centres engaged in trade. There were other urban centres too in ancient times, such as Pataliputra (Patna), Indraprastha, Agra, etc., which came up as administrative hubs. These became the capitals of kingdoms during ancient and medieval times. The third type of cities included pilgrimage centres like Mathura, Haridwar, Nashik, Allahabad, Kashi, etc.

Urbanisation caused by industrialisation with towns or cities growing up around factories and other commercial activities was quite different from the pattern that existed in the pre-industrial era. Hence, the new urbanisation was industry-centred.

The new urban centres had a higher concentration of population because of the growth of industry and its need for human labour. Urban centres faced problems of infrastructure and communication. Besides, in the absence of proper roads there was no sewerage or waste disposal facility. Drinking water too was not freely available. For example, the city of London, one of the largest urban centres during the early phase of industrialisation, was ill-equipped to cater to such a large population, especially the working poor. Around the mid-seventeenth century (1664–66), London was faced with a plague epidemic where thousands of the working poor died. The plague was mainly due to the growing population of rats that thrived on the garbage which was thrown out and there was no system of waste disposal. It was after this that the city of London initiated a sewerage and waste disposal system. In India, Mumbai was one of the early industrial cities, and it faced similar problems in the 1850s. A study by Farooqui (2006) shows that the *chawls* where the working people lived did not have proper toilets and even the night soil was collected in baskets which would frequently overflow.

DEMAND FOR NATURAL RESOURCES

Industrialisation demands greater resources from nature, such as forest and agricultural products, minerals, and oil. Since urban areas do not produce their own food, they have to depend on rural agriculture for their sustenance. This calls for greater production in agriculture to feed the urban masses. Small or marginal farmers who produce for self-consumption had to increase their production through use of irrigation and better technology. In most of the industrialised countries such as Britain, USA and those in Europe, the population in rural areas is now less than ten per cent of the total population. A large part of the traditional rural folk migrated to the cities in search of employment and in their places large farmers engaged mainly in producing for the market emerged. Hence, we will find that agriculture in these countries is in the hands of rich farmers having hundreds of acres of land. This too is a form of industrialisation of agriculture.

In India, however, the rural population is still quite high. This could be because industrialisation has proceeded at a slower pace. The 2011 Census shows that 68 per cent of the population live in rural areas, which are inhabited mainly by small or marginal farmers and agricultural labourers. There is a small number of large land-owners who, through their economic power and so-called superiority of caste, have become politically powerful and control the village economy. This is more pronounced in areas like eastern Uttar Pradesh and Bihar. The agricultural produce in rural India is largely in the hands of small and middle farmers.

The demand for natural resources increases under industrialisation because it makes greater use of energy produced through thermal power, which requires large quantities of coal, or hydroelectric power which relies on water. Petroleum products also are in great demand because of their use in automobiles, generators and certain manufacturing processes. The steel industry is important as it provides the infrastructure for most other industries and for transportation. Industrialisation has its impact on agriculture too. Fertilisers and pesticides are produced in factories. Pump sets for drawing water for irrigation need diesel/electricity and steel. For transportation too, natural products such as coal and wood as well as steel derived from iron ore are required. These factors resulted in the extension of mining, oil exploration and exploitation of forest products.

FLOW OF GOODS AND SERVICES

As we know, industrialisation requires efficient means of transport for making industrial products available in different parts of the country. This gives a boost to the transport sector. The urban areas require a large network of services for the population. These would include public transport, health care, banking, finance and other services such as recreation and entertainment under which come restaurants, electronics, television channels, etc. These in turn provide new forms of employment. In fact, as industrialisation develops, there is a decrease in the demand for labour in manufacturing which is increasingly done by machines that substitute labour. At the same time, employment in sectors other than manufacturing tends to expand.

One finds that with the growth of industrialisation the non-industrial sector proliferates and becomes a major source of employment. Thus, industrialisation leads to growth in several sectors of the economy in addition to manufacturing. However, in countries like India, where labour is cheaper than machines, growth of manufacture may not necessarily be due to higher forms of mechanisation. We will deal with this later, when we discuss the informal sector.

Use of Money

The distance between centres of manufacture and consumers created problems of exchange. Earlier, in the preindustrial barter system, goods and services could be traded in exchange. This required face-to-face interaction between the buyers and sellers. In such a situation, the buyer is also a seller, since they exchange their products in exchange for another person's products. This is a simplistic way of explaining the barter system because there were many other factors, mainly social, that determined the relationship between buyer and seller. The value of a particular product could change depending on whom it was being exchanged with. The upper classes/ castes would give less for receiving more, and the lower classes/castes would give more and receive less of the same product. For example, a barber in the village would receive different proportions of goods/services from the different clients with whom his services were exchanged for goods. A Brahmin might recite a few prayers in exchange for services throughout the year, whereas people belonging to lower castes might have to give more to receive the same barber's services. This in broad outline was what was known as the *jajmani* system.

In order to exchange goods over large distances, a simple system of barter would be insufficient. Hence, a new form of exchange had to be developed. This is where the use of money came in. Money became the medium of exchange for goods and services. For example, when a consumer in Assam buys mill-made cloth produced in Mumbai, they use money as the medium to pay for the value of the cloth. This makes exchange easier for both the producer and the consumer.

The second aspect of money is that it is a store of value. In other words, the value of all goods or services is determined by their cost in monetary terms. This does not change, irrespective of who the consumer is. We mentioned earlier that the value of services or goods in jajmani relations varied with the social status of the consumer. In the new system, this value remained unchanged. In other words, the price of a designer sari would be the same for a rich person or for a slum dweller (provided she could afford it).

The use and circulation of money was possible only after industrialisation because machines added uniformity and precision in the production of currency notes and coins. This is most needed or else there would be counterfeiting of currency if produced by hand. Mohammed-bin-Tughluq was the first to introduce coins as a medium of exchange. The idea was novel, but way ahead of its time. Since coins were handmade, they could be copied easily, and very soon the market was flooded with counterfeit coins. The difference between coins that existed in the pre-industrial period and those available now is that the worth of the metal (like silver or gold) used to be equivalent to the value attached to the coin. The present system of coinage is different; a one-rupee coin may contain metal which is worth less than its value. Similarly currency notes are also worth less than their value. Hence in the current system, units of currency are merely a medium of exchange and financial transactions and they are legal tender because they are backed by the treasury/ national bank of the country concerned.

Development of the Market

Production in a traditional society was done at the local level of the community or the village. The distribution of these products was also local, and the jajmani system is one of the ways in which it was done. In England too, villages produced goods which were consumed locally. Industrialisation increased the production of goods which could no longer be sold/exchanged locally as these were far in excess of the local needs. For example, all cloth manufactured in the textile industry in Surat is not consumed locally. Much of it is sent out of the region to different places.

We have seen how the use of money was able to overcome problems of trade and exchange. The market too, performed an important role in this regard. A market is a place where goods and services are exchanged. Modern markets may not be physical; they can be notional and we can see how goods and services are traded. There is no centralised place for this; exchange can take place through advertisements in the print media, electronic media, the Internet and so on. Markets therefore, have a wider reach. Sociologically, one of the most important features of markets today is that they integrate societies by breaking down the isolation of villages and bringing them within the ambit of the wider society. For instance, agricultural products manufactured in different corners of the country find their markets in far-off urban centres. Similarly, industrial goods produced in one place are sold all over the country.

The market has national and international features. Initially, the borders of countries are drawn and their markets operate within those boundaries. The exchange of goods in the market integrates different parts of the country into a unified whole. One can trace the growth of nationalism to the integrating role of the market. As industries and manufacturing start expanding rapidly, the boundaries of the nation-state may tend to become too restrictive. Hence, new markets are sought which are outside the national boundaries. At one time, such moves were accompanied by force and led to colonial conquests by the industrialised nations. British colonialism was extended after it underwent the industrial revolution. Since Britain, and more specifically England, is the mother of the Industrial Revolution, it was also the first country to colonise non-industrialised countries in different parts of the world. The other colonising countries like France, Portugal, the Netherlands, etc., were not industrialised when they embarked on their colonising ventures. Hence, they had influence only in the port cities because they were interested in trade rather than increasing their markets. After these countries underwent industrialisation, they started colonising whole countries. The objectives were, firstly, to use these colonies as suppliers of raw materials for industry and, secondly, to use them as markets for industrial products from the colonising country. Such ventures were imperialist in nature because they succeeded primarily by exploiting the colonised country for their own gains. After WWII, there were rapid changes globally, as many of the countries including India broke away from the yoke of colonialism.

In modern times, international trade is considered an important aspect of industrial development. Trade can be in terms of goods and services such as manpower. We also find the developed countries trying to exert control on the exports of the less developed countries, even today. They have dominated international regulatory bodies such as the General Agreement on Tariffs and Trade (GATT) and now the World Trade Organization (WTO). Many of the less developed countries find the terms of trade loaded against them. At times, the developed countries lay down conditions which are based less on economic realities than on socio-political factors. Hence the market itself may not be a perfectly egalitarian system but, given the fact that despite its limitations it is the best institution for exchange of goods and services, it survives. There are checks and balances in the markets, nationally as well as internationally. At the national level, the state plays an important role in regulating the markets. This could be in the form of framing laws that prevent any single private producer from monopolising the markets. In India, the Monopolies and Restrictive

Trade Practices Act, 1969 (replaced by the Competition Act, 2002, with effect from 1 September 2009), tried to regulate the growth of individual or family- based monopoly control of the market through its products.

Individualism

Industrialisation has witnessed the growth of individualism among the population. Individualism can be criticised because it can be interpreted as a person's being interested in their own self as opposed to the family or community interests. In the pre-industrial period, social institutions such as family, kinship and community played important roles in shaping behaviour and social interaction. It also influenced the thought processes of people. The concept of individualism is largely a result of the nature of work under industrialisation. Earlier, work was collective in nature, and could be based on family, kin or community. For instance, a weaver would produce cloth through division of labour within the family, his wife would spin the thread, and the children too would be assigned some activity, such as removing the seeds from the cotton or helping their parents generally; hence, the production of cloth was a joint effort of all the members of the family. This kept the family integrated as a social unit. The family did not operate as an isolated unit because the weaver had to depend on other people or groups such as those engaged in dyeing of cloth and shaping the cloth into garments. The same could apply to a farmer producing grain. His production was done through division of labour within the family or kin group, where the male members ploughed the field and sowed the seeds, the females were engaged in transplantation (in the case of rice) and threshing the grain after the harvest, and the children were also engaged in the different stages of agricultural production; this was a training period for them, before they could take up the gendered roles of their parents.

Though the work was collective, it was not necessarily egalitarian. In other words, all who engaged in work did not have the same social status. There was a grading of work based on who performed it. For example, in agriculture, ploughing and sowing of seeds which are tasks performed by males were considered superior to the activities performed by women. This was also true of all other types of work such as pottery, weaving, washing clothes, etc.

Factory production has changed the nature of work. Work is now done by individuals and not by social groups. The textile mill employs individual workers in its different production processes. There is now greater division of labour. The work in textile mills is broken into smaller parts, such as spinning, weaving, dyeing, folding, etc. Each of these sections (known as shops) in the factory is interlinked to each other though they are run as individual units. The worker in each of these units performs work as an individual and not as a collective though work in the factory is a joint and interlinked effort. In other words, though the shops function independently, their outputs have to be synchronised or else the total output will be affected. For example, if workers in the weaving section are efficient and produce large outputs of cloth but the dyeing section is inefficient and is unable to process the cloth on time, the total production will suffer.

A worker is employed as an individual irrespective of his social status, and a textile worker cannot take his family along to work in the textile mill as was done in the pre-industrial phase. This implies that a worker is paid a wage accordingly. In such a situation even if his wife works in the same textile factory, it is not regarded as family employment as she is a separate employee. One can see that this situation is quite different from the earlier situation of dependence on collective work.

Growth of individualism helped shape the views of society. Most importantly men and women were regarded as independent workers drawing separate wages. This sowed the seeds for the demand for equality between the sexes and challenged existing social divisions that were ascribed at birth. Since the new system demanded that workers be paid according to their skills and as individuals, it contrasted with the earlier system where the status and occupation of a person were determined at birth. Hence this system underwent what Talcott Parsons described as a shift from ascribed status to achieved status.

Gender and Caste

A major contribution of individualism is its impact on caste and gender. Individualism, which emerges from the industrial system, treats individuals irrespective of caste, gender or any other form of discrimination as independent units of work. In traditional societies, there was a fixed division of labour based on the sexes and on one's status according to one's caste. This meant that the status of women and that of the lower castes remained fixed and unchangeable because these were determined by the socio-economic system. Under industrialisation, these divisions changed. The new industrial system required more workers than those under the traditional caste system. The nature of employment was decided by the market and not by the traditional community authority. In other words, if a landlord needed more agricultural labourers, he could not ask other castes to participate in this activity. The work of each caste and the rewards they would get for their work was predetermined. Such a system could not exist in an industrialised setting. Now, it was the market that decided who was willing to work and for what wage. Hence we can see the shift in control of the working sections of the society.

In the earlier system, control over the low-level workers (serfs in Europe and the landless lower castes in India) was exercised through the entire life-cycle of the workers. In most Indian villages, residential areas were demarcated for different castes. The lower castes whose members were mainly landless labourers performing all kinds of manual tasks stayed on the outskirts of the village. There were regulations on their dress, their social behaviour and their interaction with other social castes. Control was exerted through a series of complex relations, which covered every aspect of a person's life.

Under the new system, this form of control was not necessary. The industrialists/capitalists now controlled the workers through wages. This meant that the capitalist was only interested in getting work done by anybody who was willing to work under the conditions laid down and the wage offered. In case the worker did not agree with the conditions or the wages, they had the choice of not working. In the earlier system, the lower castes did not have this choice as their castes determined the nature of work they performed. The capitalist was not interested in who their workers were and what their social background was. All they were interested in is that the person employed should work under the conditions laid down. For example, if an industrialist wanted 500 workers in the factory, they were actually looking for 500 units willing to perform work under the terms and conditions stipulated by him/her. The capitalist was not interested in whether these workers are from upper castes or lower castes, Hindus, Muslims or any other religion or whether they were men or women. This brought in some form of egalitarianism among the workers as they were not differentiated on the basis of social categories. This provided the basis for the lower castes and women to question the existing norms of the society. It may not have happened immediately, because old values persist over a period of time, being hard to change. However, the repercussions of this new system could be felt several decades later with the anti-caste movements for justice for the lower castes and the women's movement which strives for equality between the sexes.

As industrialisation developed, conditions of the workers improved because there was less dependence on manual work as machines replaced most of the work done physically. Workers also got unionised and were able to articulate some demands for regulation of the system in their favour. For instance, May Day, celebrated annually on 1 May, was a landmark for the international working class movement, because for the first time, the workers in the USA raised the demand for an eight-hour working day. This is a commemoration of what happened on 4 May 1886 when workers assembled at the Haymarket in Chicago. The police dealt with them brutally and several workers were killed. Other workers tore off the blood-soaked shirts of the dead workers and used them as flags to propagate working class unity in the city. This reinforced the use of the red flag as a symbol of the working class movement all over the world, such a flag having earlier been used during the Paris Commune of 1871 as a mark of communism.

Mechanisation of work resulted in improving working conditions but it also resulted in the lay-off of workers. In such a situation, it was the women workers who bore the brunt. It was presumed that as men were heads of households, if there were to be any lay-offs in the factory, it was the women that had to sacrifice their jobs as their income was supposed to be supplementing the family income. This in turn, led women to question the rationale behind this inequality. For both women and Dalits (in the case of India), the fact that there was some form of equality at the workplace but in social life there was gross inequality triggered off questions relating to egalitarianism.

For the women's movement in particular, industrialisation plays a crucial role in setting forth the real issues. In Hindu epics and mythology, several women are shown as independent and articulate such as Draupadi, Kali, Durga, etc. They do not inspire working women as much as the industrial system does. Industrialisation with its inherent defects makes women realise that the unequal relations between the sexes are not something that is intrinsic but are created by a patriarchal society for its own benefits.

IMPACT OF INDUSTRIALISATION ON SOCIETY

Industrialisation has resulted in a wide range of changes in society and social institutions. such as family, kinship functions, marriage and community relations. We shall discuss these changes later. However, the immediate impact of industrialisation was the creation of a new class structure. This resulted in new social types such as wage workers, entrepreneurs, management, and so on. There was also a great deal of professionalism in managing these institutions. Hence, a cadre of trained managers came into existence.

Industrialisation also resulted in changes in work orientation and the concept of time. Workers working on machines had to keep pace with the way the machines functioned; this is known as machine-pacing. It results in short-cycle work; in other words, the same action is repeated over and over again, keeping pace with the machine. This type of short-cycle work existed even before the industrial revolution. Women engaged in transplanting of rice performed short-cycle work as their actions were repetitive. Similarly, weavers, potters and other artisans had to repeat the same types of actions in sync with their tools of work. However, all these were controlled by the people concerned; the weavers' loom or the potter's wheel was controlled by the person operating it. Under industrialisation, the short-cycle work is a result of machine-pacing and these machines are controlled not by the worker performing the work, but by the supervisors who operated those through inanimate power (electricity or steam).

Rationality as a Social Value

An important aspect of industrialisation was the development of rationality as a social value. This meant that human behaviour was interpreted through rational actions rather than blind faith. Rationality also meant that people questioned the existing systems based on tradition or some form of faith in the supernatural. The role of religion had become important in earlier societies because all actions and thought were determined through religious interpretations. Social hierarchies, inequalities and even injustices which prevailed were attributed to the will of a divine entity. Hence, it was god or some other supernatural power that determined the fates of human beings and not their own actions. For instance, the caste system in

India was supposedly not based on inequalities arising out of human actions but was attributed to the workings of a divine being. Hindu mythology holds that the four *varnas* sprang out of different parts of Lord Vishnu's body, which again symbolises what type of work they were to do. Similarly, in nineteenth-century England, there was an Anglican hymn (also popular with other Christian denominations) the third verse of which read:

> The rich man in his castle,
> The poor man at his gate,
> God made them high and lowly
> And ordered their estate.

This meant that differences in society were decided by a supernatural power (known as God) and not because of inequalities with a human origin. In such a situation, those who are oppressed will never challenge the system because of the belief that this would mean challenging the word of God. Hence, religion and 'the fear of God' determined social stratification and also justified social inequalities.

Industrialisation required a new system of stratification. If the old system of having landlords and serfs in the case of Europe, and upper castes and lower castes in India, was replicated in the industrial system in terms of owners/managers (upper castes or landlords), and workers (lower castes), it would never survive. We can see that the new class of entrepreneurs/capitalists did not necessarily come from the upper castes or classes, but mainly from the middle ones (like the trading communities in India as also in Britain). Similarly, many from the upper castes could become workers in factories. Hence, the traditional system of stratification started changing. The old system of conforming to traditional norms was being challenged. This is when rationality as one of the values was developed and the new form of stratification was based on rationally developed ideas. In such a system, the different strata were not rigid or watertight compartments as there could be mobility between them. The basis for these strata was ability and skill rather than status at birth. This gave opportunities to different strata, especially those lower in the hierarchy, to change their social status. For example, it is possible for a worker to become an industrialist, if they have the potential for it. Similarly, it is possible for an entrepreneur whose venture has failed to become a paid worker. This was not possible in the traditional system where hierarchies were rigid.

The basis of rationality, in this context, was egalitarianism. The system tried to provide equal opportunity to all, though it may not have happened in reality. Inequalities in such societies were quite high, perhaps even more than the inequalities in the pre-industrial system. The gap between the rich and the poor increased considerably. In terms of status too there were more layers such as the super-rich, rich, upper middle class, middle class, lower middle class, and the working poor. However, there was a difference between the two systems. Even though the extent of inequalities may have been less in the pre-industrial system and there were greater differences in the industrial system, the latter operated on the basis of inequalities but within the framework of egalitarianism, for all had an even chance, at least in theory.

INDUSTRIALISATION AND SOCIAL INSTITUTIONS

Industrialisation has an impact on the structure of the family. Since industrialisation led to migration, the structure of the family changed from joint or extended families in the rural areas to nuclear families in the urban centres. The need for the nuclear family in the industrial age was stressed by sociologists like Émile Durkheim, Ferdinand Tönnies, Georg Simmel and Karl Mannheim. They viewed families as isolated units which were important centres of socialisation for the young as well as for providing emotional support to the working males. Parsons (1980) stated that the nuclear family was necessary to meet the needs of industrial urban society. When a person from a rural background migrates to urban areas for employment, he finds himself in an alien environment. His source of support was earlier his extended family in a rural area. It was not possible to bring the entire family to his new place of work for reasons of space and economy. Instead, his nuclear family (comprising husband, wife and unmarried children) becomes the unit of migration.

Urban areas have larger numbers of nuclear families. This helps the working male to adjust to his new environment. It also provides him emotional support in terms of his wife and children being with him. Parsons stresses on the traditional roles in the family as being functional. He argues that the urban nuclear family demarcates these roles clearly. This would include the male breadwinner as head of the household, and the female, the wife, as the caretaker of the home and the children. Parsons further explains that in the earlier system, tasks performed by women such as household work and childcare were shared by all the women in the family. In the nuclear family, the wife performs the specific role of the homemaker and takes care of the initial socialisation of the child. These are the skills that she acquires within the nuclear family. Though this argument may sound traditional and may be flawed, the positive side of it is that, for the first time, a sociologist talked about separate skills within the family. This could be interpreted as the starting point for a discussion on issues such as unpaid family work performed by female members.

The other argument is that since the family does not perform its traditional roles, its necessity as a social institution decreases considerably. The traditional roles of the family include:

i. Socialisation;
ii. Marriage and legitimacy of children;
iii. Sexual gratification and emotional support;
iv. Economic dependence of the wife on her spouse; and
v. Domestic work performed by women in the family such as cooking, cleaning and childcare.

Each of the above could be met outside the family. As far as socialisation is concerned, the family does play a role even now. However, its role was much more important in the traditional system because children learnt the social norms and rules of behaviour from elders in the family. In other words, a Dalit child was taught to behave in different ways with different castes not by people of other castes but by his own family and community. The skills and knowledge of occupations which existed for each caste group were passed down by the elders in the family to the young. In other words, the son of a potter or a farmer learnt the skills of his trade only from the elders in his family.

The role of the family in socialisation has been reduced considerably. The main institution of socialisation for children now is not the home but the school. Parsons stresses the importance of school for the role it plays in preparing children for citizenship. When the child is in the family, it feels that it is at the centre of all the love and affection. The child also feels that they are different from others because of the love and care they receive from parents. However, when the same child goes to a day care centre, primary school or some other educational institution, they realise that there are other children similar to them. This experience becomes the first step towards a sense of citizenship. Further, the school also lays down the guidelines not merely for accumulation of knowledge but also behaviour in public. Durkheim in his work, *Moral Education,* argued that the discipline and the values taught in school are important for the student when they go out to seek a living. Apart from imparting knowledge, the school also teaches the child to respect elders (teachers), be punctual, and so on. These qualities are essential for citizenship. Durkheim also says that the spirit of nationalism and national pride is inculcated through the subjects taught in school, such as history, civics, etc. In fact, schools are important institutions for inculcating values such as secularism and multiculturalism.

Sexual gratification can be found even outside marriage which is not its only source, and it is not uncommon for urban people in particular to have extra-marital relationships. The issue of legitimacy of children too, is not very important in most developed countries, which has witnessed the growth of the phenomenon of single mothers. This was more apparent after WWII in places where the population of males declined. Many women who could not get married opted for motherhood by having a child outside marriage and as single mothers. This in turn led to a decline in the sanctity of marriage.

Moreover, women have become independent earners, which in turn reduces their economic dependence on their spouses. A married couple, both of whom have jobs, and who together contribute to the family income is substantially different from traditional society where males and females in the family combined to perform the work. In that case, it was joint work which fetched joint returns, whereas in the case of the husband and wife who are both independent individual workers, the income of one is in no way influenced by that of the other. The so-called domestic work which is supposed to be the wife's prerogative may not be something sacrosanct because this can be done by hiring employees or it can be shared with the husband, and childcare can be delegated to childcare centres.

Role of the Family in Indian Society

In the section above, we have shown how industrialisation affects the nature of the traditional family. There is a preference for the nuclear family in urban centres. This may hold true in the case of developed industrial countries such as USA, UK and other European countries. In the case of India, where industrialisation developed in a limited way due to colonialism, the situation may not be the same. Industrialisation in India was restricted to only certain areas because the products were meant for the colonising country (Britain), rather than for domestic consumption. Industrialisation in India began in the 1850s with the establishment of textile mills in what was then Bombay and jute mills in what used to be Calcutta. Those industries were situated in port cities to facilitate their exports. There was little or no industrialisation in other parts of the country as colonial rule did not permit this to happen.

Around this time, there was large-scale pauperisation in the rural areas because import of goods from Britain had replaced the need for traditional village artisans. These people joined the ranks of agricultural labourers. The industries were started precisely because there was a possibility of cheap labour from these impoverished sections. The wages were so low that it was not possible for families holding no land to migrate to urban centres. Hence the first workers to join the textile mills in Mumbai were those who had small, low-productivity portions of land, which perhaps provided the basic food requirement in the family and nothing else. In these circumstances it was possible for one member of the family to migrate to the city and work there on the low wages offered. A major part of these wages would go for consumption of the worker, but he could save a small part for his family in the village for purchasing other essential commodities. It was possible for fairly large-scale migration to take place mainly because of the joint or extended families which these workers came from. The worker's wife and children were looked after by the extended family back in the village.

The above holds true not just for workers migrating to Mumbai and Kolkata,but also in other areas such as the coal mines in Bihar/ Jharkhand. Jan Breman (1998) discusses the specific role of the extended family in promoting industrial labour by citing the works of Kalpana Ram on labour in the coal mines. We find that in all cases, whether jute, textile industry or coal mines, the joint/extended family in the villages actually promoted the growth of a labour force in the urban centres. It is also found that when workers fell ill, they went back home for treatment (instead of depending on their employers for medical care). In many cases, workers also brought a sack of food grains from their villages when they returned to their workplaces. These factors made it possible for the workers to exist under the prevailing low wages. Therefore in India, it is the extended family that provided for migration as opposed to the nuclear family in the West. It is also because of the extended family in the village that the industries were able to get their supply of cheap labour. Therefore one must keep in mind the basic differences in the roles of the family in developed countries and India. This does not mean that there are no nuclear families in urban areas. They do exist, but these families too have strong ties with the larger extended families in the village. One should not mechanically presume that rural areas have joint families and urban areas have nuclear families.

Kinship

It can be argued in the same way as in the case of the family that kinship ties tend to loosen with migration under industrialisation. The loosening of kinship ties can be due to

i. Distance: Kinship ties are strongest when there are face-to-face interactions. When kin members migrate to far-off places, these ties tend to be disrupted.
ii. Wealth of individual opportunities: Employment in the industrialised societies is based on the skills and merits of a person and not on their ascribed status. Hence the support of kin groups for procuring employment will not be very strong, because individual capacities are more important than kinship support.

Marvin B. Sussman and Lee G. Burchinal (1980) in their study on kinship networks in USA show that the above assumptions are not necessarily correct. In fact they argue that it is because of distance and isolation that kinship ties become necessary. Normally, kinsfolk keep in touch with each other through exchange of gifts during certain festivals and they also exchange greeting cards and brief notes which keep each other updated on the developments within the family.

Money may also be given to younger members of the family. The authors find that such ties exist more among the middle and lower-middle classes. They observed that when a person needs money, it is their kinsfolk from different parts of the country that contribute. Hence they argue that though America has nuclear families, they do not exist as isolated atomised bodies. The nuclear family exists within the kinship network. Hence we can see that kinship ties do not wither away due to industrialisation.

The situation may be slightly different in India. Sociologist David Pocock developed the concept of a rural-urban continuum in the context of India. The concept was originally developed by Robert Redfield in his study in Mexico. Pocock argued that the fundamental structural features such as caste and kinship find full expression among the migrant urban population. The migrants feel insecure in the urban environment and they depend on their caste and kinship ties for their basic requirements such as employment and help during times of illness. Another study by anthropologist Mark Holmstorm (1976) on industrial workers in Bangalore shows that when workers come to an alien environment they depend on their kinsfolk for support. He argues that the ritualistic aspects of kinship (such as observing common festivals and religious ceremonies) may slacken due to distance. However, the other aspects such as providing emotional and financial support in an alien environment continue. His study shows that many of the workers have got their jobs in factories due to kinship ties. They may have a relative who is already working in the factory and puts in a good word for them. Normally, when questioned, no worker will admit that he got the job because of his networks: he will insist that he got it because of his abilities. Holmstorm spent several months in the residences of the workers and got his information because of this closeness to them.

Social Control: Growing Role of the State

The growth of urban centres under industrialisation necessitated new types of social control. Urbanisation as a result of industrialisation led to large-scale migration from rural areas to the urban centres. In traditional societies, social control was exercised through fixed agencies like the community, caste panchayats, and the village panchayat. In the urban areas, the system had to change because migration meant that diverse types of people were settling in these areas. They had their own notions of social control based on the areas from where they had migrated. Moreover, this complexity required that there should be an independent central authority to deal with the various issues of control. Control is much more complicated in industrialised societies because there are several dimensions involved. Firstly, there is a need to control the diverse types of people who settle in the industrial centres in terms of law and order. The industries, too, need to be regulated and also there should be some planning for urban development. All these necessitate a centralised authority for governance. This institution came to be known as the state. As society progressed, there was greater need for this type of a centralised regulation, and hence the significance of the state increased.

The normative structure laid down by traditional societies in the institutions mentioned above exerted control in a region or more specifically in a village. The state exercises greater control over a larger area. It occupies a territory, and its defining feature is its exclusive right of using coercive methods for making its citizens comply with its rules. Max Weber referred to this as rational legal authority. Coercion could be used outside the state too, but this would not be legal. It would amount to non-legitimate behaviour which could be punishable, as the law says that only the state has the authority to apply force. Herein lies the difference between power and authority. Power is the ability of a person to impose their will on others even in the face of opposition, and can be legal or illegal. When it is legitimate power, i.e., power derived from a body like the state, it becomes authority.

The role of the state can be seen in different aspects of our lives. The state regulates business, industry, education, etc., through the laws that it lays down. Even individual action comes under the purview of the state. The rules within the family, the legitimacy of marriage and social relations are all regulated by the state. For instance, if a parent cannot take care of their child, the state is obliged to do so, through its orphanages or other such institutions. Even violence within the family is illegal, which means that a parent cannot use coercive measures against their children. Earlier, these issues were decided locally according to the traditional laws which were oral and not codified. In modern times, however, all laws are codified and the state has a separate branch to interpret the implementation of these laws. This is known as the judiciary. The other branches of the state include the legislature which frames laws, and the executive which comprises the bureaucracy which is expected to enforce the laws.

Key Concepts/Definitions

Spatial juxtaposition A large number of people from different regions being placed close together in a comparatively small area.

***Jajmani* system** Mutually dependent division of labour between castes, with unequal relations where upper castes are at an advantage over the other caste groups.

Machine-pacing Workers working on machines keep pace with the way the machines function. The same action is repeated over and over again, keeping pace with the machine.

Rural-urban continuum (Pocock) Fundamental structural features such as caste and kinship find full expression among the migrant urban population.

References and Readings

Anderson, Michael, ed. 1980. *Sociology of the Family*. Harmondsworth (UK): Penguin.

Burns, Tom, ed. 1977. *Industrial Man*. Harmondsworth: Penguin.

Breman, J. et al., eds. 1998. *Industrial Labour in India*. Delhi: Sage India.

Farooqui, Amar. 2006. *Opium City: The Making of Early Victorian Bombay*. Delhi: Three Essays Collective.

Holmstrom, Mark. 1976. *South Indian Factory Workers*. Cambridge: Cambridge University Press.

Moore, Wilbert. 1971. *The Impact of Industry*. Delhi: Prentice Hall.

Parsons, T. 1980. 'The Family in Urban-Industrial America'. In *Sociology of the Family*, ed. Michael Anderson. Harmondsworth (UK): Penguin.

Sheth, N. R. 1995. *Social Framework of an Indian Factory*. Delhi: Hindustan Publishing Co.

Sussman, Marvin B., and Lee G. Burchinal. 1980. 'Kinship in Urban Industrial America'. In *Sociology of the Family*, ed. Michael Anderson. Harmondsworth (UK): Penguin.

2

SOCIAL ORGANISATION OF INDUSTRY

Chapter Highlights

- » Definition of social organisations
- » Hierarchy
- » Three types of authority structure
- » Bureaucracy
- » Scientific management
- » Human relations

The American sociologist and specialist in organisational studies, Amitai Etzioni, wrote, 'Our society is an organisational society' (Etzioni 1972). We are born in hospitals, educated in schools employed in business firms, government agencies, universities, etc. We join trade unions or professional associations, go to hospitals when we are ill and when we die, we are taken to crematoriums which are run by the municipality or burial grounds run by a church or a mosque. Therefore, in sickness or in health, at work and at play, life in modern industrial society is conducted in organisational settings.

WHAT ARE SOCIAL ORGANISATIONS?

Organisations are social units which are predominantly oriented to the attainment of specific goals. They differ from other social units like family, friendship groups, community groups, etc., because they are designed to realise clearly defined goals. For example, schools are designed to transmit knowledge, hospitals to treat the sick, industrial units for manufacturing goods, etc.

Social organisations are not new entities that came into existence because of factory production. But factories or industrial units particularly need organisations for ensuring that work is done in a systematic manner. Without organisations, there would be chaos which in turn would affect production. Every factory or hospital or school has certain rules for conducting its activities. Though there may be common features in these organisations there are also differences. One cannot run a hospital the way one runs a factory. This is a controversial issue because the earlier scholars stressed on common features of all organisations (to be discussed).

Let us return to the historical aspects of organisations. As suggested above, it may not be an exaggeration to say that organisations have been in existence since the birth of human civilisation. Primitive human beings who depended on hunting and gathering for their survival searched for food by organising themselves into functional groups which they formed so that they could undertake their tasks more efficiently. In the case of hunting, a group of humans would encircle a prey and kill it when it was trapped. Some animals hunt alone. Tigers do not go in herds to hunt; similarly, carnivorous animals such as leopards, panthers, etc., hunt alone. An exception is found in the case of lions or rather lionesses who hunt their prey in a group (called a pride) through coordination between two or more lionesses. Other animals that are mainly herbivorous move in herds. These include different types of deer, wild buffaloes, zebras, etc. They do so mainly for protection from any carnivorous animal that preys on them.

The difference between organisations of animals and humans is that while the former are similar as animals have instinctive behaviour, the organisations of humans change according to the situation. Technology is the main instrument that leads to change, the prime motivating factor for human development. In primitive times, humans would encircle their prey and stone it with their bare hands. When humans invented the spear the organisation of hunting changed; the group would not need to surround the animal but they could position themselves in front of it and throw spears to slay it. Later, with the invention of the bow and arrow the group function again changed. The hunters could stalk their prey from a greater distance with less chance of the animal's attacking them. We can thus see that group functions of humans changed with the progress of technology.

Technology in effect distinguishes human beings from other animals. Technology is not something static but changes and improves over time. These changes are due to human efforts. For example, following the invention of the spear to help in hunting, further changes were found necessary. The energy used in throwing a spear was limited. In order to make it more effective it became necessary to transform this energy to some other form. The catapult could be an effective human tool; the missile (usually a stone) travels with greater force and speed and it requires less human effort than throwing a spear. Further innovations led to the invention of the bow and arrow. Here too with less effort the missile (arrow in this case) could travel with greater speed and hit its mark with greater force; we can think of other inventions that are more effective in killing the prey.

All technologies are not used for killing as man has moved beyond the hunting stage. There could be forms of technology starting with primitive types of production and after centuries becoming more and more sophisticated. The basic necessities of life are food, clothing and shelter. We can see in all cases how human endeavour improves with the invention of newer and more efficient technology. Let us take the example of making cloth. In earlier times, women used to weave cloth with a loom that was attached to their waists. They wove while sitting on the floor and the shuttle they used was operated by hand. This was a cumbersome and time-consuming task. The invention of the shuttle loom (known as handloom) was more efficient as it wove cloth at a faster pace. When power was introduced after the industrial revolution, the handloom was upgraded to the power loom which was more efficient. A redesigning of the spindles by making more of them operate in unison helped to create the textile mill. From this there was a shift to an even more efficient air-jet loom. We can thus see how with the advancement of technology, there has been a rapid increase in production.

Along with technology, another factor for the spread of organisations is the growing division of labour in society. At the primitive stage when there was a low level of technology in use, human beings performed the same type of activities. All human beings were engaged in attaining the same three objectives of living, namely, food, clothing and shelter. They jointly collected food or hunted, the garments they wore were obtained either from the skins of animals or the bark of trees and leaves, and their shelter consisted of crude dwellings that could be easily constructed. Since the level of technology was low, it was possible to replicate these activities. There was no division of labour as everyone performed the same types of work.

With improvements in technology, it was possible to have division of labour. In other words, some people could specialise in some types of activities. For example, some people could exclusively make pots and other earthenware for household needs, others could weave cloth and some could be involved in agricultural work. This type of division of labour needed to be coordinated or else it would give rise to a chaotic situation where people did work in a haphazard manner. The coordination of these activities required what we call 'social organisation'. Hence we can see that organisations coordinate the activities of large numbers of people aimed at a common objective.

In ancient times, huge monuments were constructed which exist even today. These included the pyramids of Egypt, the Sphinx, large palaces and temples. A large number of labourers were used for such construction. Work on these sites had to be coordinated properly in order to ensure that work was done efficiently. Similarly, at war, armies were organised to be efficient so that they could effectively fight the enemy. In its absence, armies were likely to be defeated because of lack of coordinated effort. We can take the example from history of the first battle of Panipat (1526) which was fought by the invading army of Babur against Ibrahim Lodi, the last to rule over the Delhi Sultanate. It is said that Lodi had a huge army of 1,00,000 foot soldiers and several thousand soldiers on elephants and horses. Babur, on the other hand, had only around 30,000 soldiers on horseback. Despite a smaller force, Babur was able to defeat the vast army of Lodi. The reason, we are told, is organisational coordination and efficiency of Babur's army. Lodi's large army, on the other hand, was deficient in this regard. Hence, when Babur's force attacked them, they did not know how to retaliate. Moreover, the elephants which were not given any commands ran helter-skelter, and, in most cases, trampled their own people. Amidst the chaos, Babur's army was able to defeat Lodi's men. This illustrates how effective organisations are necessary for achieving objectives.

The spread of organisations was related to the division of labour. The French sociologist Durkheim (1947) mentions that solidarity was the basis for human society. There were basically two types of solidarity, namely, mechanical and organic. The simpler societies had little or no division of labour, but there was solidarity among the members. The members grouped together for various reasons, the most important being the need for protection against wild animals and other elements of nature like fires, floods, rain and so on. This is what Durkheim terms as mechanical solidarity. In such societies, there was hardly any need for superior organisational framework because of similarities among the members.

As division of labour increased, we could find differences arising in occupations. For example, there were peasants, ironsmiths, potters, weavers, priests, cobblers, merchants, etc. In modern societies, the division is even more extensive. People have different professions such as those of lawyers, doctors, teachers, business executives, industrialists, workers, etc. The solidarity which is seen in such societies is based on differences among the people. Yet, each of these different occupations is important for the functioning of the society. Hence, one finds that societies with such differences come together because of organic solidarity. These two types of solidarities depict the differences between simple and complex organisations.

Hierarchy

The other aspect which needs to be stressed is that the differences which occur in societies are not based on equality but on hierarchy. This means that some individuals or groups are superior, and others are inferior. The difference, for instance, between the employer and the employee shows that the employee is lower in hierarchy as compared to the employer. This form of hierarchy is based on rules that govern society. In sociological terms, the hierarchy is based on social values or shared beliefs which all members of society, whether high or low, have that hierarchy is necessary for the effective functioning of society. Hierarchies can also be based on specialisation. Specialist tasks require direction and coordination if they are to be combined to produce the end product, and a wide range of specialised tasks needs coordination and also a hierarchy of authority. When these factors are combined in the pursuit of a specific goal, an organisation is formed.

We can examine the work of another sociologist, Max Weber, as an important starting point. Weber's theory of authority structures characterises organisations in terms of authority relations. The main question which Weber tries to tackle is: why do individuals obey commands? In order to deal with this problem, Weber made a distinction between power and authority. Power is defined as the ability to impose one's will over others even when there is opposition to it. Hence, power has a coercive element in it. However, power can be of different types and many times it could be exercised through the use of brute force of through fear. Weber states that when orders are obeyed voluntarily it becomes authority. Under authority, the receiver of orders (the subordinates) sees it as legitimate in receiving orders from the super-ordinate.

Power encompasses authority only if it is legitimate. There can be two ways of imposing one's will over others. A local goon through his use of force and other means of coercion can force people to obey his commands, he may even collect rent from them which they give to him not willingly but because they are afraid of the consequences if they fail to do so; this is power that is not legitimate. However, when the police use authority to quell a mob, or to arrest this goon who along with his supporters is terrorising the locality, it is understood as authority. The police may use the same form of brutality as that of the goon, but they do so because their actions are treated as legitimate by the people. Just as the goon collects rent from the people, the state too collects taxes for its functioning. But the difference is that people pay rent to the goon because they are afraid of him and his gang, whereas the same people would pay taxes to the state because they think it is legitimate. Hence, two similar actions can be viewed differently in terms of legitimacy.

Weber explained that the nature of legitimatisation of authority determines the nature of the organisation. There are three types of organisations with three different types of authority structures; these are the traditional, rational-legal and charismatic structures. Each has its peculiar administrative apparatus. Let us deal with each of these types separately.

Traditional Authority Structure

In organisations with a traditional authority structure, the leader has authority by virtue of the status they have inherited. The extent of the authority is also fixed by custom, in other words, tradition. In feudal systems, the authority enjoyed by the king is by virtue of the status he has inherited from his predecessors, a result of the privileges and the customs associated with his office. Traditional leadership is usually found in pre-industrial societies. One finds that even positions in villages are hereditary; if the father is a headman of the village, he will most probably be succeeded by his son and not by any other person, no matter how competent the person is. Similarly, the son of a ruler will succeed his father irrespective of his shortcomings.

However, there can be occasions where modern business organisations may adopt traditional leadership and succession. Managerial positions are often handed down from father to son and this is quite often legitimised by the fact that a competent father can produce a competent son. Many firms establish their own dynasties based on hereditary succession. In these cases, the selection and appointment in superior positions are based on kinship ties rather than on expertise. This is observed in most of the larger industrial houses in the country. Normally, large dynastic companies induct the children of the top management but not merely on the basis of heredity, for in many cases, the incumbent would have acquired specialised skills such as a management or engineering degree from a reputed university at home or abroad. This tends to justify their induction.

Rational-Legal Authority Structure

This type of organisation is based on bureaucratic principles strictly on a person's abilities to pursue organisational tasks. Weber saw this as a dominant institution of modern society. The organisation is rational because it is designed to meet specific goals; it is like a well-designed machine in that respect. Every part of that machine contributes to the attainment of the highest performance. The organisation is legal because authority is exercised by means of a system of rules and procedures through the office that an individual occupies at a particular time. The power that this organisation or its leadership exerts over the others is legitimate and hence its rules are accepted willingly.

Charismatic Authority Structure

This comes from the Greek word *kharisma*, which implies that the personality of the individual sets them apart from others because of exceptional qualities, which could be rated as 'superhuman' or 'supernatural'. This type of leadership is typically found in religious or political movements.

In the case of quite a few organisations, their founders were charismatic leaders. These could include pioneering industrialists like Henry Ford, Jamshedji Tata and G. D. Birla, among others. Social and political leaders like Mohandas Karamchand Gandhi, Indira Gandhi and Dr Babasaheb Ambedkar were also regarded as charismatic.

In such cases, the basis of authority lies in the characteristics of one person, and what they say and stand for is an inspiration to many. Such organisations often have a built-in instability because they attain their peak during the tenure of the charismatic leader, after whose death there is instability and sometimes a struggle for succession. Often, there may be infighting even if the leader nominates his/her successor who may lack the leader's charisma. If succession is hereditary, the organisation becomes traditional in form while if succession is determined by rules, it develops into a bureaucratic organisation. The problematic part of Weber's analysis is that charisma can be both positive and negative; Mahatma Gandhi was a charismatic leader and so was Hitler but Weber fails to make a qualitative difference between different types of charismatic personalities.

While looking at the three types of organisations, one finds that they cannot be viewed in watertight compartments for there is considerable overlap. For instance, industrial houses were often founded by personalities who had charisma; at the same time, these organisations were rational-legal because they were run on bureaucratic principles and the succession also resembles the structure of traditional authority. Hence, all three types of organisation are prevalent in the major industrial houses in our country especially those that are run as family businesses.

BUREAUCRACY

This is an important institution in the organisation of work. The idea of bureaucracy was developed and theorised by Weber in his study, *Theory of Social and Economic Organization* (1947). Weber believed that bureaucratic organisations were the most dominant institutions of industrial society because they are designed rationally to coordinate the efforts of a large number of individuals working in a wide range of activities.

Weber stated that the distinguishing feature of modern capitalism was 'the rational organisation of free labour'. Capitalism is based on the pursuit of private gain. This ensures that the system makes profit as a measure of its success. Weber notes that the pursuit of private gain was known in many earlier societies but what distinguishes capitalism from that is the peculiar organisation of the production unit. This was done on the lines of a bureaucracy.

In dealing with bureaucracy, Weber stressed on social relations within the work organisation. He also observed that though bureaucracy is a result of capitalism, it is not solely limited to it for it could be found in other economic systems or organisations as well. These would include government, the Christian church or any organisation that is large and involves a number of personnel.

Weber felt that a bureaucratic structure would be the natural choice of any large-scale organisation because it was superior in precision, in stability, in stringency of discipline and in reliability in comparison with any other form of administration. Furthermore, the functioning of an efficient bureaucracy makes it possible for a high degree of calculability of results. In other words, the goal set by organisations can be achieved with accuracy. Due to these qualities, bureaucracy is capable of application to all kinds of administrative tasks.

A bureaucracy can be defined as a type of organisation which is designed rationally to coordinate the work of many individuals in the pursuit of large scale administrative tasks. The word originates from 'bureau', a large desk with shelves or pigeonholes where files and papers could be stored. Hence the person who worked at the desk had shelves or boxes in which he could store files, and there was a cover which could be locked so that the contents would be safe even after the person left office.

Besides written directions regarding work, there is also clear division of labour among the people in the organisation. Each person performs a specific task or tasks that can be distinguished from the others. In modern organisations, a person who is employed is given an appointment letter which, besides informing them that they have been appointed, clearly states what their work will be. There are also other written rules and guidelines that further clarify the duties and responsibilities of each employee.

An important aspect of the bureaucracy is that the offices within it do not have similar status. On the contrary, there is a distinct hierarchy where the offices and the people are ranked one above the other. The differences between consecutive tiers in the hierarchy are based on access to power. The ones with lesser access to power are at the bottom and those with greater access are in the upper tiers. The higher offices therefore embrace or subsume those below them.

Most organisations have a pyramid-like structure; the base is broad while the top is narrow. Those at the base are the menial workers such as peons, messengers, watchmen, sweepers, etc. Workers in a factory too occupy this position. These people have no power in the sense that they only receive orders, which they have to execute. Those above them such as supervisors or foremen give them orders. These people, in turn, receive orders from those above and they pass the instructions to those below. This goes on in a similar way till it reaches the person at the top—the chief executive officer/ managing director or someone in a similar position. Such a person only gives orders and does not receive orders from anyone as there is no one superior. Hence we see that all tiers in the hierarchy receive and give orders to those below, the exceptions being those at the bottom, who only receive orders, and the one on the top who only gives orders.

If we look merely at the giving and receiving of orders it will appear that the bureaucracy is like a relay race, where the baton is passed from one runner to the other. This is, of course, not true. Those in senior positions do not merely issue orders but also have other jobs to do, which could include planning, and ensuring the smooth functioning of the work. Though people in similar positions in the hierarchy enjoy equal power/authority, they do not perform identical work. Let us consider some examples.

The administration in a university comprises peons, security guards, etc., who form the lowest tier. Above them are clerks, senior clerks, superintendents, assistant registrars, deputy registrars, and the registrar whose job, as the head, is to supervise the administration. People in the same tier do not have similar access to power nor do they perform the same tasks. Let us consider the post of deputy registrar (DR). A university may have several DRs and each is in charge of a specific area of work. The DR in charge of academic activities will do only that work, just as the DR of the decision-making bodies (Academic Council, Senate, Executive Council, etc.) has control over the staff engaged in these sections. Students seeking clarification regarding the admission process will have to meet only the DR Academic. They cannot go to any other DR to seek clarifications, as this will not be their responsibility. Hence, each office and each person in the office has specific functions based on the division of labour. Each DR has some assistant registrars (ARs) working under them. The DR Academic will have ARs, each of whom is in charge of specific activities such as undergraduate studies, post-graduate studies, technical subjects, etc.; similarly, each AR will have superintendents working under them and clerks and stenographers who receive instructions from the superintendent. We can thus see that the higher office subsumes the lower ones and the officer concerned has specific activities or roles to perform.

The procedures in a bureaucracy are written and recorded and these records are preserved for further reference. We notice a difference here between traditional administration and a bureaucracy. In the former, records are hardly ever maintained, and in most cases, procedures are oral, which those holding power use to instruct those working under them based on their understanding or judgement of the situation. There is hardly any reference to the past cases as these are not recorded; if at all there is a mention of the past, it is based on the memory of the elderly.

The administrative staff have specialisation and have also undergone training. Clerks and officers are selected on the basis of their expertise and nature of specialisation. A clerk must be well-versed in the language of the administration and must also have some typing or, at present, computer skills. A major aspect of bureaucracy is that members of the staff are selected principally based on their skills. There is a separation between personal affairs and business matters, which means that, within legal limits, employees cannot be penalised for their personal activities. For example, if they are divorced legally, this will not affect their job or career. However, if an officer or clerk commits an illegal act such as rape, he can be removed from his job.

We can contrast this with traditional administration where personal and business affairs go hand in hand. For example, if the minister of a king married outside his caste, especially one that is lower than his, he may be dismissed by the king. The same cannot hold true now. If a government officer marries outside his caste, it will not affect his job. This means that incumbents will be judged solely by their work and *not* their personal life.

A person occupying public office is expected to be neutral to all pressures and not be influenced by anything other than the merits of the case that they are dealing with. Weber (1947) believed that, in order that the official remains neutral, the relations between the official and their clients should be impersonal. He felt that this was important because the official should not develop personal relations with the client as the official may then favour one client over others, which would indicate partiality. The officer has to treat all clients on an equal footing. This can be done if officials distance themselves from the clients through impersonal relations.

As mentioned earlier, the authority embedded in the tier of the hierarchy distinguishes the status of each incumbent in the bureaucratic organisation. The authority enjoyed by the official is based on the office and not on personal status, which means that an official draws authority from the office they are appointed to. A DR in the university administration has authority not because he is anybody in particular, but by virtue of being a DR. When he leaves that position, he no longer enjoys that authority. Weber wanted to show the difference between bureaucracy and traditional organisations, in the latter, authority being embedded in the person and in the position. For example, a king has authority and he derives this from his lineage, and therefore he cannot be removed from office, unless he is dethroned by opponents.

Unlike traditional authority which is embedded in the person, the authority enjoyed by an official can change. It can increase or decrease according to the position they occupy. An important aspect is that employment constitutes a career. The official is appointed through a selection process which may include written tests, interviews, etc.; once appointed, the official is permanent in the bureaucracy and they enjoy a regular salary and increments. More importantly, the official does not stagnate in one position but can be promoted based on his/her performance. This provides an incentive to the official/incumbent to work better and also ensures that he/she has a stake in the organisation. This is true not only of senior officials but also others such as those in the lower tiers. All of them receive increments in their salaries and they can also be promoted to higher posts if they prove themselves meritorious. Weber thought that these incentives make a bureaucratic organisation efficient in its activities.

The last point that Weber raises is regarding the appointment of the officials. He stresses the fact that the appointment of officials must be done by those placed above; in other words, the appointment of a DR has to be done through a selection process and the appointment letter is issued by their superior, namely, the Registrar. This happens in all cases in an administration, where the head of the administration appoints people in various posts. This ensures that the incumbent is loyal to the organisation. Weber mentions this point specifically because in some cases bureaucrats were appointed through elections. He was especially cynical about appointments of administrators such as sheriffs and even judges through elections as was done in the United States. He felt that this actually weakened the bureaucratic system because the bureaucrat would then be loyal to the electorate and not to the system. This implied that the relations between the official and the client would not be impersonal but would be influenced by the mood of the electorate.

Bureaucracy: An Assessment

Weber's construction of a bureaucracy is that of an ideal type. He has built up a model that may or may not exist in reality. An ideal type could be termed as a method of investigation which may or may not exist but is something that is *expected* or is *desirable*. Thus Weber's formulation of a bureaucracy is not based on the features of existing administrative structures; on the contrary, he envisages a bureaucratic structure based on those features that he thinks are rational or go together in a rational way. While dealing with bureaucracy, Weber was inspired by the administration in Germany (Prussia). It was a powerful state in Europe then and had a strong administration. All well-run and efficient governments have strong administrations. Capitalism, or the spirit of industrialisation, created centralisation of production and consequently in distribution (please see Chapter 1). This shift to centralisation requires strong administrative and managerial skills. Traditional (pre-capitalist) forms of administration were based on localised structures. These could not fulfil the needs of a capitalist form of production. Weber built his model of bureaucracy as a contrast to the traditional means of control. He stressed that bureaucracy could tackle complex problems thrown up by a complex society, which needed centralised administration. In other words, his model of a bureaucracy was used as a means of comparing it with the existing administrations. One can examine the strengths and weaknesses of these organisations when compared to the rational construct of the ideal type. As the ideal type does not exist, criticism of Weber's bureaucracy cannot be based on reality. The criticism therefore has to be on whether the features that he highlights are real or not. The two main arguments against bureaucracy are on the issue of rationality and that of impersonal relations.

Weber himself saw the dangers of 'over-bureaucratisation'. He expressed his misgivings in an article written some years after he had developed bureaucracy as in ideal type of organisation or administration (Etzioni and Etzioni 1971). He reiterated that bureaucracy was an essential form of administration and that it could not be done away with. At the same time, there was a need to evolve means to control its consequences. He felt that the feature that a bureaucracy provides a career for the official as it includes a fixed salary, increments and also promotions may help in gaining commitment but it may also lead to complacency, where the official knows that whether he works or not he will get his benefits. Weber was also critical of the promotions aspect, as it might lead to officials becoming over-ambitious. Each official would want to reach higher and higher in the hierarchy and all would want to reach the top. Weber wrote that they were like small cogs of the machine having ambitions of becoming the machine itself. He dreaded the day when this would happen.

He also noted that too much stability produced men who became nervous about unstable conditions. These people would not want to confront such situations by being bold and taking risks. Instead, they would try to hide behind rules. Suppose a critically injured person is brought to a hospital. The doctor in charge knows that he has to be treated immediately or else he will die. However, it is found that the person does not have medical insurance and the hospital needs proof that he will clear the bills. There are two possible solutions. First, the doctor treats the patient as he is critical, but if the patient fails to clear the bills the higher authorities will blame the doctor for this lapse; the doctor takes the risk of treating the patient and he will deal with the consequences later. The second possibility is that the doctor goes by the rules and refuses to treat the patient until he has proof of his financial condition; the patient may die in the meanwhile but the doctor may not be penalised as he was following the procedures and the rules. Weber was afraid that the second situation would be more common.

Besides Weber, there were other sociologists who were critical of his construction of bureaucracy. Robert K. Merton, in his article

'Bureaucratic Structure and Personality', believes that bureaucracy should not apply the same yardstick to all, as it tends to do because of its stress on *impersonal relations,* which means that the bureaucrat must behave similarly in all situations: an official in a hospital would behave in exactly the same impersonal manner as an official in a prison. This could have ridiculous consequences, and such behaviour could well be harmful to the patients in the hospital. Such a situation may however arise in a government organisation where the official has to deal with the public at large, where he cannot and should not show any form of partiality to some people or discriminate against others. Merton (1972) says that in other settings, such as in an employment exchange, impersonal relations may not be the ideal way of dealing with people. The clients here do not have jobs and they are already in a depressed state of mind; the official should be more understanding and his behaviour towards his unemployed client could be personalised. Similarly, in other places, like a hospital, impersonality may actually harm the interests of the clients. This happens because the bureaucrat has not been encouraged to improvise and innovate. In fact, as Weber has shown, he may be afraid to do so. His career incentives such as promotions and higher salary are designed to reward discipline and conformity to rules rather than empathetic behaviour.

Another American sociologist, Alvin Gouldner, in *Wildcat Strike,* his study of a gypsum factory, criticised the excessive dependence on formal rules (1954). He found that when the management did not stress unduly on rules and allowed workers to improvise, the work improved considerably and the workers were more relaxed; production also increased. Some time later a new management assumed charge, which was much more formal and it compelled the workers to strictly follow the rules; rule-breaking by workers was to be reported to the higher management and strict action was taken against those guilty. The workers were also not allowed to move around the factory at will as they had done in the past. While management was successful in increasing the degree of bureaucratisation in the plant, it was not so successful in the mines. The attempts of the management to impose a strict bureaucratic system were opposed effectively by the miners. Gouldner observes that this section of the workforce expressed greater solidarity because they worked underground and in hazardous conditions. They also believed that they should be exempted from some of the rules because of the dangers involved in their jobs.

The new management tried hard to discipline the miners under its bureaucratic code, but their resistance prevented it from doing so. Gouldner concludes that the management must avoid adopting rigid bureaucratic norms as this may encourage rebellion from the workers which would in turn affect productivity.

Peter Blau, a specialist in the sociology of organisations, criticised Weber for stressing only the formal structure of bureaucracy (1965). He says that there are also informal relations within the bureaucracy, which actually help in the smooth functioning of the organisation. Blau had studied the functioning of a law enforcement agency. The officials were expected to examine the standards of employment and whether laws dealing with employment had been broken. After completing the inspections, the officials had to write their reports. The agency's rules stated that the officials should not confer with each other on their cases because the reports they had collected from the employers were confidential, and in case of doubt they should consult their supervisor. The problem with this was that if they consulted their supervisor too often, it would be construed as being inefficient and lacking the skills of analysis, which would affect their chances of promotion. Hence, despite the rules, the officials frequently consulted each other in private while writing out their case reports. Blau shows that the informal relations led to greater efficiency in the system.

It can be seen that the very basis of Weber's contention that strict adherence to rules helps in improving efficiency does not appear to be realistic. In real life informal relations actually help in running a bureaucracy efficiently. It is the improvisations in the relations among the incumbents that enable a bureaucracy to function efficiently. For example, we observe that if in any office the incumbents were to follow the rules strictly, work would be hampered. For example, any customer going to a bank (in the recent past) to cash a cheque needed to deposit the cheque at the counter designated for the bank account number. The clerk would accept the cheque and after verifying the balance in the account would pass it on to the officer sitting behind for checking the signature. The peons/messengers in the bank were expected to take this and other cheques and deposit them before the officer, who after completing his work, would hand these cheques over to a peon for delivery to the cash counter. In case of a shortage of peons in the bank, the clerk at the front desk would hand over the cheque to the officer, who in turn might carry the scrutinised cheques to the cash counter. All this was done so that the bank functioned properly and the customers were not delayed or harassed. If the bank employees were to follow rules strictly, the clerk would allow the cheques to accumulate on his table, in case no peon was available to carry these cheques. In that case, the efficiency of the bank would be considerably reduced.

It is evident that if rules are followed strictly, little or no work may be done. For example, bus drivers are expected to ensure that all equipment essential for driving is in working order. In reality, it happens quite often that some of the equipment or instruments like the speedometer, the petrol gauge, a rear-view mirror, are not in working order. In normal circumstances, the driver does not protest as he is quite sure that he can drive the bus without these appendages. Now let us picture a case when bus drivers decide that they would not drive the buses until all the equipment were in working order. We may in fact find that on that day over half the buses, if not all, would not be plying on the streets.

Such a situation did take place in 1974, when the railways in Britain were on strike. The motormen in the tube (underground rail) did not operate any trains because of a minor provision in the rules. The strike took place in the middle of winter, in January. According to that rule, motormen were to remove their overcoats when they were in the cabin driving the train because heavy overcoats would obstruct their manoeuvrability. They were expected to hang their coats up on a clothes hanger in the cabin, but none of the cabins had such hangers. In the normal course, the motormen would remove their coats and possibly drape it on their chairs. But in this case, all motormen decided that since there were no hangers, they could not remove their coats and hang them: if they couldn't remove their coats, they could not operate the trains. Hence, though all of them reported for duty, none of them would operate a train. This shows that strict observance of rules might actually result in no work being done. In fact one of the effective means of trade union struggle is by declaring 'work-to-rule'. Invariably, this leads to stoppage of work.

Management Perspectives

Despite its shortcomings, bureaucracy undoubtedly had a big impact on the evolution of organisations. In many cases, the location of power and the exercise of authority were crucial in understanding an organisational setup. Thus we can say that bureaucracy formed the basis of managerial innovations. In this section, we shall deal with some cases of management of organisations. The first study of management of industries is found in the works of Frederick Winslow Taylor (1856–1915). This was known as 'Taylorism' or 'Scientific Management'.

Scientific Management

The nineteenth and early twentieth centuries saw rapid industrial expansion in the USA. However, the organisation of work was often not conducted in a rational or scientific manner. In most cases, it was left to the relations between foremen and the workers. Work was highly personalised. A factory worker who owned his own tools would carry these in his toolbox to the workplace. There he worked according to the use of his tools and the speed of the machines he was working with. The foreman was the centre of work-relations. He hired or fired workers according to his understanding of the situation. The rigour of work and the rest periods were all dependent on the understanding of the foreman. In such a situation, work was mainly haphazard and to a large extent, inefficient. For example, workers in an automobile factory would work in groups in building an automobile, getting together with their tools and starting to assemble the vehicle according to their efficiency. A car factory therefore consisted of several such groups of workers who were jointly engaged in the manufacture of cars. Such a system showed variants in speed, skill and also levels of quality of the end product. This meant that there was little uniformity in the output. Moreover, the process was expensive and time consuming because how work was to be done was left largely to the efficiency of the group and the control of the foreman.

Taylor was the first manager who tried to raise the efficiency of work by using a scientific time-and-motion study. He was an engineer by training who had, however, worked as a labourer in Midvale Steelworks out of choice. He felt that he should know the work in a factory at every level. Taylor was obsessed with the study of how to conserve energy in order to increase efficiency. In fact, one of his little-known contributions was the design of the spoon-shaped tennis racquet which is used even now; the earlier tennis racquets were round like lollipops. Taylor found that in those round racquets greater resistance was created by the wind, i.e., the tennis player had to use more energy while playing with a racquet of that type. The racquet that he designed reduced the resistance to wind and thereby conserved the player's energy throughout the game.

The same eye for detail led to Taylor's formulation of scientific management. When he rose to the rank of a supervisor at Midvale, he observed that a change in the work implements and efficiency of physical movements could result in increase in production. Taylor was given charge of workers who had to shovel pig iron into rail wagons, which were to be transported later to the steel factory. Each worker could shovel twelve and a half tonnes of iron ore every day. The company believed that the optimum amount could be around 25 tonnes but Taylor was not convinced. He felt that with proper guidance and conservation of energy, much more could be achieved. He chose a tall, well-built Dutch worker and told him that he would have to perform work in exactly the way Taylor instructed him. His movements would be guided by Taylor and so also his periods of rest. He allowed the worker to work for a couple of hours and then asked him to take rest for some time; after that, the worker would again resume his duties. Taylor ensured that he not only performed work strictly according to his instructions but he also took time to rest after a short period of vigorous activity. At the end of the day it was found that this worker had shovelled 47.5 tonnes. For the factory, this seemed like a miracle, but for Taylor this was just proof of his contention that efficiency of work could be increased substantially with the proper conservation of energy and check on the physical movements. This became the origin of time-and-motion studies.

Taylor rose to the rank of consultant for Bethlehem Steel (in the state of Pennsylvania, once the second-largest steel producer in the USA). In 1911, he wrote a book titled *Principles of Scientific Management* in which he explained his views on how to achieve maximum efficiency and productivity at the workplace (1947). Taylorism enjoined: (i) select the best man for the job, (ii) instruct him extensively on his work or how he should perform his work; this meant that the supervisor/manager should study how best there could be an economy of movement which would conserve the workers' energy for working over a long period of time, and (iii) use the carrot-and-stick approach by persuading people to try harder by offering them a reward if they did, or punishing them if they did not. This meant that management should provide incentives to the worker for doing his work well and disincentive for failing to come up to standards. The basic assumption of scientific management was that the worker should obey the instructions of his supervisor unquestioningly. Time-and-motion studies were based on instructing workers on their movements, ensuring that workers do not face fatigue, and that the physical environment of work is clean and healthy. All these factors encouraged the workers to achieve their optimum productivity. Scientific management has similarities with Weber's bureaucracy in the sense that it stresses that orders/instructions have to come from the top to those at the bottom.

Taylor explained that the true science of work deals with the issue of a fair day's work. There is a difference in the perception of employers and employees. The former wants more work while the latter wants less, but for Taylor this was not an issue. He was not interested in what could constitute a fair day's work; he was more interested in the result. Therefore, he suggested that the management must find a large daily task which would be performed under optimum conditions. This implied that workers showing greater productivity should be paid more than the average worker in unscientific workplaces. This would attract the better workers to the factory. At the same time, he advocated wage cuts if the worker failed to perform. The workmen must be selected in a scientific manner so that they possess the physical and intellectual qualities for the tasks to be performed. They should be trained systematically so that they can improve their performance and become 'first class workers'. Taylor even suggested that good workers could be lured by offering them advances in pay.

Taylor was critical of the management. He felt that in most cases inefficiency in work was the outcome of an unscientific approach of the management. He even stated that there has to be a mental revolution in management to accept a scientific system. He found that workers were willing to accept it but managements took more time to understand its implications. According to him, scientific management could succeed only if there was cooperation between management and workmen, and there was equal division of work among them. This implied that both workers and management had to be subjected to the same rigorous discipline or else the scheme could never be successful. This means that if there is a highly motivated workforce coupled with an indifferent management, productivity would fall. The converse too holds true, that if the management is highly motivated but it is unable to inspire workers in the same way, productivity would suffer.

The major drawback of Taylorism is that it treats individuals (workers) as isolated units which are viewed apart from their group. Later studies showed that incentives to individuals without taking into account the performance of the group inevitably ends in failure. The group which the worker belongs to exerts as much if not more influence on the worker's attitude towards work. We will discuss the importance of the workgroup in a later section.Taylor has been criticised because he viewed the efficiency of a worker in terms of how well he could take and execute orders unquestioningly. This fact creates a separation of physical and mental labour, hence the conception of work being done by the management whereas the execution is done by the workers. This results in the dehumanising of work as the worker is deemed to be just an instrument in the production process and not a human being. In the long run, such an attitude could lead to frustration and rebellion.

It may seem from the above discussion that Taylorism is a thing of the past. This is far from the truth. Many Indian companies use Tayloristic methods in their organisation of work. One can find Taylorism even in work involving high technology. An example is the call centres where the activity of the agents is regulated by their supervisors. These agents perform mental labour, which is as unquestioning as Taylor's approach to physical labour. They have to react to questions in a standard manner as instructed by the supervisors or trainers, and as there is little scope for any creativity in this work, being largely mechanical and repetitive. In factories we find that Taylorism plays an important role in increasing productivity.

A positive aspect of Taylorism is that it raised the issue of fatigue among the workmen. Taylor had stressed on the role of rest and the conservation of energy. In most cases, we find that these aspects are overlooked by employers or supervisors in factories. Taylor had suggested that factory workers should get a brief rest period after a couple of hours so that they can recuperate and work more efficiently. This is hardly observed in our workplaces. The Factories Act, 1948, laid down that there should be an eight-hour work period with half an hour's recess for meals. A worker practically has to work for at least four hours before he gets some rest. Taylor would have argued that this would result in lowering the worker's efficiency. He also emphasised other aspects of factory life, such as a clean and healthy environment which would encourage the workers to work harder. This too, is violated in most factories.

Fordism

This is a production process that was initiated by Henry Ford, founder of Ford Motors. Ford used this technique for manufacturing his Model T cars. This later came to be known as mass production. The technique increased the production of cars besides drastically decreasing costs of production. Hence cars could be affordable for middle-class consumers in the USA, and later elsewhere (Rose 1994).

Earlier, a group of workers using their own tools would be engaged in the production process, while the foreman/supervisor would direct the work performed. In the automobile manufacturing industry, a group of workers would be engaged in putting together a car, which might take a few days. Henry Ford thought of a new form of work organisation that would boost the production process. He was impressed by scientific management and adapted its techniques in building his model. Mass production basically split up the production process into small parts. Instead of a group of workers putting together a car, Ford split these activities into smaller parts. He used the assembly line as the means for putting together the different components to make the whole. The workers stood in a line, one next to the other, a conveyor belt ran in front of them and each worker had the components he had to attach to the machine. The first worker (in the division that manufactured engines) would fit a component to the basic machine, and the conveyor belt would take this to the next worker, who in turn would fix another component. In this way, the machine would travel to each worker and at the end of the conveyor belt, the final product would be ready.

Ford used the time-and-motion approach of scientific management. In order to achieve the highest degree of efficiency, the worker had to control his movements which were repetitive and performed according to the pace of the conveyor belt or the needs of production. If production were to be increased, the worker's actions had to be faster. The work on the assembly line was designed in a way that though workers worked close to each other, they did not have any physical or verbal communication among themselves for that would distract them and reduce their pace. The only communication they had was with the supervisor who instructed them to increase or lower the pace of work and who also reprimanded a worker for not keeping pace with the others. The worker was thus reduced to being a machine. He could not use his discretion while at work and he had to simply follow orders.

Ford realised that assembly-line work could be monotonous for the workers. He therefore compensated this with high wages. His workers were paid US$ 5 a day when the prevailing wage rate was in the range of US$ 2–2.5. This did work in his favour because he was able to achieve higher levels of productivity, which in turn compensated for the high labour costs. Ford thus provided workers with high wages, and consequently rising levels of consumption, in exchange for an intensified work regime.

There were other factors too that were related. Ford's method of production could be called vertical assimilation. He ensured that all inputs required for producing his cars were a part of the production process. He bought coal and iron ore mines and steel plants to process these so that he was ensured that there was a steady flow of raw materials for his production. He also reorganised the marketing and advertising of his products. Since these were mass-produced, thus less expensive than the other cars in the market, advertising had to target a larger segment of consumers rather than just the elite, as done by the other manufacturers.

Ford achieved tremendous success in his business and forced his competitors and all other manufacturers to switch to his techniques. Soon, America became a land for assembly-line manufacturing for all products.

Fordism: An Assessment

The term 'Fordism' was coined in 1936 by Antonio Gramsci, an Italian intellectual who was general secretary of the Italian Communist Party during WWII. Italy was then under Mussolini's Fascist party and he tried to regiment factory workers on the lines of mass production. Gramsci identified Fordism as a hegemonic form of industrial organisation. According to him, Fordism ensured that the workers were dominated by the capitalists through control over wages and also over the labour process.

Both Fordism and Taylorism have their strengths and weaknesses. Both revolutionised production and also ensured that there was greater discipline in the workforce. These techniques proved that extensive physical labour is not needed to increase production. A worker can be physically more productive not by increasing energy levels but by preserving them. Another common aspect is that the two systems did not lay stress merely on increasing productivity but also on adequately rewarding workers for doing good work.

The assembly line in effect changed the nature of work through its extensive division of labour. The worker was engaged in just one act of production and had little connection with the end product. In the early days of automobile production, workers knew how many cars they had manufactured; the assembly line worker in the Ford factory, however, could not tell how many cars he had produced as, far from being associated in the total production process, he was engaged in only one aspect of production. This had other implications. Under assembly-line production, workers were no longer specialists in the true sense; their 'specialisation' now lay in taking orders from their supervisors and translating them into work. Hence there could be no categories such as steel workers, textile workers or auto workers. A worker in a steel plant could also work in a shoe factory, because in both cases, they were performing only one action.

At the same time, work became more mechanical and involved only physical labour. Under assembly-line production, work was carried out at such a fast pace that workers did not have time to think—they just performed their work mechanically. This was bound to lead to frustration even if wages were increased periodically. In fact most of the labour unrest in the post-WWII period was attributed to the nature of work in the factory.

In the 1970s and 80s, Fordism was replaced by 'post-Fordism' which introduced a degree of flexibility among workers. This became known as flexible specialisation. In the following section, we shall see how another system developed to cope with the failures of scientific management.

Human Relations (HR)

The Human Relations (HR) approach is in some ways a contrast to the two approaches discussed earlier. This grew out of investigations at the Hawthorne plant of the Western Electric Company at Chicago. The study was conducted by a team of social scientists headed by Elton Mayo, the sociologist regarded as the founder of industrial sociology, who was a professor of Industrial Relations at the Harvard Business School.

The huge Hawthorne plant of Western Electric had adopted Tayloristic practices in totality. Workers were guided in their work by supervisors, and they were rewarded when productivity increased. They were given proper rest and the dining facilities were good and reasonably priced. Despite all these facilities, it was found that productivity was falling. Whenever some facilities were provided or the existing facilities were improved, productivity showed an increase. However, after a few weeks or months, the situation was back to square one.

The management was quite confused about this. They had tried various positive measures but these helped only for a short period of time. It then decided to approach Prof. Mayo to help them out. The study was known as the Hawthorne experiment. Mayo and his team started their work in 1927 and ended in 1932. During this period, the team had many hits and misses in their investigations.

Mayo's team started with the assumptions of scientific management. They tried to improve the work environment and also provide incentives to workers for raising production. A group of workers was selected and the lighting was improved. It was found that soon after this change, productivity increased. However, shortly afterwards, it was found that productivity of workers in other groups also increased. This appeared puzzling for the team. They tried to establish a relationship between other factors such as length and frequency of rest periods, monetary incentives, better meals, etc. The results were inconclusive because there seemed to be no clear relation between productivity and the incentives offered.

The team then selected two girls working on the assembly line manufacturing electrical components. They asked these girls to form their own working groups and start work. Changes were introduced in the working conditions. The rest periods were increased and the workers were also given the freedom to improvise on their activities. Facilities such as free meals, better lighting, etc., were introduced. This resulted in an increase in productivity. The next task was of trying to isolate the factor(s) responsible for this increase. This was sought to be done by withdrawing all facilities for a specific period. The work could be then observed and after the period was over, the facilities could be reintroduced one by one. This would help in finding out which of the facilities were responsible for the increase in productivity.

The production team withdrew the facilities for a period of twelve weeks. To their bewilderment, they found that despite the withdrawal, productivity continued to rise. It later dawned on them that since the girls could form their own team, their enthusiasm had increased. They were more at ease while doing their work, because they were also allowed to improvise. Hence, to them, work was no longer a monotonous carrying out of the supervisor's orders: they could think of themselves as responsible human beings. This was an important lesson that the team learnt. Mayo then changed the direction of his research and, instead of stressing on the principles of scientific management, examined the workers' attitude towards work and their behaviour as members of informal work groups.

The first experiment was carried out in the bank wiring observation room, 'bank wiring' referring to the attachment of wires to switches for certain parts of telephone equipment. This comprised wiremen who connected wires to the terminals and solderers who each soldered the work of the wiremen. In addition, there were two inspectors who tested and completed the job. The output of each person was carefully measured and tests were conducted to measure their skills and mental abilities. The researchers were surprised to note that there was no connection between the results of the tests and the output of the workers. A similar experiment was carried out with regard to the workers' pay. The team introduced the concept of incentives to the group. The pay of each worker was in accordance with the efficiency of his group: the more productive the group, the higher would be the pay. They found that this experiment too failed. They had assumed that each individual worker could maximise their output in terms of their capabilities. In reality, it was observed that the individual worker restricted their output so as to maintain a uniform weekly rate of production for the group.

The team also found that each group set up its own norms of production based on what it defined as the basic wage. In other words, it was the income which each worker defined as a fair day's wage. The workers' groups did not follow the standards set by management for increasing production and wages; it was their standards that determined the output. In such a situation, providing incentives to individuals would fail. The individual worker was more loyal to the informal group and was governed by the norms set by the group. Hence if the group decided that the productivity would increase, all its members would follow suit. If any member disobeyed these norms, s/he would be ostracised as a 'chiseller' (one who hinders the group's production standards). Similarly, if the group decided on a particular target and one worker worked harder to achieve more, they would be called 'rate-buster'. In both cases, the concerned workers were defying the norms set by the group.

The team came to the conclusion that productivity was determined not through incentives to individual workers but by respecting the work-group. The main incentive given to the work-group was in terms of consultation and assessing what their aspirations were. The study realised the importance of the informal group in the production process. This was an important lesson because the worker should not be looked at as some instrument in production, but as a thinking individual whose ideas are determined by the interactions they have with their co-workers. This also meant that management must consult workers in matters relating to production. Later, when Mayo wrote his book, *Social Problems of an Industrial Civilization*, he emphasised that consultation with workers regarding the work hours, rest, and improvement in working conditions was absolutely necessary for maintaining industrial harmony and higher productivity. These activities would increase the sense of belonging of the worker.

Stuart Chase, a member of the Human Relations team, wrote in his book, *Men at Work*, that the factory performs two major tasks. The economic task was of producing goods (Rose 1994). Every factory would like to increase its production and this is a very important economic task. The second task was a social one. He stressed that an equally important role of the factory was of creating and distributing human satisfaction among the various people in it. Unfortunately, he asserted, managerial experts spent more time in analysing factors related to production. The Hawthorne experiment showed that the two were inseparable.

F. J. Roethlisberger and W. J. Dickson who were also part of the team wrote a detailed report in their book, *Management and Worker* (ibid). They stressed that the behaviour of individual workers 'could not be understood without considering the informal organising of the group.' Informal groups are important as they meet many of these needs and the workers should also become a part in the decision-making process. The informal organisation becomes important to the worker as it formulates norms which the workers abide by which may be different from formal norms but they regulate performance of the workers. The worker is thus dependent on other members of their group for meeting the needs of production.

Both Taylorism and Fordism had focused their attention on improving the individual worker. They assumed that the individual worker would work harder if he/she was assured that he/she would be rewarded for this. The Hawthorne experiment showed that this was incorrect. It was not the individual but the group which decided on the workers' behaviour. Rewards given to individual workers would have no effect unless these are ratified by the group.

Basic Characteristics of Human Relations

Based on the elaboration of the HR approach in the above section, we can summarise it in the following manner:

1. Managers and workers have a mutual interest in promoting production. These interests are not identical in the sense that both hold the same interest for there may be conflict between the two, as also between groups of workers. Hence, neither side should assume that their aims and goals are identical. They must accept that there is commonality but not 'commonness'. The main point is that if both sides agree that there are common goals, this would create grounds for solving problems together instead of creating problems for each other.
2. Though HR stresses the role of the work group, it does not deny the role of the individual worker. The group cannot act on its own for it is not a collective that can take decisions on its own. Leadership in a group is important, because it is the leader who encourages others to take initiatives. The leader shapes the group's behaviour and helps to initiate new steps by motivating the group members. This is a vital aspect of group behaviour. There could be differences among individuals but these could be sorted out by the leadership. Therefore another key point of the HR approach is the role of the leadership within the group.

3. The third aspect of HR is motivation which is directly related to goal analysis. The company has a goal or several goals. This idea may be shared by the management, since it shapes the goal. Workers, on the other hand, may not be aware of the goal/s. In order to have inclusive development in the company, management must inspire the workers to share the goal(s). Workers must be motivated so as to create the desire to achieve a planned goal. The goal could mean anything from an increase in production by a certain percentage by a specific period to the industry's wanting to be the leader and excelling in superior sales practices. Whatever the goal, it cannot be achieved if workers are not actively involved with management in attaining it.
4. Finally, HR suggests that the most important aspect of work is maintaining human dignity. People, more so the workers, want to be treated with respect and dignity. One of the ways of achieving this is by ensuring that supervision of work is employee-centred and not job-centred. The supervisor must treat workers with dignity, only then will the workers be motivated enough to get involved in the goals of management. Job-centred supervision implies that completing the job is more important than looking at issues concerning employee satisfaction. The earlier methods such as Taylorism and Fordism were job-centred where supervisors were only interested in attaining the production targets set by management. They were told that all problems could be solved through monetary incentives. HR has proved this incorrect.

Criticism of HR

Though HR looks like an improvement over the other two approaches, there are certain problems in its implementation. The positive aspect of HR is that it emphasises the role of the informal group in industrial relations. However, the worker cannot be seen only within the precincts of the factory. Just as the group influences the workers' behaviour and choices, the workers' life outside the factory too influences their behaviour. Workers are members of larger communities. They have families; they interact with their community and with kinsfolk. They could be a member of a club or a political party. Life in the workplace is just one type of the different experiences they undergo. All these collectively shape their consciousness. The reaction of workers to the goals may not be the same for each one of them. Some may be influenced by the common goals set by the management, others may be suspicious of these motives. What happened in the Hawthorne plant may not be replicated elsewhere because of these issues. In fact, this is precisely what happened. This approach had mixed responses when it was replicated in other factories. In some cases, it succeeded, but in most cases, it failed.

From the above discussion, it seems that the major assumption of the HR approach is that workers accept management goals and they can be manipulated by the management. This may not be correct. Workers in general are not so gullible. Even if they themselves cannot understand a situation, there are other influences that determine their conduct. The major drawback of this approach is that it fails to take into account the role of trade unions in the workers' lives. Mayo could have considered it because he was conducting his researches when the trade union movement was taking shape in the United States but the earlier two approaches may have ignored trade unions as they did not exist in the US at that time. Mayo somehow ignored the existence of these bodies. The trade union as we know exerts a great deal of influence on the workers' perception of work. Hence, if we have a situation where the group decides on a certain path and the trade union takes a totally different view, in all likelihood the workers will follow the directions of the trade union rather than the group. In fact, the work-group itself would depend for directions from the trade union and not from the management in deciding the nature and pace of work.

Related to this issue of trade unions is the issue of collective bargaining and industrial conflict. Conflict resolution in most industrial societies can be attained through the intervention of management and the union. Similarly, in the case of collective bargaining, it is not the collective of the workers that bargains with the management for certain facilities including better pay, lighter work, etc., but the trade union which becomes the mouthpiece of the workers at such times. Hence, the idealised situation put forth by the Hawthorne team may not reflect reality.

Finally, the premise of HR is to treat workers with dignity. This may lead to more pleasant social conditions. Workers may temporarily feel that they have been treated appropriately, but it does not reduce the tediousness of the work itself. Hence, the HR approach basically tries to change the relations between worker and management without changing the nature of work.

Key Concepts/Definitions

Social organisations Social units predominantly oriented to the attainment of specific goals.

Power and authority Power is the ability of a person to impose their will on others even in the face of opposition, and can be legal or illegal. When it is legitimate power, i.e., power derived from a body like the state, it becomes authority.

Bureaucracy A type of organisation which is designed rationally to coordinate the work of many individuals in the pursuit of large-scale administrative tasks.

The Hawthorne Experiments These were a set of studies conducted by Elton Mayo and his team at the Western Electric plant at Hawthorne. The findings showed that workers' attitudes towards work were shaped by the informal group. Hence it was necessary to motivate the group rather than individual workers. This was different from the principles of scientific management and Fordism that stressed on motivating individual workers through inducement from management.

References and Readings

Blau, Peter M. 1965. *Dynamics of Bureaucracy*. Chicago: Chicago University Press.

Brown, J. A. C. 1970. *The Social Psychology of Industry*. Harmondsworth: Penguin.

Durkheim, E. 1947. *The Division of Labour in Society*. New York: Free Press.

Etzioni, A., and A. Etzioni, eds. 1971. *Social Change: Sources, Patterns and Consequences*. New York: Basic Books.

Etzioni, A. 1972. *Modern Organisations*. Delhi: Prentice Hall.

Gouldner, Alvin. 1954. *Wildcat Strike*. Yellow Springs, USA: Antioch Press.

Rose, Michael. 1994. *Industrial Behaviour: Theoretical Developments since Taylor*. Harmondsworth: Penguin.

Merton, Robert. 1972. *Social Theory and Social Structure*. Delhi: Prentice Hall.

Taylor, Frederick W. 1947. *Principles of Scientific Management*. New York: Harper and Row.

Weber, Max. 1947. *Theory of Social and Economic Organisation*. New York: Free Press.

3

WORKERS' PARTICIPATION IN MANAGEMENT AND SELF-MANAGEMENT

Chapter Highlights

» Working class movement
» Women's movement
» 'Co-determination'
» Works committees
» Joint management councils
» Indian labour conference
» Worker cooperatives

INTRODUCTION

Any form of management in work organisations involves interaction between employees and management. Work can be done only through such interactions. In the case of collective bargaining, groups representing different sides negotiate to find common grounds for solutions to issues of conflict. Another means of finding solutions is through cooperation between the two. This can happen if both parties, employees and management, cooperate and jointly manage issues. When such cooperation is for managing the enterprise, it is called workers' participation in management (WPM).

An important aim of WPM is to enable both sides to come together in order to increase productivity. Another aim is that of having peaceful industrial relations.

WPM was first introduced in Britain during the First World War (WWI, 1914–18), or the Great War as it was known then. There was an urgent need for increasing production to meet the war effort. The war required greater production of industrial goods for the armed forces. The government appointed a committee headed by Lord

Whitley, an expert on industrial and labour issues, to examine the matter of increasing production. He conducted extensive studies and had discussions with various people connected with industry and labour. He recommended that management must consult labour on issues relating to production. This would lead to greater involvement and commitment of labour in promoting industrial production. He suggested that factories and other workplaces should form works committees comprising equal representatives from both sides to devise means to increase productivity through workers' participation.

Whitley's suggestions were implemented by the government and works committees were set up in all factories. Soon, Britain witnessed a rapid increase in production. Workers' participation in management therefore had scored a strong point. These works committees continued till the war was over. After the war, production became normal as there was no need for stocking industrial goods. Managements immediately disbanded the works committees, which were successful when there was a need to increase production. In other words, management did not think it necessary to consult labour on issues that were defined as prerogatives of the management. It seemed that the workers were used by management in order to achieve its short-term goals.

After the works committees were disbanded, industrial unrest increased and the trade union movement grew stronger. However, there was no talk of consultation with the workers nor was there any move for institutional recognition of workers' participation.

The next major step was taken after the Second World War (WWII, 1939–45), which was much more extensive than the earlier war as almost all nations were involved in some way or the other. The war caused havoc to the lives of people and also led to the questioning of certain traditional beliefs. For example, when men went to war, production and factories had to be managed by someone in order to meet the increased needs caused by the war. It was then that women started manning the factories and exploring for coal and iron ore in the mines. This gave greater confidence to women that they were competent to work in these industrial areas though the ILO had earlier passed conventions that prevented women from working in factories at night and in working underground in the mines. Similarly, workers too became a part of the movement to defend their country against the onslaught of the Nazis. This in turn made workers feel that they played a positive role in society and were not mere cogs in the wheels of industry. These factors had important effects on the working class movement as well as the women's movement in the post-war period.

Till then, democracy in Britain was restricted to granting voting rights to a select population, usually males who had property rights. Women and those without property, which included workers, did not have the right to vote. After WWII, there were movements by women and workers demanding universal adult suffrage, i.e., voting rights for all above a particular age (either eighteen or twenty-one), which was eventually granted in Britain. This in turn led to movements for democratising the workplace. The argument put forth was that if workers were competent to elect governments, why could they not take part in the functioning of their factories? Thus began a new phase in the movement for workers' participation in management. The new move was qualitatively different from that of the works committees proposed by Whitley. The workers now demanded the right to formulate policies along with the management.

In Germany, in the WWI period, the working class demanded that there must be equal partnership of management and labour in running industries. The trade union movement in post-war Germany assumed militant overtones and strong socialist undertones in defending and fighting for the rights of the working class. The state had to find a middle path and 'co-determination' was introduced as a middle way between socialism and capitalism. Here, workers' committees operated at different levels in the workplace in order to enable a large number of workers to take part in decision-making. The system of co-determination was a form of workers' participation in management practised in West Germany after 1951. Employees have the legal right to participate not just in the management of the workplace but also in that of the company as a whole. This was done through elected board representatives. This model has inspired schemes in other European countries.

WORKERS' PARTICIPATION IN MANAGEMENT IN INDIA

In India, workers' participation is a far cry from what it encompasses in Western countries. There have been schemes for including workers but these are mainly at the peripheral levels. The first form of participation was seen in the Works Committees (WC) under the

Industrial Disputes Act, 1947, Section 3 of which stated that Central and state governments have the right to declare the formation of works committees in industrial establishments that employ 100 or more workers. These WCs would have equal number of representatives from labour and management. There would be a chairperson, vice-chairperson, secretary and a joint secretary for every committee. If the chairperson was a representative of the workers, then the vice-chairperson would be from the management's side; similarly, if the secretary was from the management's side, the joint secretary would be from the workers' side.

Though WCs were formed in some industries, there were no clear-cut rules as to what their functions were. In fact it was ironic that though the committee itself was set up by law, its functions were never defined. In the 17th Indian Labour Conference held in 1959, a tripartite committee was formed to examine the working of the WCs, and its suggestions were endorsed in the 19th Conference in 1961. The list of items covered was:

a. Conditions of work, such as ventilation, lighting, hygiene;
b. Amenities such as drinking water, canteen, crèches, medical and health facilities;
c. Safety and accident prevention: occupational diseases and Personal Protective Equipment (PPE);
d. Festivals and holidays: the committee would decide on which national events and festivals could be given as holidays;
e. Educational and recreational activities: libraries, reading rooms, sports, games, community welfare and celebrations;
f. Promotion of thrift and savings; and
g. Implementation and review of the above decisions.

It was made clear that WCs could not encroach on the functions of trade unions. Hence, they could *not* cover the following items:

a. Wages and allowances;
b. Bonus and profit-sharing schemes;
c. Rationalisation of work and fixing of workload;
d. Fixing of standard labour force, i.e., decision on number of workers required per shift;
e. Planning and development of work;
f. Retrenchment and layoffs;

g. Victimisation for trade union membership/ activities;
h. Provident fund, gratuity and retirement benefits;
i. Incentive schemes; and
j. Housing and transport.

In addition, decision on holidays for festivals and national events was removed from the functions of the WC and included in the list stated above.

Joint Management Councils (JMCs)

The wave of WPM had spread over Europe by the mid-1950s. In India too, this was discussed by the unions and the state. WCs committees were not fully geared to workers' participation. The Industrial Policy Resolution of 1956 stressed the need for labour being a partner in the common task of development and recommended that labour should participate in this process with enthusiasm. The resolution mentioned that joint consultations should be held by management and workers and technicians to deal with managerial problems. The Second Five Year Plan (1956–61), which is also known as the Mahalanobis plan (after noted statistician, P. C. Mahalanobis), laid the blueprint for industrialisation in India. Under this plan, large public sector undertakings came up in different parts of the country, mostly in backward regions. These included steel plants, heavy electrical and engineering, power generation industries, etc. The plan recognised that large-scale industrialisation which was undertaken mainly by the state in collaboration with foreign countries could not function smoothly unless all parties were involved. The plan, hence, suggested that workers were pivotal for the growth of industry and they must be given their dues by including their suggestions in managerial activities. It therefore suggested that councils of management should be established in these industries in order to ensure smooth functioning.

Before any policies or guidelines could be drawn up about the formation and operation of JMCs, Parliament decided to appoint a committee of MPs who would visit countries in Europe to examine how they had implemented schemes of WPM. They visited Sweden, France, Belgium, West Germany and Yugoslavia as these countries had statutory models for WPM. The committee also visited Britain, and they were warned then that a statutory approach may not be ideal as it would be legally binding for all parties through an act of parliament. Hence, if the scheme was to evolve according to the needs of the people, they should adopt a non-statutory approach. The committee returned and prepared some guidelines. Their recommendations were placed before the 15th Indian Labour Conference (1957). It was decided that there should be JMCs comprising representatives of management and labour who would decide some of the managerial functions in the industry. The labour representatives suggested that the government should frame legislation on this. The employers on the other hand insisted that since this was a unanimous decision, there was no need for any legislation. According to them, all three parties, namely management, labour and the state, were fully convinced of the need for JMCs.

The main objectives of JMCs were to promote joint consultations between management and labour which in turn would lead to trust between the two. JMCs were also responsible for adopting productivity standards and securing welfare and other facilities. They also had a responsibility of promoting training and skill development. On looking at these objectives carefully, the critics of JMCs pointed out that increase in labour productivity was the main underlying factor for introducing these bodies. Unlike the bodies in industrialised countries, the roles of JMCs were limited to the above-mentioned objectives. In those countries, the councils had a much wider role, which involved decision-making on production and marketing.

The composition of the JMCs was similar to those of the WCs. There would be equal representatives from both sides and if the chairperson belonged to labour, the vice-chairperson would be from the management, while if the secretary was from management, the joint secretary would be from labour. There was also a provision of nominating outsiders (managerial experts or trade union leaders from outside), but their number had to be restricted to twenty-five per cent of the total membership. The JMCs could also set up technical committees or sub-committees to decide on specific issues. The composition of these committees and whether outsiders should be taken in as members could be decided by the JMCs.

The JMCs had three basic functions. Firstly, consultation was a must. The council could advise or be consulted by management on issues relating to administration, standing orders, new methods of production, re-deployment of workers, etc. Secondly, it would receive information and could make suggestions after due discussion. This information could be based on the profitability of the company, the market situation, the situation in sales, the need for expansion of production, etc.; the JMCs could deliberate on these issues and give suggestions to the management. Thirdly, JMCs had to implement and monitor welfare schemes. They could also discuss issues relating to rifts in industrial relations and how to improve them. Many of the radical trade unions felt that JMCs tried to divert the attention of the workers from their basic issues of wages, bonus, allowances, etc. However, it was clearly understood that the JMCs could not replace the functioning of the trade unions.

DIVERSITY IN WPM

The JMCs could comprise shop councils or joint councils. Shop councils are those that exist at the shop-floor level where approximately 500 workers are employed. Large factories normally have several shops. The shop councils could be viewed as the grassroots form of representation. A large number of disputes over work and its regulation originate in the shop-floor level. Hence this council, if given enough authority, could go a long way towards resolving problems of workers. The shop councils were to assist managements in achieving production targets and improving overall productivity. They could also identify low-productivity areas and suggest corrective steps. Absenteeism was another issue to be dealt with at the shop-floor level. Besides these, there were issues relating to discipline, lighting, ventilation, noise, dust and reduction of fatigue (health issues concerning workers). JMCs were the larger bodies representing the industrial unit as a whole. Its composition would be the same as the others but the chairperson was the chief executive of the unit. It was expected to meet at least once a quarter and discuss issues similar to those of shop councils.

Worker Directors

In 1970, the government introduced the scheme of Worker Director (WD) on the boards of public sector companies and nationalised banks. The government considered this scheme as a step forward as a part of workers' participation. The largest union of bank employees,

All India Bank Employees Association, refused to nominate its members on the boards. Later, it relented on condition that the WD would participate in discussions only if they involved issues relating to employees.

The issue of WDs is regarded as the weakest of all programmes for WPM. Having just one worker representative on the board does not change decisions, even if these involve employees. Moreover, the member is bound by the oath of secrecy, so s/he cannot disclose all issues discussed in the board. These are issues that could help competitors if they are made public at inappropriate times. In the case of banks, where this is most widely prevalent, it is found that these directors are ineffective when it comes to putting across the employees' views to the board. In most cases, the unions have been more successful in making gains for their employees. The union the WD belongs to is usually the one that organises protests and strikes in the bank when the board takes decisions that are not in the favour of employees.

The scheme of WD can be successful only if the organisation had other schemes for WPM such as JMCs. Banks, being commercial establishments and not factories, are outside the ambit of JMCs. Commercial and service establishments in the public sector were covered by WPM schemes after 1977. Having just one member to represent workers in a large establishment cannot deal with the interests of the workers. The Indian National Trade Union Congress (INTUC) had pointed out that the scheme could be workable only if workers are given proportional representation on the board, explaining that this meant that half of the board members should be workers and the other half could represent shareholders.

There were other schemes for WPM in the 1970s. When a state of emergency was declared in June 1974, the Central government came out with a 20-point programme that was meant to form the basis of the country's development. WPM was extended to all units engaged in manufacturing or mining in the private or public sector employing 500 or more workers. The scheme provided for establishment of shop councils at the shop/ department level and joint councils at the enterprise level. Basically, the composition of the shop council and the joint council was the same, as in the other schemes, namely equal representation from both sides. The government stated it would watch the progress of these councils for a few years and would then decide on whether it should enact legislation. This never happened. The government, however, inserted a clause in the Directive Principles of State Policy that the state has to promote workers' participation in management in all industries.

In 1989, the United Front government of opposition parties was voted into power at the Centre. Ram Vilas Paswan was minister for labour and he framed a bill called Participation of Workers in Management Bill that was introduced in the Rajya Sabha in May 1990. The bill could never become an Act because the United Front government led by V. P. Singh collapsed after BJP withdrew support from outside. However, this was the first time that government thought of an Act to make workers' participation mandatory. The structure envisioned in the bill was different from earlier schemes because it had suggested a three-tier system instead of the two-tier system. There would be the shop-floor council, where both workers and supervisors would be represented to deal with day-to-day problems of the workers. The next level was the establishment council comprising a few shop-floor councils. This would provide greater representation of both workers and management in different levels of the administration. At the highest would be the board of management consisting of representatives of shop-floor and establishment level councils. Membership to all these committees would be determined by secret ballot. The labour inspector would ensure that there would be a monitoring committee to supervise the elections in an objective manner.

The Planning Commission too took a great deal of initiative in promoting WPM. The Five Year Plans, beginning with the second plan, had devoted at least one paragraph to the importance of WPM in increasing productivity. It had usually stressed that workers had to be encouraged to play a major role in the country's future. Growth of industrialisation was important for economic and social development and one of the most effective ways of achieving greater industrialisation was by making workers partners in this process. This seems possible only when the country had a planned and protected economy, with the public sector playing a major role in the country's development. After 1985, when the first seeds of liberalisation were sown, we find that the plans hardly made a mention of WPM. In fact, the seventh plan had only half a sentence devoted to it.

WPM: AN ASSESSMENT

The issue of WPM was important for involving workers in the production process. It would also empower them to make independent decisions and be more confident about their own capabilities. Most of the schemes in the developed industrialised countries of Europe gave much more opportunities to workers to get involved in different aspects of management, including planning sales targets, marketing, and improving labour productivity. In fact, many specialists have commented that the successes of these countries were due to WPM.

WPM in India was not even half as inclusive as its European counterparts. Most of the schemes were restricted to merely helping boost productivity and maintaining discipline. Objectively, when unions and workers realised that their only contribution lay in ensuring industrial harmony and nothing else, they lost interest in these schemes. Earlier studies conducted by the Institute of Public Enterprises in Hyderabad had found that in different participatory bodies, the worker representatives were much better prepared for the meetings, but the management representatives were casual and appeared not to take these bodies seriously. This shows that the schemes of WPM had created a lot of enthusiasm in the working class. They saw in it a means of participating in the future of their company. Their hopes were soon belied when they found that neither government nor management gave these bodies the importance they deserved. The fact that schemes for WPM were not statutory requirements made matters worse because it was not mandatory for employers to allow WPM. By the 1970s, it was not surprising to find that there were less than a hundred instances of WPM in the public sector. The number fell drastically after 1985.

It was said that the public sector was different from the private sector because everyone from top to bottom was an employee and not an owner. This has been reiterated by public sector managers in many forums and seminars on the subject. At the same time, senior officials were wary of allowing workers to participate beyond issues relating to discipline and productivity. Their excuse was that many of these issues involved decisions which were confidential and should not be known to the rivals or they were too technical for workers to understand. Hence, workers could not be trusted nor did they have the competence of dealing with areas that included decision-making and policy strategies. Therefore, it should not be believed that just because people were employees, they would all be treated as equals. In the private sector, there may be a vested interest of owners who would like to keep their ownership rights intact and not share these with workers or others. At the same time, the issue is not just of ownership but more so of power. Public sector officials who boast that they are not owners but employees are highly conscious of the power that they wield. Hence, just as families controlling private enterprises do not want to share authority with the workers and other officials, those in the top echelons of the public sector too show similar tendencies of not sharing with the workers the authority they enjoy due to their positions. We find that the lure of power is the main issue that prevents effective WPM. This could also be because we have inherited a feudal system that refuses to accept as equal with the rest those that are defined as being in lower positions. Perhaps the influence of the caste system has a bearing on such attitudes. The rigid hierarchy of this system that has existed for several centuries has had a long-lasting effect on our society, despite the changes taking place. The caste system believes in exclusion of the lower class because they are 'impure'; similarly, we rigidly believe that workers too need to be excluded from managerial practices because of their low status.

Multi-unionism is another factor that goes against the interests of participation. In India we have a large number of trade unions operating in a single factory or workplace. The infighting among unions can hamper WPM. Some public sector undertakings try to overcome this by having secret ballot for election to the different committees. The union getting the highest (above fifty per cent) of votes becomes the representative. In other undertakings, such as Bharat Electronics, the top two unions are taken as representative. This does not prevent other unions from wielding their power. The Industrial Disputes Act allows any union to raise any issue relating to work. This union, even though a minority, can take up issues of workers in the labour office and the courts. We do not have a system of determining the representative union (see Chapter 5 on labour movement in India).

WORKERS' SELF-MANAGEMENT THROUGH WORKER COOPERATIVES

Worker cooperatives are industrial or commercial organisations which are owned and controlled by employees of these organisations. Such cooperatives are fairly recent in India as compared to their long history in the more developed countries, especially Britain and other countries in Europe. There are a few instances of worker cooperatives in plantations, mines and industrial units. The workers of Sonali Tea Estate, a tea plantation employing around 500 workers in the Jalpaiguri district in West Bengal, established the first worker cooperative in plantations in 1974. In Tripura, five tea plantations are being run successfully by their workers since the early 1980s. In Dalli Rajhara, near Bhilai Steel Plant in Madhya Pradesh, there are around half a dozen worker cooperatives operating in the open cast iron ore mines. In Calcutta, now Kolkata, there are at least twenty industrial units that are managed by worker co-operatives since the early 1980s. The fact that these cooperatives have survived for more than two decades is itself a measure of their success.

Worker Cooperatives and Empowerment

Before discussing the role of worker cooperatives in empowerment, it is necessary to define these institutions and delimit their scope. Derek Jones, an American economist who studied worker cooperatives, noted five distinguishing attributes that could serve as a definition. These are:

i) They are autonomous organisations and not subsidiaries of another firm;
ii) Workers are able to become members of the enterprise, usually by nominal holdings of share capital;
iii) Formal provision exists for direct and indirect participation in decision-making by worker members at all levels;
iv) Worker-members, by virtue of their functional role as workers, share in the income remaining after payment of all other costs of production; and
v) The cooperative principles of 'one member-one vote' and 'limited return on capital' apply.

There are aspects of the above-mentioned definition that need to be stressed in the assessment of worker cooperatives. In these cooperatives, the workers are not only co-owners but they are also actively involved in the management of the organisation. Hence, while assessing the success of a cooperative these aspects must be kept in mind. One has to draw a distinction between ownership and control. The workers in a worker cooperative may be co-owners in the sense that they jointly hold the shares of the enterprise. However, the more important question that arises is: are they also in control of their organisation? Ownership does not necessarily imply control. It is possible that though ownership is with the workers, the actual decision-making powers may lie elsewhere. For example, in several government-sponsored cooperatives we find that the officials of the Cooperative Department exert greater control over decision-making than the members. Hence, though the members are joint owners they may not have effective control as major decisions are taken elsewhere. These cooperatives thus function not as independent decision-making bodies but as appendages of the government. The same may be said of cooperatives that are controlled by other agencies external to their membership. Such cooperatives may be controlled by political parties or trade unions. There are instances of cooperatives meant for the underprivileged sections being usurped by unscrupulous industrialists. In 1996, a massive cooperative scam came to light.[1] It was found that a few large leather companies had floated primary cooperatives of leather workers in order to corner the funds provided to these institutions as their members belonged to the scheduled castes. However, despite these aberrations, when cooperatives, which are directed towards the uplift of the weaker sections of society, are autonomous and run on democratic lines they can play a positive role in the empowerment of these sections. Some of the studies presented in this chapter underline this view.

Cooperatives and Social Uplift

Cooperation as a form of human organisation has been in existence since the beginning of civilisation. In a broad sense, the different types of exchange and reciprocal relations which existed in pre-industrial societies and which were crucial for survival of its members could be

[1] This information is based on newspaper reports at the time.

regarded as cooperative action. For example, the jajmani relations in Indian villages were forms of economic cooperation. Every caste in the village entered into a relationship based on reciprocity with other caste groups where the goods produced or services rendered by each caste were exchanged with members of the other castes. The village economy was able to function in this manner. These relations were not aimed at altering the existing economic relations in the society they operated in. On the contrary, they played a functional role and contributed towards perpetuating the system. Hence these types of cooperation are different from what we understand as the cooperative movement.

The origins of cooperation as a movement for changing and improving the economic and social conditions of the less-developed sections of society can be traced to the first half of the nineteenth century in the philosophy of Robert Owen. The first cooperative was started in England in 1844: a cooperative store set up by a handful of unemployed weavers at Toad Lane in Rochdale, Lancashire. The group was known as the Equitable Pioneers of Rochdale and its objective was to provide consumer goods to workers at fair prices. The Rochdale Pioneers saw cooperatives as a step towards a larger goal, namely, a socialist society characterised by economic democracy. Rochdale served as a model for many other cooperatives in England, the United States and the rest of Europe. The basic principles governing the functioning of this cooperative were adopted by the cooperative movement all over the world. These were: one vote for each member (and not for each share as in the case of joint stock companies), sale at market prices, division of profits among the shareholders on the basis of the shares each held, and limited interest on share capital.

The cooperative movement thus grew out of a need to change the existing society through an ideology based on egalitarianism, and it could not be equated with the traditional forms of cooperation. The early cooperators such as the Rochdale Pioneers and Robert Owen in England and Franz Schulze and F. W. Raiffeissen in Germany propagated the cooperative movement as an alternative to the exploitative nature of capitalist society in nineteenth-century Europe. Cooperation for them was a vehicle through which capitalist exploitation could be replaced by an egalitarian and just society. They envisioned cooperatives not as bodies that were functional to their respective societies but as instruments for transforming their societies. In this way, the objectives of cooperatives differ not only from those of private enterprise but also from traditional forms of exchange and reciprocal relations.

Cooperatives are not expected to function merely as mutual benefit societies. They have in addition certain social obligations which are spelt out in the principles of co-operation. While elaborating on this aspect, the Commission on Cooperative Principles, appointed by the International Cooperative Alliance, noted in 1966: 'Cooperation at its best aims at something beyond promotion of interests of individual members ... Its object is rather to promote the progress and welfare of humanity. It is this aim that makes a co-operative society something different from an ordinary economic enterprise and justifies its being tested not simply from the standpoint of its moral and social values which elevate human life above the merely material.'

Principles of Cooperation

Based on these objectives, the International Co-operative Alliance, the official representative body of countries having cooperatives (its membership comprising countries and not cooperatives), with headquarters in London, formulated six basic principles of cooperation that have been accepted by the cooperative movement all over the world. These are: voluntary membership, democratic administration, limited interest on share capital, equitable division of surplus, cooperative education and mutual co-operation among co-operatives (Ibid: 10). We shall restrict ourselves to those principles concerning participation and social change.

The principle of voluntary membership stipulates that any person who fulfils the basic requirements of the cooperative and who is willing to abide by its objectives should be allowed membership. A cooperative cannot discriminate among its membership as it is expected to include all those who are eligible. Similarly, a cooperative cannot force people to become its members. It is expected that the members of a cooperative are those who have understood and accepted its objectives. In cases of cooperatives of the underprivileged and marginalised sections of society, it is necessary for the members to understand the objectives and the functioning of the institutions. If they do not understand these, they will not be able to participate effectively. Hence this principle also presumes that cooperative education is essential for ensuring greater participation. This principle is frequently violated, especially in the government-sponsored cooperatives meant for the poorer sections. Over-enthusiastic government officers may force people to become members in order to increase the membership. The efficiency of an official of the cooperative department of the government is judged by the number of cooperatives he can initiate and the number of members he has inducted. This drives many of them to embark on mass membership without making these members aware of what the cooperative stands for and how it functions. In such cases, the general members remain passive and detached from the functioning of the cooperative. Either a coterie of interested members takes over the cooperative's functions or the government officials more often than not usurp these.

The principle of democratic administration tries to ensure that all members have an effective say in the functioning of the cooperative. This is the most significant principle of cooperation as it distinguishes these organisations from other enterprises. The objectives of the cooperative movement do not limit themselves only to securing economic benefits for its members. The movement is also expected to inculcate a sense of participation by building democratic institutions of equal partners. It can be distinguished from joint stock companies by its principle of 'one vote for each member' and not each share. Therefore, even if a member has a large number of shares he has only one vote. The attempt here is to ensure that control of the organisation does not lie in the hands of a few people who manage to corner a large number of shares. Thus in principle the status of all members is equal and all have equal opportunities for participating in the decision-making process. The Commission on Cooperative Principles observed that democratisation is important because a cooperative 'exists in order to place the common people in effective control of the mechanism of modern economic life. ... it must give the individual (only too often reduced to the role of a cog in that machine) a chance to express himself, a voice in the affairs and destinies of his co-operative and scope to exercise his own judgement (NCUI 1969).'

Democratic control of a cooperative is not restricted to exercising one's franchise during elections. It is a continuous process which is expected to encourage all members of the cooperative to actively participate in its functioning. The social implications of these could be far-reaching. For developing countries such as India, cooperatives can provide scope for increasing the self-confidence of the socially marginalised sections of society such as agricultural workers and workers in the unorganised sector. These sections have for long been isolated from the decision-making process because of the belief that they are incapable of deciding what is good for themselves. Cooperatives have the potential of institutionalising the democratic process whereby it becomes a continuous involvement of the people in its management. They can increase the self-confidence of their members by making them realise that they are capable of dealing with complex problems of management.

Collectivist Organisations

Building cooperatives as participatory organisations is not an easy task. Cooperatives are contrary to mainstream organisations if they are truly democratic in nature. Mainstream organisations follow the bureaucratic model where authority is derived from the top. The incumbents in the various offices in the organisation's hierarchy derive their authority from those superior to them. Decisions are taken by those at the top and the orders are carried out by those below (see Chapter 2).

The authority structure in a cooperative is expected to be substantially different, if not the reverse of, normal bureaucratic structures. Here the ultimate authority rests with the general body of its members. The entire administration of a cooperative is responsible to its general body and not to its highest executive authority. The Commission on Co-operative Principles observed: 'Since it is the members who bring a co-operative into existence and whose constant adhesion and support keeps it alive, those who administer its affairs and in particular, conduct its day-to-day business must be chosen directly and indirectly by the members and enjoy their confidence. It follows further that the administrators and managers, who are accountable to the members for their stewardship, report regularly in a business-like manner on their activities and submit the results to the members' judgement. If members are not satisfied, they have the authority and power to criticise, to object and in extreme cases, to dismiss and replace their officers and officials (NCUI 1969).'

A democratic organisation is something intrinsic to a cooperative. Authority is vested in the members who elect or appoint their representatives or officials to run the cooperative. These people have the power to exercise authority or take decisions, but this power is delegated to them by the members and not by a higher bureaucratic authority. While drawing a distinction between collectivist and bureaucratic organisations, Rothschild-Whitt observe: 'Perhaps more than anything else, it is the basis of authority that distinguishes a collectivist organisation from any variant of bureaucracy. The collectivist-democratic organisation rejects bureaucratic justification for authority. Here authority rests not with the individual, whether on the basis of incumbency of office or expertise, but resides in the collectivity (1987).' They admit that this may lead to a chaotic situation where each member may hold opinions which differ from those of the others. The authors explain that organisations 'cannot be made up of a collection of autonomous wills, each pursuing its own personal ends. Some decisions must be binding on the group. Decisions become authoritarian and binding in collectivist organisations to the extent they arise from a process in which all members have the right to full and equal participation.'

Organising collectivist organisations where power is decentralised is not an easy task. It is easier to organise in an authoritarian manner, as it requires less effort; decisions are taken by a few at the top and these are implemented by those below. A participatory organisation is more complex because before any decision is implemented discussions have to be held at every level and a general approval obtained. This is why in most cases cooperatives tend to take the easy way out by evolving an authoritarian and bureaucratic pattern of organisation. Decisions are taken by a few at the top (the managing committee or even a government-appointed administrator) and, instead of being a continuous process, the democratic process is restricted to the periodic election of managing committee members. This defeats the basic purpose of cooperation. A cooperative, as noted earlier, is not merely an economic organisation but it is above all a democratic institution in which ordinary members must have a say in the decisions. When this aspect is subordinated, there arises a contradiction in the cooperative movement, besides the violation of its basic principles as espoused by the Commission on Co-operative Principles. In such cases there is a distinction between ownership and control.

The owners, namely, the members, do not exercise effective control. Hence even if such organisations were financially successful they would still not qualify as being real cooperatives. In the case of worker takeovers, the problem is not so much of appropriation of power by the collective of workers as this is done soon after the takeover. We will find that this is true for most of the cooperatives, which we will discuss later. The main problem is of retaining power within the collective after the takeover. After the cooperative stabilises, there are possibilities of bureaucratic tendencies developing within the organisation. In most cases it may be found that the promoter of the takeover or the union leader (in several cases they are the same person) becomes the centre of power. Democratic functioning within the cooperative suffers, and soon the rank-and-file members become indifferent to its functioning.

From the above discussion we can see that democratic control by the collective is a crucial attribute in a worker cooperative. The main means of achieving this control is through worker-members' participation at every level of decision-making. This can be achieved partly by educating the worker-members on the principles of cooperation and the objectives of the cooperative movement. Cooperative education will help the workers understand the significance of the cooperative in changing their lives; in transforming them from mere executors of orders passed from the top to becoming empowered to give the orders which are to be followed by all. At the same time it should be noted that there can be no cut-and-dried system of democratic control. Each cooperative needs to evolve its own means of involving its rank and file in its decision-making process. These means can be worked out through the concrete situation of the cooperative and its members. In other words, there can be no magic formula or any standardised technique for ensuring democratic functioning within cooperatives. The cooperatives themselves have to come up with their own ways of ensuring that their organisational structures are conducive to a decentralised pattern of decision-making through which members at every level of the organisation can participate. This aspect should not be underestimated as the very existence of a cooperative or, by extension, the cooperative movement, depends on democratic functioning and participative management as these will ensure the effective involvement of the ordinary members.

At the same time, this task may not be as difficult as it appears. A system of collective decision-making exists in all types of organisations. This is however restricted to the upper levels of the hierarchy. In all organisations where power is located at the top and is delegated to those below, whether in the state sector or private corporate sector, decisions are not taken by individuals alone. Instead, small committees are formed among the senior managers which discuss the various issues before coming to any decision. However, as one goes down the ladder, collective decision-making gives way to an authoritarian system wherein orders flow from the top and are executed by those below. The point to note is that the basic unit of decision-making is not the individual but the small face-to-face groups that rule the corporate and bureaucratic worlds: the boards, sub-committees, executive councils, etc., which meet regularly to plan and execute decisions. The problem is thus of designing organisations which are technically competent but which also encourage decision-making throughout the organisation. Rather than being top-heavy, organisations must embody group structure throughout so that the different groups at various levels are coterminous with each other.

Conditions for Survival

In this section, we will discuss some of the instances where workers have taken over production and management of their enterprise by forming cooperatives. When a firm becomes sick, the main sufferers are its workers as they are left without any means of livelihood. They therefore take up the challenge of running the establishment and, in the process, maintaining production, through their own initiatives in order to save their jobs. There is some truth in this observation but it does not answer an obvious question: why are similar attempts not made in all firms that are sick or closed? Sickness alone cannot be the main reason for starting such ventures, and there are several other conditions that give rise to worker cooperatives. In most cases in India it is found that the objective conditions for their formation and survival are based to three factors. Firstly, the respective trade unions played a crucial role in mooting the idea and later in helping the workers run their enterprises. Secondly, the workers themselves responded positively to the idea and evolved their own structures of management and control of the enterprise. Thirdly, the state played a significant role in encouraging their formation. There are other factors too such as marketing of the products, and competition from private enterprise, among others. We shall examine each of these factors through the cases of cooperatives in tea plantations and other industries.

Cooperatives in Tea Plantations

The tea plantation industry in India is one of the largest employers in the organised manufacturing sector. Tea plantations employ around a million permanent workers and around half that number as casual labour. A little more than half the workers are women. Being in the organised sector, workers in this industry have permanent employment and are covered by the relevant protective legislation. At the same time, their relative isolation within the plantations, their low levels of literacy and the low wages paid contribute towards making these workers the less developed section of the organised industrial labour force. Yet we find that the most successful attempts at workers' control are found in this industry. These cooperatives provide interesting cases of how workers who may not be as developed as other sections of the working class are able to manage their organisations successfully.

The Saongaon Tea and Allied Plantation Workers' Co-operative Society in the Jalpaiguri district of West Bengal is the first workers' cooperative in tea in the country.[2] It was formed in September 1974 and comprises workers of Sonali Tea Estate who number about 500. The plantation has 500 acres under tea cultivation. It had been running at a loss for several years and its owners had closed it prior to the takeover by the cooperative. The board of directors had passed a resolution soon after the closure handing over ownership of the plantation to its workers along with all liabilities. Though no deed for transfer was executed, the cooperative was registered on the basis of the intention expressed in the resolution. The cooperative managed the plantation till 1979 during which time the plantation witnessed unprecedented developments. Inputs of fertilisers, pesticides and weedicides were increased and the workers took greater care in maintaining the tea bushes. The area under tea was increased by 10 acres in 1976 which cost the cooperative Rs 40,000. These steps helped in increasing production. The plantation's average yield used to be 850,000 kg green tea leaves and its highest recorded yield prior to the takeover was 900,000 kg. The cooperative achieved this yield in 1977 and in the following year it recorded a yield of 1,043,000 kg. It should be noted that unlike other new cooperatives Saongaon received no loans, grants or subsidies from any quarter and all the

[2] All the information regarding the Saongaon Tea and Allied Plantation Workers' Cooperative Society is based on the author's study.

above-mentioned development activities were carried out from the cooperative's income from sale of green tea leaves. At the same time it was able to accumulate savings of Rs 700,000, purchase a diesel jeep and a tractor, and build a warehouse on its premises. An unfortunate feature of this venture was that despite its impressive record the cooperative did not get any support from the Left Front government in the state of West Bengal when it came to power in 1977. In fact, in 1978 the cooperative had to stop its activities because of an interim order from a lower court as there was a petition by one claiming to be the new owner of the plantation. This case continued till 1998 when the Supreme Court finally disposed of the matter. Though the so-called owner was evicted, the cooperative was unable to take control as the state government had temporarily taken over the management through one of its corporations.

Tea is the only organised industry in the state of Tripura in north-east India and is important for the state's economy. Unfortunately, the industry has been in financial doldrums for long as the productivity of the plantations was low primarily due to bad management. When the Left Front government was voted to power in the state in 1978 with a huge majority it was faced with a number of closed tea plantations. The government was not in a position to take over these plantations as it did not have the necessary finances to do so. It therefore opted for workers' takeover instead. The idea for this came from Bhakta Bhattacharya, the general secretary of the Tripura Tea Workers' Union. He started the first cooperative in December 1979 called Tea Plantation Workers' Cooperative Society which set up a new tea plantation called Tachai in North Tripura district. Its members were retrenched workers from the region. After its establishment, Bhattacharya convinced the state government that some of the closed tea plantations could be revived through workers' takeover. The government decided in 1980 to allow workers of three tea plantations which were closed for over two years to take over their respective plantations after forming cooperatives. These were Durgabari in West Tripura district, and Ludua and Lilagarh in South Tripura district. In 1983, another tea plantation, Darangdilla in North Tripura district, was taken over by its workers, and in 1986, four more plantations were taken over by their workers. All these plantations, with the exception of Tachai, had been abandoned by their owners and were in a shambles at the time of takeover. All these cooperatives required financial assistance in the form of loans and subsidies for their survival. Their output was initially low and investments were needed for their revival. An unfortunate development was that when the Left Front lost to the Congress in the state elections in 1988 and a new government was formed, financial assistance to the cooperatives stopped because they were viewed as creations of the previous government. As a result, the four cooperatives set up in 1986 had to close down, as they had no resources left, but five other cooperatives started between 1979 and 1983 were in a better financial position and they were able to continue their activities despite the financial stringency, having become economically viable within five years of their existence. This is remarkable considering that three of these (Durgabari, Ludua and Lilagarh) were closed for more than two years prior to their takeover and the fourth (Darangdilla) was running at losses since 1973. These cooperatives were running at moderate profits even after repaying their loans. Their success in terms of increase in financial independence and production is noteworthy when one takes into account the condition of the tea industry in the state. These cooperatives showed that workers' initiatives can help in reviving sick and closed units despite financial hardships.

An underlying feature in all these cooperatives is that their unions at the unit level backed the workers in their efforts. It was the unions which mooted the idea of forming cooperatives in order to take over production. The unions in the plantations in Tripura were affiliated to the Centre of Indian Trade Unions (CITU), allied to the Communist Party of India (Marxist) (CPM), and the union at Sonali Tea Estate was affiliated to All India Trade Union Congress (AITUC) which has links with the Communist Party of India. After the cooperatives were formed, the union leaders helped and guided the workers in their efforts. A significant fact was that the level of participation of the general workers in the functioning of their units was high and efforts were made by their leaders to ensure this. The cooperatives in Tripura were comparatively small in size as the number of their workers varied from 100 to 150. Each cooperative had a managing committee comprising seven or nine members who were elected from among the general body of members. The local trade union leader acted as secretary of this committee, and all decisions relating to the functioning of the plantations were taken by these committees. Besides, the local leaders held regular discussions with the workers regarding the financial and production aspects of their plantations.

Their opinions were sought when important issues such as new schemes of finance or production were to be implemented.

The experiences of these cooperatives demonstrate in a striking manner that even illiterate and less-developed sections of the working class are capable of managing their own affairs when they are given the opportunity and the encouragement. Indeed, workers, for whom servility and submission to the management's authority had almost become a way of life, have been able to manage their plantations more efficiently than most professional managers. It may be recalled that the sickness of these plantations can be traced to professional management. It is ironic that the setback of the Saongaon cooperative (Sonali) was the precursor to its success. Had it not failed, the so-called owners would not have made a bid to displace it.

Cooperatives of Industrial Workers

Kolkata is the third largest city in India and is the capital of the state of West Bengal. This state was ruled by an elected communist party-headed government for over thirty years, which was replaced by the Trinamool Congress in June 2011 by a huge majority. This city had a number of worker cooperatives. A study conducted by Professor Alok Bhaumik noted that at least twenty industrial units of varying sizes were run by their workers, including a ship-building and repairing factory, a bakery, two printing presses, two publishing companies, a factory manufacturing spindles for jute mills, two factories connected with making high tension wires, and a unit manufacturing batteries for rail compartments, among others. All these units, with the exception of one, were taken over by their workers after their owners were unable to manage them, the sole exception being a cooperative unit manufacturing hosiery products. This venture was initiated by a minister of the Left Front government and its members were retrenched hosiery workers in the vicinity.

For the first ten years of their existence, most of the cooperatives were doing well in the sense that they were not making losses, though their profits were low or non-existent. All these cooperatives lacked working capital. For a decade after they started in the late 1970s, they could get loans for working capital from banks because the state government acted as guarantor. All cooperatives had repaid the loans before their terms ended. After ten years, the state government decided not to become guarantor for the cooperatives. The latter started facing problems because without working capital they could not sustain their business. Some of them depended on advances provided by their clients. Four of these cooperatives were dependent on government undertakings for their market for they supplied products to different government departments such as the railways, state electricity boards and other undertakings. According to the leaders of the cooperatives, they faced problems in recovering their money because of corruption; the officers wanted their palms to be greased before they would release their dues.

There were some common features among these cooperatives. Firstly, all of them were initiated by their trade unions, invariably affiliated with CITU, a wing of the CPM which was the main constituent of the Left Front. The support of trade unions is vital for the formation of workers' cooperatives. In all cases (the exception being the hosiery cooperative), the trade union leaders proposed that the workers should take over the units after their managements had shut them. The lead taken by the trade union leaders provided a broader perspective for the movement. The unions were able to draw in other sections of the working class in support of these workers. They could also negotiate with the government. The workers in these units could have not done all this on their own. The position of the unions was ambivalent in the beginning. They had favoured the idea of forming cooperatives as an immediate measure of relief. Union leaders were primarily trying to contain the problem of unemployment resulting from the closures but they also believed that this was a prelude to takeover by the state government. The workers too believed this but this never happened.

After its initial support, the state government became indifferent to the fate of the cooperatives. This was a result of changes in the Left Front government's orientation. When the Left Front was elected for the first time in 1977, it adopted a pro-labour policy. After 1987, when it was elected for the third time, its attitude changed. The government then tried to create an atmosphere in the state that would be congenial to foreign investment. This basically meant that the unions would have to show restraint in their dealings with management. It repeatedly assured foreign investors that labour unrest would be contained as the main constituent of the government, CPM, controlled 80 per cent of the unionised workers in the state through CITU. In this process, the interests of labour were side-lined. The workers' cooperatives were victims of the government's new policies.

This created bitterness among the workers as well as the local trade union leaders who were supporting the cooperatives in their area. These leaders, local level CPM functionaries as well, were a major source of encouragement to the workers despite the lack of support of the CPM-led Left Front government.

One positive outcome of this situation was that the cooperatives learned to depend on their own strength for survival, rather than on an external agency like the state government. Despite adversities, some of the cooperatives continued to exist, but at least half of them ceased to function. The reasons for the failures were varied but in three cases infighting among workers had led to intense rivalry among the worker-members.

Besides support of trade unions, another major factor for the existence of these cooperatives was internal democracy. Here, too, the union leaders played a positive role. The leaders met the workers frequently and explained the problems to them. Dissemination of information is the basis of internal democracy. In the aforesaid three cooperatives, the leaders tried to keep the members informed on all aspects of their functioning. The day-to-day activities and policy matters were handled through consensus. This ensured that all workers would participate actively in the cooperative's functioning. The successful cooperatives practised cooperative democracy. The formal means was through the General Body Meetings where reports were placed for discussion and policies were finalised. Elections to the Managing Committee (Board of Directors) were held regularly. The informal means were of holding regular meetings with the workers and discussing the problems faced and the possible solutions. Workers got more involved in trying to make their ventures successful.

The problems facing cooperatives are lack of adequate working capital and trained personnel, and the corruption involved in procuring contracts. Three cooperatives could not get loans from the banks because they needed guarantors. Though the state government had initially agreed to stand guarantor for bank loans, it later backed out. If these cooperatives had had access to greater liquidity they could have increased their production and employed more workers.

Corruption, involving kickbacks, is a problem these cooperatives faced in their dealings. The elected members have said that soon after they had started functioning, the cooperatives found that they would have to pay bribes to various state agencies for procuring orders and also for collecting payments after the orders were executed. Four of these cooperatives that were largely dependent on orders from government agencies were the worst sufferers as their payments were held up for several months at a time for they did not bribe the officials concerned to speed up payment of their dues. This meant that their working capital was blocked for a long period of time. All four had to close down eventually. By 2010, only two of the cooperatives, a printing and publishing unit and a factory manufacturing aluminium cables, were in operation.

We have seen that new types of management practices involving direct participation of workers did not last for a very long time—twenty-five years at the most. However, it cannot be deduced that these experiments were totally unsuccessful. Most of them failed because of forces beyond their control, such as, lack of working capital, lack of support from the government, and corruption. Some, like the ones that were victims of inter-group rivalries, were themselves responsible for their failures. Had the government provided greater support a few of the cooperatives could have survived.

Key Concepts/Definitions

Workers' Participation in Management (WPM) Cooperation between employees and management in order to jointly manage the firm.

Works committees Organisations comprising equal representation of management and labour representatives for deciding certain (non-trade union) issues in factories employing more than 100 workers.

Worker cooperatives Industrial or commercial organisations which are owned and controlled by employees of these organisations.

References and Readings

Bhowmik, Sharit, and Kanchan Sarker. 2002. 'Worker Cooperatives as Alternative Production Processes: A Study in Kolkata'. In *Work and Occupations*, 29 (4), Nashville, November, 460–482.

National Cooperative Union of India (NCUI). 1969. 'Report of the Commission on Co-operative Principles Appointed by the International Co-operative Alliance'. New Delhi.

Pylee, M. V. 1997. *Workers' Participation in Management*. Delhi: Vikas Publishing House.

Rothschild-Whitt, Joyce. 1987. *The Cooperative Workplace*. New York: Cambridge University Press.

4

TRADE UNIONS

Chapter Highlights

- The writings of the Webbs, Cole and Engels
- History of trade unions
- Systems Theory and Pluralist Theory
- Marxist view of trade unions

TOWARDS A DEFINITION

Trade unions are a product of the Industrial Revolution. They bear no connection with any earlier organisation. They were a healthy outcome of the needs of the workers and, as Allan Flanders (1970) noted, they arose out of the need to protect workers. Theory did not play a role in its formation. Unions have emerged as an important factor in production and distribution systems the world over. At present, they are looked at with suspicion by the middle class and by sections of the media precisely because they are so powerful in representing the interests of the working class. We must realise that trade unions are not homogeneous bodies in the sense that there are differences in the approaches of different trade unions. This is to a large extent governed by the ideology of the trade union. There are some political ideologies that believe that the interests of labour and capital are the same and there are others that believe that they are opposed to each other and there can be nothing in common between the two. We will examine these views later in this chapter.

Sidney Webb with his wife Beatrice Webb is regarded as the doyen of trade union history. They were academics who were actively involved in the trade union movement in Britain. Their definition of trade unions was regarded as ideal at the turn of the 1900s. In their book, *A History of Trade Unionism*, they defined a trade union as 'a continuous association of wage earners for the purpose of maintaining the conditions of their working lives.'

Another academic, also highly regarded for his study of trade unions, G. D. H. Cole, wrote in his book, *Introduction to Trade Unions,* that a trade union is 'a continuing organisation of employees established for the purpose of protecting or improving, through collective action, the economic and social status of its members.'

Though both definitions seem quite satisfactory, there are some problems. First of all, why is there a need for trade unions to improve the conditions of workers? In the traditional sense, this should be the responsibility of the employer. Hence it can be deduced from both definitions given above that employers on their own do not initiate improvement in the living and working conditions of their workers. The definitions should have included the role of employers too. Employers are to a large extent responsible for the conditions of their workers but not solely for there is another powerful institution that influences the lives of all citizens—the state. Both workers and employers have to function within the regulations of the state. The legal framework provided by the state forms the guidelines for relations between employers and workers. Hence we can say that the most powerful factor in guiding industrial relations is the state. Neither definition takes these two factors into account. This may be because the three writers (the Webbs and Cole) were ideologically syndicalists who believed that labour and capital were partners in development. Hence employers were never considered as an opposing force. We can attempt a more comprehensive definition.

According to this, trade unions are organisations of workers that attempt to protect their interests against the power of the employers and the state and its institutions. In a general sense, the objective of a union is to secure better living and working conditions for workers. In order to achieve this, trade unions must secure the rights of the workers. These rights could comprise seeking fair wages to better working conditions and perhaps facilities relating to work and retirement. Besides securing these rights, it is also necessary to protect them. Trade unions need to ensure that these rights are not depleted or eroded by other forces. In this way, trade unions try to lessen the burden of exploitation.

In his study, *Conditions of the Working Class in England in 1844,* Friedrich Engels tried to trace the origins of trade unions in England.

He noted that in the early nineteenth century, the labour market was unorganised and had little or no interventions from the state to protect workers. Factory production had replaced the artisans in the villages. Craftspeople such as weavers, ironsmiths, potters, etc., became redundant. These people flocked to the industrial cities to seek employment. In the cities, the number of job-seekers outnumbered by far the jobs available. Hence, there was a sharp competition for jobs. In such a situation, if some workers felt that the nature of the work and the wages offered were lower than their expectations, they knew that, if they refused, there would be at least double the number of workers willing to work at wages lower than those offered.

According to Engels, workers realised that their wages were depressed because of competition with each other, and that instead of competing with each other, they should unify and oppose the tactics of the management. They could not do this at the early stages because initiating any form of collective action was deemed illegal and punishable with imprisonment. Their activities had to be carried out under strict secrecy. This meant that these organisations could not disclose their identity. This restricted their growth. Secrecy impeded their spread as they could not be mass-based. The state would have suppressed them with brutality as collective action against employers would not be countenanced.

Finally the state realised that these sporadic and secret actions were harming production. It reluctantly allowed the formation of associations of workers by passing the Freedom of Association Act in 1824. After this, trade unions spread rapidly across the industrial townships of Britain.

A BRIEF HISTORY

The period from the beginning of the Industrial Revolution till the Freedom of Association Act of 1824 was rough and arduous for the working class. Any forms of association of workers were regarded as a conspiracy against the state and were dealt with harshly. This was true not only for Britain but also for other industrialising countries such as France, Germany and USA in the nineteenth century. The British parliament had passed two laws in 1799 and 1800 known as the Combination Acts which laid down that any combination of workmen was illegal and needed to be put down. The state used brutal methods for breaking these movements. These combinations were defined as associations of ungrateful employees who were bent on causing harm to their employers. It was difficult for workers, who were made to work in gloomy and unhygienic surroundings in the factories, to protest against their employers.

Despite obstacles, associations continued to grow clandestinely. These associations had some inherent shortcomings. Since they functioned underground, they could not cover a large number of workers, and those who were involved had to have strong ties among them as this would ensure their secrecy of functioning. In most cases, members were from the same community and could be bound together by strong ties. In USA, the most famous of these underground combinations were the Molly Maguires who were mine workers of Irish origin. They used violence against supervisors who were harsh on workers. These clandestine organisations were not democratic in their functioning. Since they could not openly protest they showed their anger by destroying machines, or beating up managers or supervisors in dark alleys where they could not be identified easily. These moves were effective in the sense that the state realised that it could not continue to subdue workers' protests by suppressing them. By the turn of the nineteenth century, the British Government started tolerating them, or at least it did not put down these moves with brutal force. There was a general acceptance that the Combinations Acts had to be repealed and they were replaced by the Freedom of Association Act.

THEORIES OF TRADE UNIONS

We have noted earlier that trade unions were a healthy, spontaneous outcome of the industrial revolution and that theory played no role in their formation. Though there was no predetermined design for forming trade unions, after they were established they could be interpreted theoretically. Theory deals with the diversity of trade unions and examines how they react to industrial conflict.

Systems Theory

The Systems Theory was put forth by John Dunlop. He developed the theory on the functionalist model, and the thrust was on maintaining industrial stability. Dunlop's basic contention was that both parties—employers/management and labour—want stability and they want industry to prosper, and this is beneficial for all.

The Systems Theory emphasised the internal properties of trade unions and the mechanisms that maintain stability. Dunlop adopted the structural-functionalist model of Parsons, who stressed that components in any social structure (in this case, the industrial structure) performed functions that contributed to maintaining stability in the structure. According to Parsons, the notion of stability is not merely a shared belief of management and workers. He stresses that stability involves a complex set of functions which when acting together can achieve the shared common goal of stability and integration. He noted that there were four sub-systems corresponding to four functional imperatives, in the form of Adaptation, Goal Gratification, Integration and Latent Pattern Maintenance (AGIL). Let us examine each on of these in detail.

Adaptation

Adaptation to the industrial way of life is crucial for successful functioning of industry. We discussed in Chapter 1 the changes in social relations caused by industrialisation. The industrial environment requires a new set of norms based on the changed social values. Adaptation as a functional pre-requisite deals with how unions and management take to the industrial system.

An important way of maintaining stability in the organisation is through rule making. Rules lead to regulation of behaviour and they also facilitate maintaining stability. The Systems Theory looks at rules in the same manner as the functional theorists assume that norms set the basis for social behaviour. In functionalism, social values determine the norms, while in industrial society, the new values that emerge are the basis of rule making. Hence, rules in industrial relations are those norms that are needed for maintaining peace and stability in the industrial system.

For Systems theorists, rules are mutually agreed instruments. The theory does not delve into how rules came into being but presumes that rules are an outcome of the need for all parties in the industrial system to want stability. There could be different categories of rules. Some rules dealing with relations between management and labour could be based on the expected behaviour of the two sides in the industrial system. These rules follow the guidelines set for interaction between labour and management. For example, there could be problems relating to labour; if the management is prudent, it will set aside one day in a week or month when these problems are discussed with the union. The problems from the workers' side could relate to issues regarding work or wages; the workload in a section may be high, or workers in another section may have been redeployed and they have problems or the shift timings may not be suitable to some. From the management's side, there could be issues relating to falling productivity and how to increase it, absenteeism, problems relating to punctuality, and so on. These problems need to be sorted out through dialogue because if they accumulate, they could burst out into the open and make the system dysfunctional. The discussions have to be based on mutually accepted rules. One such rule could be that industrial peace must be maintained for the good of all parties concerned. Hence we find trade unions in such organisations that take great pride in maintaining that they have never organised any labour unrest.

The main function of trade unions under the Systems approach is of maintaining order in the industry. They play an important role in serving as the voice of the workers. There are hundreds of workers in a factory with their own problems which, if not tended to, will cause discontent. Trade unions channel these different views and place them before the management. As it is impossible for the management to know the views of all workers, trade unions act on their behalf by putting forward their views.

Goal Gratification

Goal gratification deals with the way workers view the industry through their unions. The aim of each worker is to work hard so that they can get some success in their lives. This goal can be achieved only if there is stability in industrial relations. Unstable systems may cause frustration to the workers because they are drawn away from their main objective of achieving maximum satisfaction. How can this stability be achieved? The Systems theorists believed that there are political functions that deal with distribution of power. The hierarchies in the industrial system are based on power relations (please refer to section on Bureaucracy in Chapter 2). These hierarchies are necessary as they help the actors attain their goals.

Most workers seek to improve their position within the industry. If this goal is not achieved, it could lead to chaos in the system. Each actor would like to be better than the others irrespective of the costs, resulting in unhealthy competition between the actors. A regulated industrial system, where the hierarchy in industrial relations is based on mutually agreed rules is the answer to chaos. In such a system, the goals of the individual can be maintained in an orderly and organised manner. Hence this functional pre-requisite too stresses on stability and the rules of governance.

Integration

The problem of solidarity is a critical issue facing the industrial system. It implies that management and labour cooperate with each other, which results in integration between the two. The industrial system runs as a smooth conflict-free apparatus. Integration could be achieved through shared understanding and common ideology of the system.

It is important to see how individual roles relate to the hierarchy, and how hierarchies relate to each other. The industrial system does not comprise a single hierarchy. There are line organisations and staff organisations as well as functional organisations. The line organisation comprises the hierarchy from top to the bottom, while the staff organisation and functional organisations are vertical entities in the hierarchy. In other words, they may be occupying the same positions in the power structure, but at the same time, there could be tensions in these relations. One section of the staff, say, the engineers, may feel that they are superior to the generalists, which include people in public relations, advertising, etc. There are others in the hierarchy too, such as the medical personnel who many may regard as outsiders, as they do not play a direct role in the production or distribution process.

Among workers, there may be competition between departments. For example, in a textile mill, workers in the weaving section may feel that they perform a more important task as compared to the spinning or dyeing sections. In the army, officials in the stores section may be regarded as inferior to those who are involved in battlefield operations though they may occupy positions at the same level within the hierarchy. The main task before the management would be to integrate these sections so that it does not lead to conflicting situations.

Other problems of integration could be those of perceptions of authority concerning individual players. A union leader may assume the role of directing managers on how to conduct their affairs or there could be cases of those who are lower in the hierarchy wanting to play a bigger role. This could strain the process of integration. What should the management's role be in issues relating to participation of workers in managerial functions? These are issues that management has to solve with the help of the union.

Latent Pattern Maintenance

Latent Pattern Maintenance preserves the system against cultural and notional pressures. The culture of society may be contrary to industrial values. We can see this in the case of countries that started industrialisation long after the Industrial Revolution. Industry, as we had pointed out in Chapter 1, gives rise to new cultural practices and hierarchies. The ranking of hierarchies in pre-industrial societies was based on the social position one had at the time of birth. One's position in the hierarchy remained unchanged throughout one's life and this also was true for the future generations. In industrial societies, one's social status is determined through one's achievements. There could be a basic contradiction in these societies on these issues. The pre-industrial ideologies could permeate the industrial system, which could either lead to conflicting situations or to acceptance of the social values. Thus, in India, caste defines social status through ascription, but the caste system could lead to conflict within the industrial hierarchy as it is in many ways contradictory to it. A worker of a higher caste may not want to take orders from his supervisor from a lower caste because he feels he is socially superior.

Conflict in values could be seen through the working of textile mills in Mumbai in the 1930s, which is found in the work of Morris, the economic historian. Textile workers graded their positions in the hierarchy according to the type of work they did. Hazardous work, such as that in the spinning section where cotton lint could fly and be inhaled by the workers or in the dyeing section where workers come in contact with chemicals, was done by workers of the lower castes. These workers were prevented from working in the weaving section which became the exclusive right of higher-caste workers. They developed an ingenious way of preventing workers from lower castes from entering their section. They said that cloth made by any worker belonging to an untouchable caste was 'polluted' and hence they would not touch it. The reason they gave was that while putting the thread into the spindle, one has to wet it with one's spit and if the spit from a low-caste touched the thread, the entire cloth would get polluted. In this manner, we see how pre-industrial agencies such as caste permeated the industrial system which was expected to be different from caste hierarchies and where the notions of ritual purity or pollution were not supposed to exist.

However, another study conducted by sociologist N. R. Sheth in a Gujarat factory in the 1950s, shows something opposite to what has been discussed above. At that time, it was believed by Western sociologists that traditional Indian values such as caste were contradictory to the industrial culture. Sheth's study showed that the management belonged to castes that were higher than those of the workers. Even among the workers, there was a division of castes. He found that workers followed the management's orders because of the traditional belief that they should obey orders from the upper caste. Moreover, he found that among the workers, caste was used as an idiom to justify the success of some and rationalise the failures of the others. In other words, when some workers were promoted, the others did not envy them; because they were from castes higher than theirs, they deserved it. In this way, they also rationalised their own failures. According to Sheth, this led to stability and conflict-free situations.

Criticism

The most important shortcoming of the Systems Theory is that it deals with systems that are static. This is the common criticism of functionalism. However, we know that the industrial system is dynamic. By making the system static, the theory tends to focus on structures and ignore processes. Let us examine this is in detail.

Since the theory concentrates only on structure, it does not take into account what happens when structures fail in their objectives of achieving solidarity and industrial peace. The system is not free from conflict or dissidence. If managerial policies become aggressive towards the workers, there will be conflict sooner or later. Trade unions cannot doggedly stick to their position of avoiding conflict. Unfortunately, the Systems Theory with its emphasis on stability does not take such situations into account.

The stress on rule making has its shortcomings too. The stress is on formal rules, and informal organisation and its rules are overlooked. These are equally important if not more important for industrial relations. The Hawthorne experiment brought this aspect to the fore. We also dealt with this while elaborating on the criticism of bureaucracy.

Collective bargaining is not governed only by formal rules, for the bargaining process is influenced by other forces too. These could be outside the workplace or within it. For example, if there is a change in government and the new government takes a pro-labour position, the nature of collective bargaining may change. Unions may be more aggressive in their demands. The state of the economy may be another external factor. If the economy is booming, the union may press for higher demands. Besides these factors that are related to the attitude of the state and the condition of the economy, there are a host of other factors as well. These could be ethnic or religious factors that may divide a union, or a political party may vociferously campaign for removal of workers from outside the state. This could affect the relations inside the factory. The functioning of the union may change depending on the stand it takes. In such cases both sides, union and management, may adhere strictly to rules.

The final criticism relates to the belief that both sides share the same goals. This has been found to be incorrect. The goals of workers may be different from those of the management. Workers may want greater rest, less work and a decent life, and management may be opposed to that. The unions' negotiation reflects the aspirations of the workers. Industrial relations have to exist in this environment of opposition.

Pluralist Theory

The Pluralist Theory is in some ways the opposite of the Systems Theory. It stresses on decentralisation of power. The basic premise is that there are competing social forces, which have to be accepted by all; only then can they avoid chaos in the system. Pluralism is a combination of British liberalism and the views of Durkheim on ethics, values and social justice.

The Systems Theory had stressed on functional stability. The power structure was oriented from the top, just like in a bureaucracy; pluralism, on the other hand, is opposed to absolute domination by either management or labour for it recognises that unregulated behaviour will lead to chaos. It suggests that there must be a system of competing social forces which prevent total dominance and thereby helps avoid chaos.

This theory is influenced by Durkheim in some ways. These factors are:

(i) **Significance of ethics, values and social justice as opposed to coercive integration:** The Systems Theory and Pluralist Theory both believe in an integrated industrial relations systems. However, the difference between the two is that while the Systems Theory stresses integration as a vital principle, pluralism emphasises the ethical basis of participation. In case this is missing, integration will be through coercive means. Such a form of integration is self-defeating.

(ii) **Division of labour as a cardinal force in shaping social evolution:** Division of labour in industry should be based on ethics and values. Pluralism lays stress on the fact that conflict is essential for maintaining the system, and open conflict can be tackled or regulated through mediation. Flanders (1970), one of the founders of the theory of Pluralism, had emphasised the ethical basis of rule making. This emerges through conflict and the struggles of trade unions. It is not something given by the management through mutual consultation as asserted by the Systems Theory. For example, the benefits granted to workers such as health facilities, leave with pay, protection of employment and post-retirement benefits were achieved because of concerted movements/struggles of workers under the leadership of their trade unions. The demands, which later became rules, were regularised through workers' struggles and not through the benevolence of the management or generosity of the state. Both the management and the state regularised these measures because of pressure from the union. By fighting for the rights of the workers, the trade union protects their status and their self-respect. This, the Pluralists believe, leads to decentralisation of decision-making.

The Pluralist Theory holds that trade unions help in introducing order in industry. Labour and management keep checks on each other and together they construct rules and institutions for regulating conflict.

Trade union behaviour is influenced by institutional interests of the organisation: this includes the survival and growth of the organisation and the long-term view of its members' interests:

(i) **Economic environment and market conditions:** If the market is positive, trade unions will press for greater demands. The economic environment too is important. Both together contribute to the nature of labour unrest.

(ii) **Political Environment:** This shows that industrial relations are not restricted only to interactions between labour and management for the political environment plays a role as well. If the state is indifferent to the problems of labour, it may lead to two types of action. Trade unions may shy away from confronting the government, or they may take up a confrontational stand and intensify their struggles for protecting the rights of labour. On the other hand, if the state is pro-labour, unions may become more active as they may feel that even if the employer takes a harsh stand and is hostile, the state will come to their rescue.

(iii) **Technology and production:** Technology, as discussed in Chapter 1, is an important factor in influencing economic and social relations. Technological change is the key to changes in the organisation of work and in the increase of production. The trade union has to take this into account and see how best the interests of the workers are protected. Technological changes may lead to layoffs as some workers may become redundant, while others, who retain their work, may be redeployed. The union needs to discuss all these issues with the management. A lot depends on the stand of the management and that of the union. If either of them opposes the other, it could lead to labour unrest. Unions may resist new technology because it displaces labour, whereas management wants new technology because it is more efficient and thus cost-effective. If the union takes a rigid stand that is opposed to new technology and will not allow it at any cost, it could resist the change for some time. However, sooner or later, this technology will be introduced and at that time, the union will not be consulted for redeployment. The workers will lose out because their problems will remain unattended. Many unions, especially the Trades Union Congress (TUC) in UK, decided not to oppose new technology blindly. The TUC prepared a checklist which was followed by its member unions. The issues are many and complicated. If there is retrenchment, who should be retrenched—the senior workers or the new ones? If seniors are retrenched, the union can fight for a better compensation package. The younger workers could be redeployed in other sections. Hence, the key to settling problems is negotiations and not confrontation, at least in the initial phase.

(iv) **Accepted social norms and cultural values:** This means that Industrial Relations (IR) and trade union behaviour should function within a socially accepted framework, which can differ between social environments. In some countries such as France and Brazil, where trade unions are more militant than in, say, Britain, employers would expect militant trade unionism and would be prepared for its consequences.

Criticism

Though the Pluralist Theory critiques the Systems Theory as being static and not taking into account the informal organisation, it too has been critically assessed because of some shortfalls.

(i) A significant criticism of the Pluralist theory is that it assumed the power of all parties to be equal. This is not correct. The power of the workers does not equal that of the employers, which means that the bargaining power of the unions is lower than that of the employers. Equal power on both sides would presume that bargaining would be on equal terms. Pluralism has somehow based its analysis on this misconception. For example, if relations between the union and management turn sour, and the union declares a strike, this could express the power of the union. At the same time, if the employers are adamant and refuse to negotiate, the workers may be put to hardship as their ability to exist without wage or work is limited. Similarly, if the workers refuse to negotiate with the employers or the state, the strike may continue and it would test the staying power of both sides in coming to a settlement. In April 1981, workers in the textile industry of Bombay (now Mumbai) numbering about 2,50,000 went on a strike that continued for eighteen months. This was the longest strike involving the largest number of workers. However, apart from breaking records, the strike achieved little else. The workers had to lose because the employers were able to withstand the pressure for a longer period. An aspect of this issue of equal power is that there is an assumption that the state is neutral, which is far from the truth. In most cases of conflict between labour and management, especially the major ones, the state does not play a role in supporting one side or the other. In very few cases does it support the employees. The textile strike mentioned above was successful for the employers mainly because of the support it got from the state. This gave a boost to the employers not to negotiate with the union on basic issues. In fact the most important issue for the workers was de-recognition of their representative union, namely, the Rashtriya Mill Mazdur Sangh (RMMS). Workers, especially the younger ones, had accused this union of not representing their interests and conniving with the employers in affecting the interests of textile mill workers adversely. Though an overwhelming majority of workers supported the strike which was initiated by a rival union, Maharashtra Girni Kamgar Union, neither the state nor the employers were willing to give in to their demand. The union was affiliated to INTUC (please see next chapter) which in turn is close to the ruling Congress Party which was in power in the state.

(ii) Pluralism does not take into account the material basis of conflict. Conflicts are not cultural or based on social prejudices but go much deeper. Social or cultural factors can be overcome and bridged but it is more difficult to resolve the material basis of conflict. The opposing interests of labour and capital are particularly difficult to bridge. Capital insists on profits, which can be achieved by increasing the pressure on labour to produce more. Labour, on the other hand, would like to decrease the workload and get more leisure time besides increasing wages. These objectives are opposed to each other. For example, if a firm wants to decrease prices of its products so that it can sell more, it will try to reduce labour costs or increase its productivity, both of which would result in sacrifices by workers, who might argue that if the firm reduces profit margins it could cut prices. The labourers' argument will run thus: why should we make sacrifices when we do not gain anything?

The above-mentioned are the fundamental differences between labour and capital which can be resolved for a short period of time but cannot be overcome. Despite this, pluralism stresses more on institutionalisation of conflict. This, the critics argue, actually results in trade unions being co-opted by management.

(iii) Pluralism lays stress on rules governing employment. Each organisation has its own source of authority and this leads to conflict as each applies pressure to persuade the other to make concessions. This is not restricted to industrial organisation but also to the wider political sphere, such as the state.

(iv) The nature of society is not considered, as the focus is on groups and their influences from within and without. Groups may be pressurised so as not to use full resources and there could be political pressures too. The nature of the political arena and the role of the state in shaping the boundaries are not considered.

The Marxist Perspective

Marx saw both danger as well as promise in the trade union movement. The danger lay in the fact that trade unions, more often than not, tend to be inward looking. They may be too preoccupied with local and immediate struggles against the might of capital, thus losing sight of the greater struggle to overthrow capitalism. In this sense, trade unions, even if they are influenced by Marxist ideology, may degenerate to economism (i.e., the reduction of all social facts to the terms of economics). Lenin in his work *What is to be Done?* made some observations on trade unions. These could be useful for understanding the Marxist perspective. Lenin noted that as long as workers fight for their rights and better conditions of employment, in individual cases, they remain involved in purely economic movements, such as demanding higher wages in a factory. They would be inward looking as they want to bring changes to their own environment. They could also ignore the problems of other workers in their own premises.

Factories or workplaces have permanent workers who are unionised. Besides, there are other categories such as temporary and contract workers. Temporary workers are those that are hired by the company for a short duration and they get neither full wages nor the security of permanent workers, while contract workers are those that are not directly employed by the company but are employed by labour contractors who are engaged by the company. They thus work as temporary workers and are not paid on par with regular workers, their remuneration being much lower. Temporary and contract workers do not have the same job security as the permanent ones.

It would be expected of trade unions to take up the cause of all workers, whether they are permanent or not. However, most trade unions prefer to defend the interests of only the permanent workers as they are their members. Normally, the temporary or contract workers are not unionised. They do not join unions because they are afraid that they may be sacked if they are engaged in collective action. A Marxist approach would presume that all workers who face exploitation are defended. When unions look towards the interests of their members and nowhere else, they are victims of economism. On the other hand, when a trade union that has its influence in one work unit joins hands with other unions to form a national or statewide alliance to change the conditions of workers throughout the country or the state, it becomes a real movement. It is a political movement because it tries to challenge the authorities of the state or it tries to modify policies. Such a movement is part of the overall struggle to control or overthrow capital.

Such movements can be seen whenever there are larger coordinated movements. They do not deal with firm or workplace-based issues. They attempt to change or modify existing policies or they seek to introduce new policies in favour of labour. For example, when workers in a factory under the leadership of their union demand a higher pay, this is economism, but when workers in the industry unite to demand a wages policy, it is a class-based movement because it attempts to introduce a new policy and in doing so they challenge the right of the capitalists to dictate terms.

The Marxist perspective looks at trade unions as having the potential of becoming organised agencies for superseding the very system of the rule of the capitalists. By undertaking class-based movements (instead of concentrating on economism), unions can help in creating class consciousness by uniting workers to struggle against the capitalists as a class.

Basis of Trade Unions

According to the Marxist perspective, there is a basic contradiction between labour and capital. One sells its labour power and the other buys it. It is through bargaining between buyer and seller of labour power that wages are determined. Labour is usually at a disadvantage. Traditionally, there was a stage in which the individual worker bargained for their wages with the employer. Trade unions, as we noted earlier, were born out of this situation. They try to unite workers as a collective unit, and not as individuals, against capital. The workers gradually understood that they had been competing with each other for getting jobs and, in the process, they were depressing the wage rate. Trade unions turned this competition into cooperation.

In some ways, any form of collective action by workers could be viewed as a positive step. Lenin in the same work quoted earlier had mentioned that when workers spontaneously oppose certain policies of management, they were not doing so in an organised and sustained manner. Organisation and sustained movement over a period of time are the two hallmarks of trade unions, and they are not necessarily creations of spontaneous action. However, Lenin explained that a collective movement that was spontaneous exhibited class consciousness in an embryonic form: the workers were upset with what they termed as injustice and they reacted to it on impulse. This however shows that the workers were willing to protest in a collective manner because they knew something was wrong with the system but they could not pinpoint what it was. This, Lenin thought, was a healthy form of collective action and it needed to be channelled through a permanent organisation like a trade union so that the protest could be sustained over a period of time.

We can thus see that criticism of the labour movement or of trade unions comes from within the Marxist perspective. It does not glorify trade unions as the sole messiah of the working class, and it makes a distinction between economism and concerted political action. Richard Hyman (1975), who used the Marxist approach to interpret trade union behaviour, is critical of trade unions because they are unable to look beyond the relations between capital and labour. Trade unions play a limited role in the class struggle, the main role being played by the political movement which tends to look beyond trade unions and mobilises all sections of the oppressed. At the same time, Hyman does not feel that trade unions can be denied their revolutionary potential of changing society. He felt that, by and large, trade unions were engaged in challenging capital but not necessarily in attempting to overthrow it.

Ralph Miliband, another Marxist sociologist, had warned that when trade unions integrate with capital, they become agents of the state which blunts their revolutionary potential. Most trade unions, even those with Marxist affiliations, are content in wresting some rewards from capital. Often, trade unions may collaborate with capital because of political reasons. Such trade unions may be co-opted by the state and they lose their power to protest. Miliband believed that trade unions must remain as protest bodies to protect labour even if the state becomes pro-labour. We can find several such instances taking place in India and in other countries. Trade unions in the former socialist countries were by and large co-opted by the state. Trade unions became bodies that educated the workers on the positive aspects of government policies. They also engaged in cultural activities like encouraging workers to see progressive plays and participate in literary circles. This might have sounded all right when the regimes were in place. However, after 1991, when the former Soviet Union and the Eastern European states started crumbling, their trade unions were confused as to what their roles should be in this changed situation. Since trade unions had ceased to protest they were unable to lead the workers against the massive restructuring of their economies that led to hundreds and thousands losing their jobs. Trade unions failed in their duties or lost their initiative to protest against government policies and so, in many of these states, the working class, in utter frustration turned to neo-fascist as also religious movements.

In India, we find that trade unions are invariably affiliated to political parties (please see Chapter 5). This affects their power to protest. For example, the INTUC, affiliated to the Congress party, is the second largest trade union federation in the country. Despite the number of its members and its size, INTUC and its affiliates rarely organise protests in states where the Congress party is in power. Similarly, the Bharatiya Mazdoor Sangh (BMS) which was formed by the Rashtriya Swayamsevak Sangh (RSS) in the 1950s is cautious in organising movements in states ruled by the Bharatiya Janata Party

(BJP). In West Bengal and Tripura, which were dominated by the Left Front led by the CPM, we notice similar trends in the trade union movement. CITU, affiliated to the CPM, is a fairly militant union in states other than West Bengal and Tripura, but in West Bengal, it rarely staged any demonstration against anti-working-class policies of the government during the long rule of the Left Front. In both states, the union collaborated with the governments to bring about industrial peace so that it would not deter those who wanted to invest there. Surprisingly, in these states, the INTUC which is normally a union that would fall under the 'pluralist' category became the militant upholder of labour rights.

We can see that the linkage of trade unions with political parties is not something exclusive to India. In most countries, trade union federations are affiliated to a political party. In the United States, the American Federation of Labor-Congress of Industrial Organizations (AFL-CIO), the largest federation of labour unions, makes no qualms about supporting and funding the Democratic Party. In Britain, the TUC is affiliated to the Labour Party. In France, the General Confederation of Workers (GCT) is affiliated to the Communist Party of France. In Italy, too, the majority federation is affiliated to the reformed communists, namely, Party of the Democratic Left. In Germany, the Confederation of German Unions (DGB) is affiliated to the Social Democrats. Hence, we can see that in developed countries too there is a strong link between politics and the trade union movement. The main difference between the situation in those countries and in India is that here, the political parties control the trade unions whereas in the West, it is the trade unions that control the policies of the political party. In Britain, for instance, when the TUC felt that the Labour Party was taking an anti-working-class stand in policy making, it decided to stop funding the party and threatened that the trade unions would publicly oppose its policies. In India, trade unions are dovetailed with political parties and hence they forgo their right to protest when the political party is not in favour of such action, something evident from the examples cited above.

A SUMMING-UP

We have tried to examine the main theories of trade unionism in this chapter. We have shown how despite appearing as opposites, the Systems Theory and Pluralist Theory have the same objectives of maintaining stability. Pluralism might appear more radical because it stresses conflict and opposing views, while Systems Theory talks of integration and stability as the prime movers of industrial relations. However, both believe that the industrial system itself should not be challenged; it can be improved but it should not be discarded. The Pluralists talk about conflict, and they also stress how conflicts can be institutionalised through new avenues such as co-opting the trade union within the industrial relations system or going in for other collaborative methods such as workers' participation in management.

The Marxist approach is often mistaken as a variation of the conflict approach. Both lay stress on conflicts that modify or challenge the existing system. However there are basic differences between the two approaches. Pluralism does not try and change the system but rather tries to preserve it. The Marxist approach, on the other hand, talks about the fundamental contradiction between labour and capital: all industrial conflicts have their roots in this contradiction. The only way, conflicts will end, they believe, is when the existing system of industrial relations based on the contradiction between labour and capital is able to operate in a system where capital is subsumed by a democratic movement of labour, which tries to overthrow it.

Methods of Settling Disputes

In most countries, especially the developed ones, industrial conflicts are resolved through interaction of labour and management. Labour is represented by trade unions. This is known as the bi-partite settlement of disputes. When a worker is punished for some fault which they may or may not be found guilty of, the union and the management try to resolve the problem through interaction of both parties. At other times, the demands of the workers are taken up collectively by the unions as they represent the workers. This is called collective bargaining.

In India, there is collective bargaining for resolving disputes but there is also a third party, the government, that calls for a tripartite settlement. The office of the labour commissioner plays an important role in resolving disputes. Dispute settlement methods are based on the provisions of the Industrial Disputes Act of 1947. There are various stages for settlement of disputes. When the management finds fault with a worker or group of workers, it initially warns them to change their ways. If this does not draw any response, the management may draft a chargesheet asking the concerned person(s) why action should not be taken against them for violating the rules. The worker/s or the trade union will reply to the chargesheet, and if the management is not satisfied with the reply the worker can be suspended and an enquiry held.

Conciliation can be done at the local level between union and management and also the government. The worker or management can take the case to the labour officer for conciliation. This is primarily a process of persuasion. Officials can only persuade both sides to agree. The labour officer cannot force its views on the parties. The process of conciliation must be complete within two weeks. If no progress is made, the labour official can submit a failure report. This report is important for any future course of action.

After failure of conciliation, there are two courses of action available to both parties, labour and management, one of which is arbitration. In this case, both parties have to agree to a person who is independent and neutral to serve as arbitrator. The latter will review the case and will give his judgement. It is expected that both parties will accept this decision as final. Arbitration is voluntary for both sides. Hence it may not be binding for the party that feels that the decision is not fair. However, once the parties agree to arbitration they cannot approach any other office for seeking justice. For the workers, if they or their union disagrees with the decision, the next course of action will be a strike. This is possible if conciliation fails and arbitration is not acceptable. The workers can opt for a strike within seven days of the failure. During this time it is mandatory that a strike ballot is held by the workers or their union/s. If the majority favour a strike, the workers must give a strike notice thirty days before it takes place.

The path that can be followed in lieu of arbitration is adjudication. This means that the dispute can be taken to the Labour Court by either party. Before seeking relief from the Labour Court, the labour department of the state government must give the go-ahead, and no dispute can go directly to the labour court without the approval of the department. This can happen only if conciliation fails.

If either party does not agree with the decision of the labour court it can go to the next level of the judiciary, viz. the High Court and then the Supreme Court.

We can see that the paths of dispute settlement are complicated and at times long-drawn. Arbitration may take less time to reach a settlement but this may not be acceptable to both sides. The path of adjudication grants more choices but it can be time-consuming. For a case to reach the Supreme Court, the worker may have to wait for ten years or more. Justice in India takes a lot of time and is not cheap as it involves lawyer's fees and a host of other expenses. This delay in getting justice hurts workers the most because they may not have the resources to fight long legal battles, while employers may have the resources to prolong the judicial process. The old saying, 'justice delayed is justice denied' may well hold true in these cases.

Key Concepts/Definitions

Trade Unions Organisation of workers set up to defend their interests against the employer, the state or any other opposing authority.

Permanent, temporary and contract workers Factories or workplaces have permanent workers who are unionised. There are other categories such as temporary and contract workers. Temporary workers are those that are hired by the company for a short duration; they get neither full wages nor the security of permanent workers. Contract workers are those that are not directly employed by the company but are employed by labour contractors who are engaged by the company. They thus work as temporary workers and are not paid on par with regular workers, their remuneration being much lower. Temporary and contract workers do not have the same job security as the permanent ones.

Collective bargaining A step taken by the trade unions on behalf of the workers to resolve conflicts with the management.

Structural-functionalist model This model looks at society as a complex system whose parts work together to promote solidarity and stability. In developing the Systems Theory (one of the theories on the basis of which trade unions were formed), Dunlop adopted the structural-functionalist model of Parsons, who stressed that components in any social structure (in this case, the industrial structure) performed functions that contributed to maintaining stability in the structure.

Line organisations, staff organisations, functional organisations The industrial system does not comprise a single hierarchy where individual roles relate to the hierarchy, and hierarchies too relate to each other. There are line organisations and staff organisations as well as functional organisations. The line organisation comprises the hierarchy from top to the bottom, while the staff organisation and functional organisations are vertical entities in the hierarchy. In other words, they may be occupying the same positions in the power structure, but at the same time, there could be tensions in these relations.

References and Readings

Clarke, T., and L. Clements. 1975. *Trade Unions Under Capitalism*. London: Fontana.

Cole, G. D. H. 1937. *Short History of the British Working Class Movement 1789–1937*. London: Allen and Unwin.

Dunlop, J. 1958. *Industrial Relations System*. Harmondsworth: Penguin.

Engles, Fredrick. 1973. *Conditions of the Working Class in England, 1844*. Moscow: Progress Publishers.

Flanders, Alan. 1970. *Trade Unions*. London: Faber and Faber.

Hyman, R. 1975. *Trade Unions: A Marxist Introduction*. London: Macmillan.

McCarthy, E. A. J., ed. 1991. *Trade Unions*. Harmondsworth: Penguin.

Polanyi, Karl. 2001. *The Great Transformation: The Political and Economic Origins of our Times*. New York: Beacon Press (reprint).

Poole, M. 1978. *Theories of Trade Unions*. London: Routledge and Kegan Paul.

Ramaswamy, E. A., and Uma Ramaswamy. 1988. *Industry and Labour.* Delhi: Oxford University Press.

Sheth, N. R. 1958. *Social Framework of an Indian Factory*. Manchester: Manchester University Press.

Webb, S., and B. Webb. 1894. *The History of Trade Unionism*. London: Longman.

5

LABOUR MOVEMENT IN INDIA

Chapter Highlights

- » Origins of industrialisation in India
- » Factory Acts
- » First trade union
- » Mahatma Gandhi's labour union
- » Industrial Disputes Act, 1947
- » Trade Union Act, 1926
- » State's role in disputes
- » Problems of the marginalised sections
- » International scenario

In this chapter, we will attempt to analyse the growth of the labour movement in India and assess its future trends. By labour movement we mean the ways and means through which labour organises itself in order to improve its working and living conditions. Trade unions are the most important organisations in this process but, given the heterogeneity of the labour force and its vast number, they have been able to mobilise only a small section of it. There are other agencies such as political parties, non-government organisations, and some grassroots organisations involved in this endeavour. We will start with a brief introduction on the trade unions and how they originated, and then deal with the key features of the trade union movement in its initial stages in India. This will serve as a background to the main discussion on the problems facing the working class, especially in the present period of structural adjustment and globalisation, and the means adopted to counteract them.

ORIGINS OF INDUSTRIALISATION IN INDIA

Factory production started in India in the early 1850s when the country was under British rule. The objective then was to export manufactured goods to markets in Britain. Factories were thus established in the port towns of Calcutta and Bombay to facilitate export—chiefly cotton textile mills in Bombay and jute mills in Calcutta. Later, factories were established in Madras, another port town. One of the reasons for setting up industries in India was that costs of production were much lower as labour was available at cheap rates. A couple of decades earlier, in 1839, tea plantations had come up in the north-eastern province of Assam, the tea being produced for consumption in Britain.

The existence of cheap labour was mainly due to two reasons. Firstly, the indigenous economy had been devastated with the introduction of colonial rule by the East India Company a hundred years earlier. During this period, the local crafts were replaced by cheaper imports of factory-produced goods from Britain. This led to the gradual ruin of the rural artisans in the country. The peasants were no better off as in many parts of the country they were forced to cultivate cash crops, in place of food crops, which were needed as raw materials for factories in Britain. Besides, the cultivators paid higher taxes due to the new types of land settlements and land revenue imposed by the colonial rulers. As a result, there was a general impoverishment of the rural population. These people served as pools of cheap labour when the factories came up. Secondly, at the initial stages of industrialisation the colonial government did not regulate work or wages. The workers were unorganised and the industrialists were able to make them work for long hours at low wages. Women and children were most affected in this system, as their wages were even lower.

The miserable plight of the textile workers, especially the children, caused concern among social workers. One of them, Shapoorjee S. Bengalee, a Parsee philanthropist and social reformer, tried to convince the government to enforce some legislation to protect children working in factories. He drafted a bill on this subject and sought the help of his friends in England for convincing the British government to pass regulations.

Meanwhile, the textile mill owners of Lancashire in England were unhappy over the state of affairs. The lack of any regulations on the textile mills in Bombay had helped the mill owners here to sell their cloth at cheap rates. The cost of production in Bombay was lower than in Lancashire mainly because labour costs were lower; the average textile worker in Bombay earned six times less than their counterpart in Lancashire. There was no regulation on working conditions or duration of work, and workers in Bombay, males, females and children, worked in the factories for *sixteen hours a day* or more. It was not possible to increase wages as there was no such provision at that time. Hence if there were restrictions on work and timings, more workers would have been hired, raising costs. The Lancashire textile mill owners pressed for government regulations on working conditions in Bombay. This move was not out of concern for the conditions of the Indian factory workers but because such regulations would lead to increase in costs of production of the textiles produced in India and help Lancashire compete.

Pressures from both sides led the Indian government to pass the Factories Act in 1881. This was the first legislation that regulated working conditions in the factories. However it had little effect. The main impact of the Act was in reducing working hours of children to nine hours a day. It provided no mechanisms for enforcing such a measure and it was left to the good offices of the owners to implement the provisions. Ten years later, in 1891, the Second Factories Act was passed that reduced the working time of children to seven hours and of women to eleven hours a day, while a half-hour recess was allowed for workers to take their meals. But there was no move to regulate the working hours of males and no regulation of wages.

Morris notes that most textile mills did not follow the regulations. The few that did resorted to paying the women and children less for the reduced time, which increased the burden on male workers as they had to work longer hours to make up for the reduction in their family income. Working hours of male workers were regulated only after passing of the Third Factories Act in 1911 which laid down that males could not be made to work for more than twelve hours in a day.

The industrial base in India remained narrow during the initial years mainly because most industries were set up for export of their products and not for the local market. Industries were thus largely concentrated in and around the three port cities of Bombay, Calcutta and Madras, and they manufactured mainly cotton textiles and jute products. The census of 1911 showed that there were around 8,00,000 workers engaged in the secondary and tertiary sectors, of whom 5,24,000 were employed in factories and plantations. The jute industry and tea plantations employed 4,00,000 workers, i.e., half the total labour force. The situation improved with the onset of WWI in

1914. The war created a need for industrial goods and the colonial government sought to meet this by expanding the engineering goods sector in India. During this period, the first steel mill was set up in Bihar in eastern India. This region has an abundance of mineral wealth. The railways, introduced in 1860s primarily to carry raw materials to the cotton textile mills in Mumbai and the jute mills in Calcutta, increased their network (Gadgil 1982).

Though the working class as a whole was exploited and subject to low wages, there were inequalities within this class based on caste. Morris notes, 'One who writes about the creation of an industrial labour force must obviously examine the relationship of caste to the process' (Morris 1976: 71). He maintains that there is paucity of material on the subject. However, he finds that the 'untouchable' castes were hardly present in the weaving section. Morris wrote, 'The explanation widely given for this situation in the weaving sheds is that whenever a weft bobbin was replaced, yarn had to be sucked into the shuttle. If untouchables were employed, other groups working with the same shuttle would have been ritually defiled' (Ibid: 79). Morris does not think that this is a convincing explanation. Besides the untouchable workers, there were Muslims who worked with Hindu workers in the weaving section and they too would be sucking the thread. Yet no Hindu thought that this defiled them. Perhaps a more plausible explanation is that workers in the weaving section were the highest paid among the mill workers. The so-called untouchable castes were late entrants to the working class in the textile mills. The others, caste Hindus and Muslims, were entrenched in these better-paid jobs and they had formed an alliance to prevent others from joining. If there were vacancies or if more workers were needed due to expansion of the mill, they wanted that their relatives should get these jobs. Hence, by raising the bogey of untouchability, the existing workers could effectively keep others out of the spinning section. However, this explanation shows there were differences among the workers based on caste.

The Problems of Labour Commitment

During the first decade or so after India's independence (1947), there were hardly any sociological studies on industry or labour. Sociologists, Indian and foreign, concentrated more on studying villages. It was only in the late 1950s that a few sociologists turned their attention to studying industrial labour. During the same time the issue of labour commitment was raised by some American sociologists. It was believed that the growth of industrialisation in developing countries was hampered by the unfamiliarity of the labour force to an industrial way of life. Two major publications, one edited by Wilbert Moore and A. S. Feldman (1960) and the other by C. Kerr et al. (1960), put forth this view. These writers argued that non-industrialised countries, like India, had features in their social structure that impeded commitment of labour to industry. These features include a closed system of stratification, emphasis on primordial loyalties, religious values, strong attachment to land, etc. Moore and Feldman noted, 'Commitment involves both performance and acceptance of the behaviour appropriate to an industrial way of life' (1960: 1). Kerr observed that a committed worker is one who stays on the job and who has severed major connections with land. These studies tried to compare the situation in developing countries with those of the developed industrialised countries, using the features of the labour force in the latter as the model.

The above propositions were general observations and were not specifically related to the labour force in India. They could apply as well to countries in Africa, South-East Asia or any other industrialising region. The implications were clear: labour in developing countries was not committed to industry because it had strong attachment to agriculture and because there existed social institutions which were particularistic and not universalistic.

A number of studies carried out in the 1960s, mainly by sociologists and social anthropologists, proved the contrary. These were all micro studies providing intensive qualitative data on the subjects studied. Richard D. Lambert (1963) studied workers in five factories in Poona (now Pune) in western India. While studying the general situation there, he found that workers, engaged in small factories where wages were low and there was hardly any social security, were prone to change their jobs. When these workers secured stable employment in large factories with higher wages, they seldom left their jobs. For these workers, factory employment implied life-time commitment; in fact, the workers were over-committed. At the same time they showed no signs of transforming their attitudes and social relations. They viewed their jobs in the same way as they viewed their traditional caste occupations where the specialist (the worker in this case) serves the patron (the industrialist). Lambert thus found that traditional culture was consistent with industrialisation.

A study by Sheth (1958) of a factory in the early 1950s, an important contribution to industrial sociology in India, was an anthropological work which viewed the factory as a composite (functional) unit. His findings were based on observations. Sheth found that rather than impede commitment, traditional culture could in fact promote it. Recruitment of the labour force was based on particularistic norms of obligation to caste and kin that were bound by personal ties. Workers accepted their responsibility towards their supervisors as a religious duty. Sheth observed that the functional stability of the system was reinforced by the caste system. He concluded that there was no contradiction between traditional values and industrialism.

There were other studies which explained the problem differently. Holmstrom (1976), in his study of workers in three factories in Bangalore, argued that the attitudes of factory workers in India are not very different from workers in developed countries. Over-commitment can be interpreted as a result of the general insecurity of getting permanent employment outside the formal sector rather than a carry over of traditional attitudes. Morris (1976), in his historical study of textile workers quoted earlier, had found that the turnover in the factories was high indicating that the labour force was unstable. However, he noted that this was mainly due to better wages offered in some of the mills and other employment opportunities in the city and not due to the pull of the countryside. Charles A. Meyers (1958) suggested that managerial policies were equally responsible for promoting or impeding labour commitment. When management adopted short-term policies of increasing profits through low wages and exploitation at work, labour turnover was high. His study of a cotton mill in south India showed that labour turnover and absenteeism dropped sharply after the management introduced welfare measures. B. R. Sharma's 1971 study of an automobile factory in Bombay found that workers who were engaged in monotonous, short-cycle work were less committed while skilled workers engaged in maintenance and tool making showed greater commitment to their work. In either case, traditional culture was not a barrier to commitment. The studies dealing with the problem of labour commitment were important contributions to understanding attitudes of workers towards work. We can now turn to other issues concerning the working class in India.

ORIGINS OF TRADE UNIONS

The origins of trade unions (TU) in India lie mired in controversy. Some believe that N. M. Lokhande started the first trade union known as The Bombay Mill Hands Association in 1880. Lokhande was originally a mill worker and all his life he fought for the improvement of working conditions of the workers. The Association he formed provided yeomen service to the poorly-paid mill workers. His crusade for improving working conditions in the textile mills earned him a place in the first Factories Commission, and the Factories Act of 1881 was passed on its recommendations. The Act, as mentioned earlier, reduced the working hours of children. There were other provisions such as better ventilation, better lighting, drinking water and toilets in the factories.

Labour historians like Chamanlal Revri and Sukomal Sen insist that the first trade union was started by B. P. Wadia, founder of the Madras Labour Union in 1918. Wadia was from an affluent family but he preferred to devote his life to the cause of the working people. He was moved by the exploitation of workers by factory owners and he decided to start a trade union on the lines of the unions in Britain. The first trade union was of workers in Buckingham and Karnataka Mills (popularly known as Binnys). His union was more organised than Lokhande's Association. While Lokhande did not recruit members nor did he charge a fee, Wadia kept a record of members, all of whom paid membership fees. This is why Revri and Sen assert that Wadia's Madras Labour Union was truly a trade union. Unfortunately, Wadia's career as a trade unionist in India was short-lived. When he organised a strike in Binnys in 1921, the employers appealed against the union in the Madras High Court. In a judgment similar to Taff Vale (please see Chapter 6), the court ordered Wadia to pay the company Rs 50,000 as compensation for causing loss through the strike, which he was unable to do. The company decided to waive the amount if Wadia gave an undertaking that he would not take part in any further trade union activity. He then went to Britain where he resumed his trade union activities.

A few months after the Madras Labour Union was formed, in August 1918, Mahatma Gandhi founded the Textile Labour

Association (TLA) or Majur Mahajan in Ahmedabad. This union is unique in many ways and it had an interesting beginning. Since August 1917, the mill owners of Ahmedabad were paying bonus to their workers of 70 per cent of their wages to compensate for the rising cost of living because of WWI; the workers used to be paid a pittance, and the bonus would avoid the issue of revision of basic pay. The bonus was treated as a form of deferred payment and it was not related to profit. In January 1918, the mill owners stopped paying bonus. This created bitterness among the workers. They demanded that they be given at least 50 per cent dearness allowance (DA) as compensation. The employers refused this demand and the workers on their own struck work. After this, the workers sought the help of Gandhi. They wanted him to intervene and strive for a compromise. He agreed to negotiate with the mill owners provided the workers scaled down their demand to 35 per cent, which they readily accepted. Gandhi, however, found that the mill owners were not in favour of any bonus or DA, but after a few rounds of talks they agreed to pay 20 per cent. This was unacceptable to the workers. Instead of continuing negotiations for a settlement, the owners declared a lockout. Gandhi then went on a fast to pressurise the owners to come for negotiations. The owners agreed to go for arbitration and in the end they raised the amount to 27.5 per cent (Revri 1958: 73).

After this incident, Gandhi decided to form a union that would work in accordance with his ideals of non-violence. The TLA was based on the ideals of trusteeship (i.e., employers and employees are trustees of capital on behalf of society) and peaceful negotiation with the employers. The union sought to protect the interests of labour through cooperation with the management rather than confrontation with them. Besides conducting its regular trade union activities, the union also conducted welfare programmes and educational activities, and provided medical facilities for the workers and the members of their families. It enlisted the support of the employers and other wealthy people in the city for funding these schemes. The union also went to the extent of supporting some of the employers or their candidates in the city's municipal elections (ibid: 75). This union had little or no influence outside the textile industry in Ahmedabad and it did not seek affiliation with any trade union federation.

Formation of AITUC

Trade unions in India grew at a fairly fast pace after 1918. Some of the nationalist leaders like Lokmanya Tilak, Lala Lajpat Rai and others wanted to draw the working class into the struggle for independence. Others like V. V. Giri and N. M. Joshi were keen to have a trade union federation that would represent the interests of labour in India in international forums. The International Labour Organization (ILO) had been started in 1919 and Indian labour could get representation if it had a federation. These two streams merged to form the All India Trade Union Congress (AITUC) on 31 October 1920.

Till the eve of Independence, AITUC remained as the representative of the working class with all shades of political forces, ranging from the communists to the liberals, under its umbrella. The federation underwent two major splits over ideological issues during this period. The first split occurred in 1929 when liberals such as Giri, Joshi and others broke away to form a separate federation over the issue of representation in the Royal Commission on Labour in India. The communists and the supporters of the Indian National Congress in the AITUC wanted to boycott the Commission but the liberals (known as the Rightists) wanted to support it. When the majority in the Executive Committee of the AITUC decided to support the move to boycott the Commission, the Rightists broke away and formed the Indian Federation of Trade Unions (IFTU). In the following year, the communists broke away to form the Red Flag Trade Union Congress. However, they re-joined the AITUC within two years and the IFTU decided to merge with the parent body in 1939 (see Sen 1979, and Revri 1958, for details).

The communists managed to gain control over the AITUC during the last few years of colonial rule. In 1942, the Indian National Congress organised the Quit India Movement. The colonial government arrested the leaders and they were imprisoned till the eve of Independence. The communists did not participate in this movement. They took advantage of the fact that Congress trade union leaders were in jail and they gained control over the AITUC. After the leaders were released from jail, they found that they had lost control over the labour movement.

Soon after Home Rule was declared in 1947, the leaders of the Congress decided that since the working class would have to play a crucial role in the new pattern of planned development, it could not allow the trade union movement to be led by those who would not fully support its policies. The Congress started another trade union centre which would rival the communist-controlled AITUC's hold over the working class. Thus the Indian National Trade Union Congress (INTUC) was formed in May 1947, three months before Independence. The remarks of Kandubhai Desai, one of the founders, make the purpose clear. While inaugurating the new federation he said, 'It is high time that those interested in building up strong trade unionism dissociate themselves from the communists if not for anything else to demonstrate to the world that whatever prestige and status the movement had was because of non-communist trade union workers' (Johri 1967: 10).

Apart from anti-communism, a more important reason was dovetailing trade union aims with the government's policies. Desai admitted, 'It is also felt by many active trade union men [sic] that with the advent of the country's independence, the trade union movement would have to play its destined and legitimate role of influencing the trends toward the elimination of political, economic and social exploitation.' The underlying meaning of this statement is that the existing federation, with its pro-communist slant, could not be a dependable ally of the Congress and its policies.

The formation of the INTUC marked the first step of the state in controlling the labour movement. Some industrial relations experts like C. K. Johri (1967: 11–12) tried to justify this by arguing that industrial peace was necessary during the period of national reconstruction, especially when there was a consensus that 'economic development must take place under the aegis of the government', implying that the government would have to play the role of employer in this system, and trade unions would have to considerably soften their role as an opposition group. Johri asserted that in such a situation the government of a newly independent country could achieve its policy objectives more easily if the trade union movement, or a major part of it, was ideologically aligned and politically close to the party in power.

The split in the AITUC in 1947 paved the way for further splits based on narrow party lines with the result it almost became mandatory for every political party to have its trade union front. When a political party splits, a division forms in its trade union front also, thereby fragmenting the working class movement further. Similarly, a new political party invariably floats its own trade union.

At the time of the formation of the INTUC, the pro-socialist group within the Congress did not support the federation and their trade unions remained with the AITUC. A year later, in 1948, this group broke away to form a new political party called the Praja Socialist Party (PSP) and decided to have its own trade union front which would attract the non-communist and non-Congress trade unions together. Thus the Hind Mazdur Panchayat (HMP) was formed in that year. The party's objective was partly realised as the Indian Federation of Labour, which was inspired by M. N. Roy, a former communist who later became severely anti-communist, merged with the HMP to form a new federation called Hind Mazdur Sabha (HMS). In 1949, the unions supported by the Revolutionary Socialist Party (RSP), a Marxist group having influence mainly in West Bengal and Kerala, which had earlier joined the HMS, decided to form their own federation, the United Trade Union Congress (UTUC). In 1952, the Bharatiya Jan Sangh a political party with a Hindu fundamentalist background, was formed and in 1955 it initiated another trade union centre known as Bharatiya Mazdur Sangh (BMS). Meanwhile, the socialists kept splitting and re-joining to form new parties. In 1965, a party comprising breakaway groups from the PSP and Socialist Party was formed known as the Samyukta Socialist Party (SSP). Its most important trade union leader, George Fernandes, broke away from the HMS to form a new Hind Mazdur Panchayat (HMP). Till the early 1970s, the most important trade union federations in the country were the INTUC, AITUC and HMS.

The split in the communist movement, in the wake of the Chinese aggression in 1962, led to the formation of another communist party, the CPI(M), or CPM, in 1964. Though initially the unions loyal to both communist parties remained with the AITUC, in 1970 the CPI(M) decided to set up another trade union body known as Centre of Indian Trade Unions (CITU) which took away a large section of unions from the AITUC, especially the ones in West Bengal and Kerala. The other pro-communist federation of trade unions, the UTUC, was also split when a splinter group within the RSP (which later became a separate political party, the Socialist Unity Centre), formed its own wing of the UTUC. The two federations are distinguished from each other by the locations of their headquarters in Calcutta (Bow Bazaar and Lenin Sarani), known as UTUC (BB) and UTUC (LS) respectively.

Apart from the working class being divided on the lines of political parties at the national level, regional parties too started forming their own trade union centres from the late 1960s. This process was started by the Dravida Munnetra Kazhagam (DMK) when it formed the state government in 1967 in Tamil Nadu (then known as Madras state) when it initiated its own trade union centre in the state. Later, when the All India Anna Dravida Munnetra Kazhagam (AIADMK) was formed in 1977, it set up a rival centre.

The year 1967 saw the birth of the Shiv Sena in Mumbai. In its early phase, the Sena claimed to represent the interests of Maharashtrians, more particularly the Marathi-speaking people in Mumbai. It was avowedly anti-south Indian and anti-communist. It formed its own labour wing, the Bharatiya Kamgar Sena (BKS). It was widely believed that the Shiv Sena and its labour wing had the backing of the industrial houses (most of which were non-Maharashtrian) in the Mumbai-Pune industrial belt to combat the communist unions which were very strong then. It managed to divide the working class in Mumbai on regional lines and it gained in strength. By the mid-1970s, BKS had become fairly strong.

The rise of the Shiv Sena was linked, to a large extent, with the deteriorating economic situation in the country. In 1966–67, the country reeled under a recession which led to a decline in production and subsequently to job losses. Mumbai, being the financial and industrial capital of India, suffered the most. The existing trade unions, including the communists, were unable to cope with this phenomenon as their traditional means of seeking redress, namely, work stoppage, mass rallies, and so on, were ineffective. The legislations granting protection to workers in the organised sector provided little solace to retrenched workers. The Shiv Sena was formed at this time. It aggressively asserted that job losses were due to the influx of south Indians into the city as these people were taking away available jobs from the local population. The Shiv Sena's influence over the organised working class based on this reasoning could not be stemmed by the traditional trade unions. It was only in the mid-1970s that Datta Samant (1933–97), a medical practitioner-turned-trade unionist, could put an effective check on the Shiv Sena. The methods used by Samant were similar to those used by the Sena unions to oust the opposition, namely, intimidation and violence.

Thus, the underlying feature of the trade union scenario is proliferation of political parties resulting in a large number of trade unions. Besides, there is a growing tendency towards unions being based on regional, communal and caste lines. There are also a number of unions created by people in order to get political mileage or other individual-centred benefits. Some enterprises, especially branches of multinational companies (MNCs), have their internal unions run by their own members. These unions are independent in the sense that they are not affiliated to any of the federations. They are called enterprise unions with their own strengths and weaknesses (see Davala 1995). While commenting on the confusing trade union scenario in India, an ILO report (qtd. in Venkat Ratnam 1994) notes: 'The early (post-Independence) splits in Indian trade unionism tended to be on ideological grounds each lined to a particular political party. Much of the recent fragmentation, however, has centred on personalities and occasionally on caste or regional considerations.'

We can see that the trade union movement, which was fairly united during colonial rule, stands badly divided. This has weakened the working class movement and deprived it of the power it has to challenge capital and the state. Quite often, inter-union rivalries are stronger than the conflicts between management and labour. Moreover, the mushrooming of unions makes it difficult for labour to get proper representation in the national policy-making bodies such as the Indian Labour Conference (ILC) and the Planning Commission. The government, in consultation with the ILC, has laid down three conditions for recognition of national trade union centres. Firstly, the centre must have a total membership of 5,00,000, secondly, its membership must be spread over at least four states, and thirdly, the membership must cover at least four industries. There are seven such centres which are recognised as national federations—INTUC, BMS, CITU, HMS, AITUC, UTUC (BB), and UTUC (LS). These unions collectively represent the overwhelming majority of the unionised labour force, but given the level of unionisation of labour, the membership is a small percentage of the country's total workforce. In the following sections, I shall discuss the problems of unionisation in the various sections of the working class.

TRADE UNION MEMBERSHIP

Apart from the problem of fragmentation of unions, the number of unionised workers is low. It is difficult to give the number of members of trade unions as there is no authentic data on this. The Registrar of Trade Unions is expected to maintain records of union membership based on the returns submitted by the registered unions. However, these figures are not reliable as there may be cases of underestimation, when unions do not send their returns regularly, or overestimation of membership. The membership of unions is restricted mainly to the 8 per cent of workers who belong to the organised sector. The rate of unionisation in the public sector, which employs 70 per cent of workers in the organised sector, is estimated to be around 80 per cent, while unionisation in the private sector is much lower. Taking into account these factors, the percentage of unionised workers in the organised sector should be around 50 per cent. Membership in unions in the unorganised sector is small, with the Self-Employed Women's Association (SEWA), the largest union, having a membership of a little over 10,00,000 in 2010, and the total percentage of unionised workers should be around 5 per cent of the labour force in this segment. The number of employees covered by collective wage agreements works out to a mere 1 per cent of the labour force (Venkat Ratnam 1994: 6). Nevertheless, the unionised section of workers in the organised sector is extremely vocal and is able to wrest more benefits from the employers as well as the government. Table 5.1 shows the trade union membership compiled by Subesh Das. The scholar has collected his data from the state labour offices and compiled them in the table. It is quite clear from the data that the total membership of 24.88 million (2.49 crore) is just a small part of the total workforce of 467 million (46.7 crore) in 2002.

Recent figures on trade union membership show that despite liberalisation the unions have experienced high increase in membership. We find from the Labour Department figures for 2002 that unions on an average have increased their membership five times over that in 1987. Besides the general increase, there have been sharp increases in membership in all the national federations. BMS had the largest numbers in the earlier verification and it has retained its position, the increase being dramatic, from around 1.48 million in 1987 to 6.22

million in 2002. It has left its nearest rival INTUC far behind with a membership of 3.95 million (from around 2.69 million members earlier). AITUC membership has grown from around 0.94 million in 1987 to 2.68 million in 2002. The other central trade union federations are HMS, CITU, UTUC and SEWA.

TABLE 5.1: Membership of Central Trade Unions, 1980–2002 (Millions)

Union/Year	1980	1989	2002
INTUC	3.51	2.69	3.95
BMS	1.88	3.12	6.22
HMS	1.84	1.48	3.34
UTUC (LS)	1.23	0.84	1.37
UTUC	0.61	0.58	0.61
NLO	0.41	0.14	0
TUCC	0.27	0.23	0.73
NFITU	0.53	0.53	0.6
AITUC	1.06	0.94	3.44
CITU	1.03	1.78	2.68
Others	–	–	1.94
Total	12.39	12.33	24.88

Source: Subesh Das 2010: 58.

STATE INTERVENTION IN THE LABOUR MOVEMENT: NATURE OF LABOUR LEGISLATIONS

The colonial government had a covert pro-employer bias. After Independence, the government tried to rectify the imbalance by passing a series of protective legislations. The Industrial Disputes Act (ID Act) of 1947 attempted to protect workers by curbing some of the rights of the employers such as the right to terminate employment, shut down establishments arbitrarily, and so on. It also recognised trade unions as an essential feature of industrial relations. In addition, a number of legislations covering minimum wages, bonus, disciplinary procedures, recruitment policies, and so on, which grant security to the workers, were passed in order to ensure that the workers, who were weaker compared to the collective strength of the employers, could get security and justice.

At the same time, government intervention, especially through the labour department, increased considerably. On viewing industrial relations in the historical context, we find that labour laws change along with the strength of the labour movement. If the labour movement is strong, there is an attempt by the state to subvert its strength or clip its wings. Thus, the ID Act, which forms the core of industrial relations in India, was based on the Defence of India Rules, framed by the British during WWII. At that time, the colonial state was interested in ensuring smooth flow of production to meet the war effort. This could be done only if labour was made to believe that means of grievance redressal existed. At the same time, care had to be taken to ensure that workers did not go on strike as that would disrupt production.

Industrial Disputes Act (1947)

The Industrial Disputes Act is important because it is the first piece of legislation that affected labour soon after India became independent. Perhaps it was the view of the new government that since India would have to reconstruct its economy, and labour would be a vital element, labour rights should be given, though they should be curbed when it came to unrest. The management was given greater leeway possibly because the new state thought that it would help in building a new India.

The ID Act provides for various methods of conciliation. For example, any dispute between labour and management may be referred to the labour officer who will try to conciliate between the two parties. If this fails, a failure report will be filed by the officer, and labour will have two options. Firstly, an arbitrator who is acceptable to both sides can be appointed but the decisions will be binding on both sides; in case the workers think that this is a risk, they can take the matter for adjudication to the labour court. If the decision of the labour court is unfavourable, the issue can be moved to the High Court and finally to the Supreme Court. Any form of strike is thus avoided during this period of grievance redressal. The legal process is long and, for the workers, expensive, unless the person is backed by the trade union which agrees to cover the cost.

The ID Act allows any trade union or an individual worker to raise a dispute before a conciliating officer with the result that any minority union, with little or no following, can intervene in a labour dispute. This practice and the issue of recognition of a trade union (see section on TU Act below) encourage multi-unionism in industries. The managements can manipulate unions and create inter-union rivalries through these methods.

One of the positive aspects of this Act is that it prevents any factory employing 100 or more workers from shutting down even if it is running at a loss. The management has to get clearance from the respective state government and its labour department before any case for winding up can be made. This clause is important because the Act tries to ensure that the workers get their dues before the factory closes.

A legal strike is extremely difficult under the Act. The trade union concerned has to prove that all methods of redressal have failed. After this, a strike ballot must be taken and a strike notice would be given one month prior to the strike. In case the strike is legal (which is almost impossible), the workers will get their wages during the strike period. If it is illegal, as is the case with most strikes, workers will forfeit their wages. A legal lockout initiated by the employers/ management is a rarity too. However, if an illegal lockout takes place (most lockouts are illegal), the management will have to pay a fine for each day of the lockout. According to the ID Act, this fine is Rs 50 per day. Hence, we can see the abject difference in the consequences of the workers' fighting for their cause and the employers' actions.

Other Acts

There were other acts too, such as the Factories Act, 1948 which broadly reflected the ideology of the ID Act. The 1948 Act had several positive aspects such as reducing the working day to eight hours with half an hour lunch break, provisions for proper lighting and ventilation, canteen facilities, crèche, toilet and drinking water facilities. The problem however lies in the definition of a factory. The Act defines a factory as a manufacturing unit having more than nine workers in case it uses power, or nineteen workers in case it does not; in other words, small-scale industries employing nine workers or less do not come under the purview of the Factories Act. It should also be noted that other acts relating to labour welfare are all applicable to factories that come under the purview of the Factories Act. These include acts relating to insurance (covering the Employees' State Insurance Corporation, or ESI), provident fund, pension and gratuity, etc. Hence, a large section of the industrial workforce that is engaged in the small factories is deprived of these benefits. One may point out that in 2009, according to official figures, there were thirty million workers engaged in small-scale industries, while, ironically, the entire formal sector employs twenty-seven million workers.

The Trade Union Act of 1926, which registers trade unions and also ensures that no legal action can be taken against them, has remained unchanged since its promulgation. It allows seven workers to come together to form a union. However, the Act only provides guidelines for registration of trade unions; it does not provide for recognition as this is left to the employer's discretion. Hence even a union representing a fraction of the total workers can get recognised as the representative union by management and it can participate in negotiations relating to the entire workers in that unit. This usually happens when the majority union disagrees with the management's directions or if it initiates a strike to put forth workers' demands, and then the management promptly derecognises the union and may recognise a union representing a small section of workers which is more likely propped up by it.

Another interesting aspect of the TU Act is that it does not distinguish between trade unions and associations of other sectors. Hence, even an association of employers can be registered as a trade union, and the Employers' Federation of India is, in fact, registered under this Act.

We have noted earlier that after Independence the government passed legislations to protect labour. It can be argued with equal emphasis that the state's policies were aimed at blunting the workers' initiatives in organising themselves against the might of capital as the state, through its bureaucracy, projected itself as the protector of the workers. This has made workers and their trade unions increasingly dependent on the government rather than on their own abilities for sorting out problems with their employers. In order to perpetuate this dependence, the state has selectively passed laws which, while granting protection to the workers, have undermined the trade unions.

It can be seen that, in general, the state's intervention in regulating industrial relations has created several problems for the workers and their trade unions. Besides the problems discussed above, the elaborate legal structure and the emphasis on the bureaucracy have placed workers in a vulnerable position. It has increased their dependence on outside leaders as workers find the complicated legal process difficult to tackle on their own. Moreover, ordinary workers, being unable to deal with the bureaucracy of the labour department, have to find leaders with the correct political contacts to do so.

The legal process for redressal of grievances is lengthy, complicated and expensive and instead of providing a framework for justice it has encouraged militancy among the workers. Workers often resort to violence or wildcat strikes to achieve their objectives. The rise of militant leaders like Datta Samant can be attributed to this. E. A. Ramaswamy's study of Mumbai's working class shows this growing impatience of the workers with the legal process. Samant (Ramaswamy 1987: 20) said, 'When the workers get something good from the lower courts the employer goes to the Supreme Court and straight away 10–15 years are lost. The workers cannot wait that long to get things changed.'

An examination of the industrial relations scene will clearly indicate that despite its projected pro-labour attitude, whenever there has been any major confrontation between labour and management, the state has intervened on behalf of the latter. Ramaswamy's 1986 study of two industrial disputes in Tamil Nadu in the 1970s, one in the textile industry and the other in the automobile industry, provides a graphic account of the state's manipulation in favouring the employers. Another significant example is the strike of textile workers in Mumbai in 1982–83 led by Datta Samant which lasted for eighteen months. For the first fifteen months, in what is regarded as the longest industry-wide strike in the country, the textile industry in the city was at a standstill. The workers put forth demands which included regularisation of casual workers, increase in wages, and so on but the most important demand was that of de-recognition of the RMMS. However, despite the display of unity by the workers and their determination to fight, the strike petered out. The government extended support to the employers, and the RMMS did all it could to break the strike (Bakshi 1987; Wersch 1992). During this period, the Chief Minister of the state, Babasaheb Bhosale, was replaced by Vasantdada Patil, who was once the president of RMMS. This was done with the intention that the new Chief Minister would be more competent in breaking the strike as he had once been a leader of textile workers.

Such instances reveal that the state has rarely taken a pro-working-class stand in cases of major labour-management conflicts. In most cases, the state has used its authority to break the workers' movement. Hence, the legal provisions regarding recognition and their effect in fragmenting trade unions may not necessarily be an act of omission.

The state fears that if the trade union movement is truly autonomous it may emerge not only as the opponent of capital but of the state (more specifically, the party in power) as well. The formation of the INTUC by the Congress as an opposition to the AITUC was a clear indication of this fear.

Problems of Marginalised Sections

Though trade unions are the most effective organisations of the working class, they also need to be sensitive to the problems of the socially marginalised sections. The two main issues which trade unions in the organised sector have overlooked are the problems of women workers and of workers belonging to the socially oppressed groups such as the scheduled castes (SCs) and marginalised groups such as the scheduled tribes (STs).

From the 1940s till the 1970s, the number of women employed in the organised sector declined drastically. This happened in industries with high levels of unionisation, such as cotton textiles in Bombay, jute mills in Calcutta, and mines in central India. In 1948, women constituted 12 per cent of the workforce in the cotton textile mills in Bombay, 8 per cent in the jute mills in Calcutta, and 15 per cent in the mines, but by 1975, the proportion of women workers had fallen to 2.5 per cent, 2 per cent, and 5 per cent respectively. This happened at a time when these industries were expanding and their labour force had increased in number. It is believed that the statutory protection given to women workers such as maternity leave, provision of crèches at the workplace, restriction from working in the night shifts and, in the case of mines, working underground made the working hours of women workers less flexible and also increased costs for the management. However, all these provisions are enforced in the plantation industry as well but this has not resulted in the reduction of women in the workforce, who continue to constitute 50 per cent of it. Apart from the attitudes of the employers, who seemed only too eager to lay off women workers, the trade unions too did not take up this issue as they were not gender-sensitive while framing union policies. Thus, trade unions, with their inherent male bias, have not been effective in safeguarding women's employment rights when the employers sought to retrench them.

A similar situation prevails in the employment of people belonging to the SCs and STs in the organised sector. Trade unions have often overlooked their specific problems of social deprivation and prejudice or have side-lined them in union activities. For example, the report of the Commissioner of Scheduled Castes and Scheduled Tribes reviewing the implementation of the job reservation policy in some public sector enterprises mentions that the employment quotas for class four (subordinate cadre) employees and factory workers are never filled up. Is it so difficult to find candidates for these categories or is it merely due to the caste bias of the senior officers in these undertakings? Similarly the promotion policy for these sections, based on the roster system, is hardly ever implemented. Both the job reservation policy and the system of promotion are statutory requirements backed by law. However, none of the national trade unions deem it necessary to take up these legal issues.

There are other problems of social discrimination which have been ignored by the trade unions. One of the more shocking incidents is that of SC workers in the textile mills in Mumbai being prevented from working in some sections in the mills because of the belief of the so-called upper-caste workers that they would pollute the thread, and hence no other worker would be willing to touch the cloth later. This happened in an industry with a high level of unionisation and militancy in trade union action. None of these unions thought it necessary to educate the workers on the evils of this issue. It is because of this indifference of trade unions to issues relating to caste and tribal affinities that often these sections form their separate associations and distance themselves from the trade unions. For example, a study of coal mine workers in the Jharia-Ranigunj belt noted that the tribal workers (Santhals) did not join the existing trade unions and instead formed '*kalyan mandals*' through which they pressed forth their demands (Bannerji 1978). The working class is thus divided on caste lines due to these actions. But the point is that such associations are formed because the trade unions are not interested in taking up issues affecting these sections of the working class and hence they are forced to form their own alliances to protect their interests.

Caste and gender differences have always existed among the workers but significantly none of the national trade union federations have thought it necessary to give due importance to these problems or even educate the tradition-bound workers on these issues. The present situation is even more complex. The divide between workers in the organised and unorganised sectors is not only based on the degree of protection or the wage levels, but also on the basis of caste and gender. Women workers are largely engaged in the unorganised sector. The 1991 Census showed that only 4.2 per cent of the female workers were in the organised sector while 10.2 per cent of the male workers were in this sector. The proportions of male and female workers in the two sectors were one female worker for every six male workers in the organised sector, and one female worker for every two plus male workers in the unorganised sector. Moreover, upper castes dominated jobs in the organised sector, while workers belonging to SCs and STs were mostly engaged in the unorganised sector. Hence, there is every possibility of this divide being exploited by caste-based organisations to create caste animosity. If this happens the tendency would then be to blame these organisations for creating casteism whereas the seeds had been sown by the caste bias which had marginalised the so-called lower castes leaving them in a vulnerable position.

CONCLUSION

The changes taking place in the economy through the policies of liberalisation pose a great challenge to the labour movement in India as these are causing job losses in the organised sector while expanding the base of the unorganised, and hence unprotected, sector. A critical problem before the working class in the present situation is one of fragmentation. Divisions within the working class have instilled in it a sense of helplessness to counteract the adverse effects of globalisation and the consequent liberalisation of the economy. The trade union movement could have countered the anti-labour policies but it has not been able to do so because it is divided. A united trade union movement is perhaps the most pressing need in the present situation. Every major trade union in the country has stressed this; yet, there seems to be no signs of it happening. Thus, the AITUC and the HMS decided to merge into one union in their respective conferences in 1992 but till date the merger has not been finalised.

Several reasons are adduced while analysing the phenomenon of fragmentation of trade unions. The most important factor is the link between trade unions and politics. It is largely true that the political role of the trade unions has overshadowed its commitment to the workers' interests. At the same time, the political role of the trade union movement cannot be ignored. Trade unions are organisations of workers formed to protect their interests. Though trade unions are expected to oppose the power of the employers at the grassroots level, they cannot do so effectively without challenging the power of the state.

Besides trying to wrest a better deal for workers from the employers, the trade union movement has to influence the state to agree to convert the gains it has made out of its struggles into legal rights. This can be done through its role in the political system which would include the support extended to political parties. Most trade unions the world over are linked with political parties. The TUC in the United Kingdom is closely linked with the Labour Party. In France, the largest trade union federation, the CGT, is linked with the Communist Party of France. A number of trade unions in European countries are associated with their respective Social Democratic Parties, or with others. In Canada, the Canadian Labour Congress has a close association with the New Democratic Party (NDP, founded in 1961). Internationally too, it is evident that trade unions are divided on the basis of ideology. The two major international trade union centres were the World Federation of Trade Unions to which most of the pro-communist trade unions were affiliated, and the International Confederation of Free Trade Unions (1949–2006) which comprised the trade unions of non-communist countries before it was merged with the World Confederation of Labour (WCL) to form the International Trade Union Confederation (ITUC).

The major difference between the international scenario and the situation in India is that trade unions here are divided not on the basis of ideology but on the basis of political parties which influence trade union policies rather than the other way around, with the result that political parties set the agenda for their trade unions. This is often based on political gains rather than the workers' interests. In the countries mentioned above, it is the trade unions which affect the policies of political parties and even oppose them if they feel that they do not serve the interests of labour. The TUC has been critical of some of the policies of the Labour party and has, at times, threatened to withdraw its support if the party did not change its stand. Similarly, the Canadian Labour Congress has often been critical of the policies of the NDP. Trade union unity is difficult in India because this would entail that the political parties supporting the trade unions too have to unite.

It would not be correct to hold political parties solely responsible for the fragmentation of trade unions. Rather, the state has played a more important role in this process. We have seen that the legal framework for industrial relations on the one hand prepares the ground for multiple unions and on the other hand makes the unions more dependent on government agencies for settlement of disputes. Moreover, the state has come out in support of the employers whenever there was a major confrontation between labour and management. The state has thus sown the seeds of disunity within the working class which is capitalised by those with narrow political interests or other elements who want to use trade unions for their own gains.

One of the positive signs in the current situation is the near-total consensus on the anti-labour aspects of the liberalisation process. Even the Congress Party-backed INTUC has joined hands with other trade unions to oppose job losses in industries. However, this unity has arisen out of opposition and as such the trade unions have not developed alternative plans which will replace the present policies. The opposition to policies comes mainly from the organised sector. One would have expected the unions to cover the unorganised sector as well, but unfortunately this has not happened. On the contrary, trade unions have become more conscious of protecting their own interests without a care for the vast sections of the unorganised sector. One can argue that unions are primarily responsible to their own members, hence they cannot organise workers who are non-members. However, under the present circumstances, ignoring workers in the unorganised sector may erode the gains of workers in the organised sector. The two sectors are linked with each other and the employers manipulate these sectors by pitting them against each other so that they can get the maximum benefits at the cost of labour. Hence, along with trade union unity, there is a need for closer links between labour in the two sectors. This will not only unite various sections of the working class but will, in addition, bring to the fore the problems of women workers and workers belonging to the socially oppressed groups.

Key Concepts/Definitions

Labour commitment (Moore and Feldman) Performance and acceptance of the behaviour appropriate to an industrial way of life.

Dearness allowance Extra payment in the salary for absorbing rising costs.

Trusteeship Gandhian belief that all profit-making organisations are held by the employers as a trust for people's benefits.

References and Readings

Bakshi, Rajani. 1987. *The Long Haul: The Bombay Textile Strike*. Bombay: Build Documentation.

Bannerji, S. 1978. Anthropological Study of Coal Mines in Jharia-Romigunj Region'. Calcutta: Anthropological Survey of India.

Das, Subesh. 2010. *Managing People at Work: Employment Relations in Globalizing India*. New Delhi: Sage.

Davala, Sarath, ed. 1992. *Unionisation and Employment in Indian Industry*. New Delhi: Friedrich Ebert Stiftung.*

——— 1995. *Unprotected Labour in India*. New Delhi: Friedrich Ebert Stiftung.

Dutt, Rudder, ed. 1997. ed. *Organising the Unorganised Workers*. New Delhi: Vikas Publishing House.

Flanders, Alan. 1970. *Trade Unions*. London: Faber and Faber.

Gadgil, D. R. 1982. *Industrial Evolution of India*. Delhi: Oxford University Press.

Holmstrom, Mark. 1987. *Industry and Inequality: The Social Anthropology of Indian Labour.* Cambridge: Cambridge University Press.

Johri, C. K. 1967. *Unionism in a Developing Economy*. Mumbai: Asia Publishing House.

Lambert, Richard D. 1963. *Workers, Factories and Social Change in India*. Princeton: Princeton University Press and Bombay: Asia Publishing House.

Meyers, Charles A. 1958. Labor Problems in the Industrialization of India. Cambridge: Cambridge University Press.

Moore, W. E., and A. S. Feldman, eds. 1960. *Labour Commitment and Social Change in Developing Areas*. New York: Social Science Research Council.

Morris, D. 1976. *Emergence of an Industrial Labour Force in India*. Bombay: Oxford University Press.

Oommen, T. K, ed. 2010. *Class, Citizenship and Inequality: Emerging Perspectives.* New Delhi: Pearson Longman.

Ramaswamy, E. A. 1986. *Power and Justice*. New Delhi: Oxford University Press.

———. 1987. *Worker Consciousness and Trade Union Response.* New Delhi: Oxford University Press.

Revri, Chamanlal. 1958. *The Trade Union Movement in India*. New Delhi: Orient Longman.

Sen, S. 1979. *Working Class Movement in India*. Calcutta: Firma K. P. Bagchi.

Sen, Sukomal. 1977. *Working Class of India: History of Emergence and Movement 1830–1970*. Kolkata: K. P. Bagchi and Company.

Sharma, B. R. 1971. *The Indian Industrial Worker, Issues in Perspective*. Delhi: Vikas Publishing House.

Sheth, N. R. 1958. *Social Framework of an Indian Factory*. Manchester: Manchester University Press.

* *Friedrich Ebert Stiftung*, or, the Friedrich Ebert Foundation, is a German political organisation associated with the Social Democratic Party of Germany, yet independent of it, and established in 1925.

Venkat Ratnam, C. S. 1994. 'Changing Role of Trade Unions in a Period of Transition'. In *Labour and Unions in a Period of Transition*, P. Sinha, C. S. Venkat Ratnam and G. Botterweck. Delhi: Friedrich Ebert Stiftung.

Wersch. H. V. 1992. *The Bombay Textile Strike, 1982–83*. Delhi: Oxford University Press.

6

INFORMAL EMPLOYMENT

Chapter Highlights

- » UN criteria for informal sector
- » Features of informal sector
- » Dualist approach
- » Structuralist theory
- » Legalist theory
- » Social security legislation

Work is divided into two basic sectors—the formal and the informal.[1] The distinction between the formal and informal sectors is crucial for understanding employment relationship. Workers in the formal sector are engaged in factories, and commercial and service establishments, and are under the purview of legal regulation. Around 70 per cent of the workers in this sector are employed in government, quasi-government and public sector enterprises. The private sector provides employment to only 31 per cent of the labour force in the formal sector (GoI 2005: 230). Wages of formal sector workers are substantially higher than those engaged in the urban informal sector. A study by the Centre for Monitoring Indian Economy shows that the average wage of a formal sector worker is four or five times the wages in the informal sector. Moreover, a range of labour laws, guaranteeing permanency of employment, health facilities and provision for retirement benefits, protect their jobs.

Though, in principle, labour laws in India are expected to apply to all sections of industrial labour, there are in-built provisions in them which exclude large sections of the labour force. The most important law regulating work in industries is the Factories Act of 1948. All other

[1] In India, formal and informal employment are known as 'organised' and 'unorganised' respectively and these terms can be interchangeably used.

laws such as Employees State Insurance Act, Workmen's Compensation Act, Provident Fund and Family Pension Act, and Payment of Gratuity Act apply only to establishments covered by the Factories Act. This Act, as we have seen, is applicable only to manufacturing units that employ a minimum of ten workers and use power in manufacturing and a minimum of twenty workers if the unit does not use power. Hence, a large section of industrial workers—those employed in smaller industrial units—do not have legal protection in their work. We can infer from this that the conditions of work of the labour force in India will show wide contrasts.

NATURE OF INDIAN LABOUR FORCE

India is the second largest country in the world with a population of over 1.2 billion. The 1991census showed that around 25 per cent of the population resided in urban areas and the rest in rural areas. The labour force in the country numbered 317 million in 1991, of whom a mere 8.5 per cent (about 27 million) were engaged in the formal sector while 290 million were engaged in the informal sector (Davala 1993: 5). Women constituted one-third of those engaged in the informal sector and one-seventh of those employed in the formal sector (ibid: 6). There were 75 million agricultural labourers and 110 million small and marginal farmers who also worked as labourers (Dutt 1997: 5). Hence, around 185 million workers were engaged in the rural informal sector. The urban informal sector comprised around 95 million workers. The 1991 Census was conducted before the policy of liberalisation was adopted (see section on Industrial Policies). The decennial census in India (first conducted nationwide in 1881) gives the population on 1 March of the year concerned. The Industrial Policy Statement of the government, which laid the foundations of economic liberalisation, was adopted in July 1991. The 2001 Census, giving a picture of the effects of liberalisation, showed that around 27 per cent of the population now resided in urban areas.

More recent statistics on employment show that the informal sector has increased considerably in size. The report of the 55th Round of the National Sample Survey (1999–2000) shows that 397 million persons were employed in the informal sector. This figure increased to 458 million in the 61st Round (2004–5). Employment in the formal sector remained almost static at around 35 million during the same period. The informal sector constitutes about 93 per cent of the Indian workforce (NCEUS 2007: 4).

Informal employment is not unique to India. To understand this phenomenon in the context of global trends, one must try to view it in a theoretical framework. The trend for informalisation may be similar to other economies though the intensity may differ. We shall examine the theoretical constructs so that we can apply these later to explain the current phenomenon.

EVOLUTION OF THE INFORMAL SECTOR

The distinction that is made between the formal and informal sectors is somewhat recent, beginning after WWII. One must remember that when industrialisation started in the mid-1750s in England and then spread to other countries in Europe and in some of the colonies, all employment was what we know today as informal employment. There were no security of jobs, no laws regulating employment, and no form of social security (see Chapter 4). This situation continued till the end of WWII (1945). During the war, production of factory-based goods had to be increased in order to meet the military requirements. Workers thus became a crucial player in this process. After the war ended, workers started realising their importance in generating wealth for the nation. Trade unions, which had gained considerable influence between the two world wars, became stronger as representatives of the working class. The state tried to provide better facilities to workers. This included social protection, improvement in the tenure of employment and regulation of work. Many countries, with the exception of USA, adopted the values of a welfare state. In other words, the state took on the responsibility for providing the basic requirements of the population. In many European countries, the state nationalised core industries such as railways and transport, health services, education, and telephones and telegraph, among others. It also took on the responsibility of assuring all people food, clothing and shelter. This notion of the welfare state helped strengthen the working class movement. As a result, till 1960, it was taken for granted that all workers in developed countries were under legal protection and, thus, in the formal sector.

After WWII, many of the colonies were liberated and they too chose a welfare state and social protection. Even though in such cases all workers were not in the formal sector, it was believed that as these countries developed, workers would be absorbed into that sector. The present situation however shows that the informal sector has grown rapidly in developing countries and it has also marked its presence in the developed ones.

Definitions

It is difficult to define the informal economy as it is varied. We can see from the above descriptions that there are different categories of people engaged in this sector and they also have different work relations. There is a difference between workers in micro/small industries and street vendors who do not have any employer. Domestic workers may have several employers and home-based workers may have no idea who their actual employers are. Hence, a single definition may not be possible for defining this sector. The United Nations Human Settlements Programme (UN-HABITAT) lays down three criteria for distinguishing informal enterprises. These are:

a. The units are not registered;
b. The small number of workers employed; and
c. Employees too are not registered.

The same criteria were also laid down by the 15th International Conference of Labour Statisticians (also known as the Delhi Group). This however, is restricted only to informal enterprises and the self-employed such as street vendors, etc. These form around two-thirds of the informal employment. But others such as day labourers, home-based workers, domestic workers, etc., are not covered by this definition. The question, therefore, is: what is the informal sector? Who are its constituents? As indicated earlier, the informal sector comprises workers who do not have any permanence of employment and who are not regulated by any of the major laws governing employment. Hence, these would include:

a. **Workers of small, unregistered or unincorporated enterprises:** In India, according to the Factories Act, 1948, only those production units that employ more than nine workers and use power in their operations or any production unit that employs more than nineteen workers and does not use power would be recognised as a factory. Hence, all others, namely, those employing nine/nineteen workers or less would not come under the formal sector. The Factories Act is crucial for determining formal employment. Workers covered under this Act are also covered under Employees' State Insurance Act (providing for medical facilities), pensions and post-retirement benefits. Hence, other factory workers would be in informal employment. In 2005, there were a total of 30 million (3 crore) workers in small-scale industries. The total employment in the formal sector was 27 million (2.7 crores).

b. **Own account operators (self-employed):** These include street vendors, micro entrepreneurs/ household industries (those employing five or less workers), domestic workers, waste recyclers (waste-pickers), home-based workers (also known as industrial out-workers) and daily-wage workers, etc.

TABLE 6.1: Percentage of Self-employed Workers in Unorganised Non-agricultural Work, 2004–5

Employment Status	Urban		
	Male	Female	Total
Own Account Worker	47.0	35.4	44.7
Employer	3.5	0.6	3.0
Unpaid Family Worker	11.1	26.1	14.0
Self Employed	61.6	62.0	61.7
All Workers	100.0	100.0	100.0

Source: NCEUS 2007: 68.

Street vendors are those who occupy space on pavements or any other open space and sell their goods to the passers-by or move from place to place carrying their goods for sale either on handcarts or on their heads. Street vending can be regarded as one of the oldest professions. Even in ancient times, there were traders who would go from house to house to sell their wares which they had brought from far-off places. This section of the employed is perhaps the most visible in the urban informal economy. Some may feel that they are too visible and their overbearing presence on the streets becomes a menace for commuters, especially for those using the pavements. Civic authorities in most metropolitan cities all over the world treat these 'intruders' on public property as a nuisance. The urban elite views them as eyesores that are a blotch on the urban scenario. On the other hand, for the urban poor, especially the working poor, street vendors are a boon. These traders provide cheap food, clothes and other items of daily use. They are also easy to access as street vendors conduct their business in convenient places in the city where a large number of commuters pass.

Household Industries (HHIs) are those small industries that employ five or fewer workers. These are small units manufacturing school bags, plastic bags, computer components, perform printing jobs, etc. They operate on small capital. The workers, many of whom may have kinship ties with the employer, are paid low wages and they do not have regular working hours. Since the profit levels are low, both workers and the employers can be included in the informal sector.

Domestic Workers are those who work in other people's houses for pay. Their tasks include cooking, cleaning the house, washing dishes and clothes, child-care, etc. A large majority of these workers are women. The ILO in its hundredth session in June 2011 passed a convention on domestic workers which seeks to protect them from physical and economic exploitation by the employers through proper legal measures in its member countries.

Waste-pickers earn their livelihood through collection, segregation and sale of scrap for recycling. They work in appalling conditions in garbage bins on the streets and at landfill sites where garbage is dumped. The Second National Commission on Labour, 2002, made the following observation on rag (waste) pickers: '…, there are 50 lakh scrap collectors in the country. The number is far greater if labourers in scrap establishments and reprocessing units are included. Waste picking ranks lowest in the hierarchy of urban informal occupations Illiterates, unskilled persons, illegal aliens and the poorest of the poor are pushed into this occupation, as they are unable to find any other kind of employment.' The Commission noted that about 92 per cent of scrap collectors were women in the age group nineteen to fifty, the mean age of entry of those in this occupation being nine to ten years. The average monthly household income is Rs 2,233 which is below the urban poverty line.

We find three distinct features of waste-pickers. Firstly, most of them are women; secondly, given the age at entry, child labour is fairly rampant; and thirdly, the income of the waste-pickers is below the poverty line. Another feature is that they are poor immigrants belonging to the lower, mainly scheduled, castes.

Home-based workers are those that work from their homes. They are engaged in a wide range of activities such as *beedi*-rolling, making of *papads*, incense, and pickles. Many of these workers do odd jobs for the larger industries such as sewing buttons on shirts and dresses and finishing work such as cutting excess threads, folding and packaging of garments for the garment industry, embellishment and embroidery work on cloth, as well as *jari* and *zardosi* work. Though home-based workers are self-employed, they work for other, in many cases, larger industries. Hence, they are also known as industrial out-workers. Just as the street vendors are the most visible section of the informal workers, home-based workers are the most invisible ones. Their numbers are not known and they could be in millions in India. The ILO passed a convention in 1997 on home-based workers in which the most important issue was of having a live register to record the number of home-based workers.

Earlier, the informal economy was popularly known as the informal sector as opposed to the formal sector, and also as the unorganised sector in India. It included all economic units and workers who were not a part of the regulated economic activities and protected employment relations (Chen 2007: 1). The term informal sector did convey, to some extent, the working conditions of those engaged in informal employment. However, to put the formal and informal into two distinct sectors would also mean that they run parallel to each other, which does not happen in reality. There would be no formal sector within the informal sector, but informal employment may exist within the formal sector. In the early post-Independence period, all workers engaged in large factories were in the formal sector. The exceptions could be those who were taken as casual labour that did not work full time and were there to fill in for permanent workers when there was absenteeism. For example, in the jute mills of Kolkata or textile mills of Mumbai, there was a category of workers called *badli* workers. These workers would stand outside the factory gate, just as the shift was about to start. If there was a shortage of permanent workers, these workers were asked to fill in for them. Another category was that of the apprentices, who were taken as trainees.

Since 1991, when the liberalisation programme was introduced in India, we have seen a growth in informal employment. Casual labour and contract labour (labourers working under a contractor) had been engaged in almost all industries. A book edited by Sarath Davala (1993) contains studies on workers in eight major industries in the country. The findings were based on surveys conducted in these industries. It was found that half the workers in the large-scale chemical industries were either casual or contract labour. In other industries, such as jute, plantations, coal, port and docks, 30 per cent of the workforce was in informal employment. Hence, the term informal employment rather than informal sector is more comprehensive in capturing the employment situation in the economy.

TABLE 6.2: Percentage Distribution of Unorganised Sector Casual and Regular Workers in Manufacturing, 2004–5

Industry Group	Casual	Regular	Casual	Regular	Casual	Regular
	Male		Female		All	
Food products and beverages	10.1	11.4	10.8	8.7	10.3	11.1
Tobacco products	2.1	0.5	10.2	18.9	3.9	2.3
Textile products	18.6	14.5	36.7	20.4	22.7	15.0
Wearing apparel	7.5	11.5	5.3	10.9	7.0	11.4
Tanning and dressing of leather	2.5	3.3	0.3	3.9	2.0	3.4
Wood and products	13.9	4.2	3.3	1.8	11.5	4.0
Chemicals and chemical products	1.3	3.0	5.1	7.2	2.1	3.4
Other non-metallic mineral products	18.6	2.3	17.8	1.4	18.4	2.2
Other manufacturing	25.4	49.3	10.4	26.8	22.0	47.1
All manufacturing	100.0	100.0	100.0	100.0	100.0	100.0

Source: NCEUS 2007: 30.

Theoretical Orientations

The concept of the informal sector was not popular till the 1970s, though this sector existed even before. For the industrially developed countries of Europe and North America, formal employment was the norm, especially in the US after the Great Depression of 1929 and the post-WWII reforms in Europe. This type of employment entitles a degree of permanence to the job and the worker is entitled to retirement benefits after they retire from work. The number of workers who were not engaged in formal employment was relatively small and merited little interest.

This idea of permanent employment being predominant in the economy was also echoed by developing countries in Asia and Africa. Though most workers in these countries were engaged in informal employment, their governments chose not to highlight their problems because employment in these countries was overwhelmingly in the agrarian sector. Modernisation of agriculture and industrialisation would surely change the situation as it had happened in developed countries.

It was only in the early 1970s that the notion of informal sector gained currency. At that time, the ILO was carrying out some major studies on the labour market in some of the countries on the continent. One of the researchers was Keith Hart, an anthropologist, who was studying the situation in Accra in the African country of Ghana in 1971. He found (1973) that quite unlike the organised markets in England, where he came from, there were workers who came from their villages in the vicinity to offer their services as day labourers. These people would assemble at certain places in the cities and wait for possible employers to hire their services. He also found that there were sharp differences in retailing in England and these countries. In the developed countries, food grains and vegetables were available in standardised packets that were sold in departmental or grocery stores. In Accra, villagers would come to the cities and sell their wares to the public at large. These were not standardised goods that were weighed and neatly packed. Instead, the street vendors who sold vegetables or food grains did so in open baskets. These were weighed in front of the customers who wanted to buy these goods. On the whole, the scenario appeared quite chaotic. There were workers who worked as day labourers and whose employers had no responsibility towards them, except for paying them their daily wage. The retail trade was equally unorganised with individual sellers rather than organised retail outlets. For lack of any other word to describe these activities, Hart labelled them as the informal sector, as compared to the formal sector.

Hart also found that there were four basic features of the informal sector that proved useful for employment in developing countries. These were:

(i) *Low levels of skill*: Most of the jobs in the informal economy are labour-intensive, involving low levels of technology. The skills required from workers are rudimentary. Developing countries have large reserves of untrained, unskilled workers who have little or no education. These people cannot hope to find work in the formal economy as they do not have the skills needed for specialised jobs in the formal sector. Hence they find employment in the informal economy. This sector therefore absorbs the surplus labour in the economy.
(ii) *Easy entry*: Because of the low skill requirements, entry to the informal sector is comparatively easy. For example, it is easier for a person with low skills and little capital to take to street vending instead of starting a venture in the formal economy such as a grocery store.
(iii) *Low-paid employment*: Wages of workers in the informal economy are low because of the low levels of skills of the workers. Moreover, easy entry in this sector is precisely because of low wages offered to the less-skilled workers.
(iv) *Largely immigrant workforce*: The labour force engaged in informal employment does not consist of local people and they are mainly immigrants. Hart presumed that migrants mainly possess low skills and that is why they can find work only in this sector. This inference is not necessarily correct because one finds a large number of local people engaged in this sector, especially in developing countries.

The Employment Mission of the ILO (1972) had noted that the traditional economic sector not only persisted along with modern enterprises but it had expanded. The mission chose to use the term 'informal sector' (coined by Hart a year earlier) rather than traditional sector. This sector included small-scale and unregistered economic activities.

Both Hart and the ILO believed that the informal sector was a transitory phase that would disappear when these countries developed. The formal sector would expand and absorb the informal sector. In other words, day labourers or workers in unregistered small factories would be absorbed as formal sector workers, and street vendors would probably be absorbed into the organised retail sector as these countries developed and expanded their formal sector. Hence, the ILO believed that these two sectors were independent of each other, and the informal sector would disappear or decrease considerably as the formal sector expanded. This approach is known as the 'dualist approach', and it is regarded as outdated considering the developments in the economy in recent years. But we find that far from disappearing, this sector has grown tremendously in all countries, even in the developed ones.

It would be unwise to throw out the entire concept of a dualistic approach. These studies were important because they brought to light some important aspects of the informal economy, especially its potential for providing employment. In developing countries, the informal economy was able to absorb surplus and untrained labour. However, it was by and large a concept that was not able to effectively understand changes in the economy or why, despite development, this sector continued to expand. This brings us to the other approach used to study informal economy, namely the structuralist theory.

The structuralist theory was developed by Manuel Castells, Alejandro Portes and Lauren Benton in late 1989 though the issue had been raised by Caroline Moser in her paper in *World Development* (Moser 1978). Portes and Castells argue that far from being independent of each other, the formal and informal sectors are related to each other. The enterprises in the formal sector use the informal sector for manufacturing components as costs are much lower, and informal sector enterprises are not subject to the laws that regulate production in the formal sector. The formal economy thus finds the informal economy as a useful means for increasing its profits. At the same time, the informal economy depends on the formal sector for its sustenance. The structuralists stress the fact that there is a close, symbiotic relationship between the two sectors. This is to a large extent true as we can see that low-paid, sweated labour in the informal sector is being used to provide inputs to the formal sector for small-scale industries are engaged in manufacture of parts that are used as inputs in the manufacture of goods produced in the formal sector. The automobile industry depends on a number of small manufacturers who supply the different components for making the vehicle. Similarly, we find that manufacturers in the developed economies outsource their production to the developing countries because manufacturing in the informal sector in these countries is much cheaper.

The structuralist approach is also relevant while examining economic growth during the phase of liberalisation (from about 1991 in India). With laws regarding setting up of industries and foreign investments becoming liberal, one can see a large number of industries in the West that outsource the manufacturing of their goods and promotion of services to the developing countries because of lower costs. Hence, vehicles manufactured in Germany have much of their parts manufactured in small- and medium-scale industries in India because labour costs are cheaper, the laws are liberal and there are no trade unions in these companies, which would have insisted on observance and maintenance of proper labour standards. Technology plays a major role in this process. The rapid expansion of information technology (IT) since the 1990s led to the expansion of this industry in India, and now much of the software used by Western companies is made in India by Indian engineers. The call centres too are an important addition, as they are set up by companies in developed countries and operated by their Indian counterparts. The only issue here is that all these industries, especially those in IT, are not self-governing in the sense that they are totally dependent on support or orders from industries in developed countries.

An important point raised by the structuralist is that the informal sector exists because of the needs of the formal sector. This implies that the informal sector is not autonomous as the dualists would want us to believe. According to the structuralist, the informal sector plays a key role in manufacture and cost reduction for the formal sector. One can see this in several industries especially in large units manufacturing consumer/personal products. There are some multinational corporations of this type in India. In the cases of manufacturing soap, beauty products, personal care products such as shaving creams and perfumes, etc., much of the production is carried out in the small-scale sector. In some cases, MNCs disband their own factories because they get greater advantages in outsourcing their products to the small-scale sector. Besides the cost advantage due to cheap labour, there is another advantage that gives them greater control over the production process that they have in their own factories. The large factories in the formal sector come under stringent rules and regulations (as discussed earlier). Moreover, in most cases, the workers are unionised and the unions are able to get considerable benefits in terms of wages for them.

The MNC has greater control over production because it places orders with small-scale industries and provides them with raw materials or cash advances to purchase the raw materials. The company, then, lays down its conditions which include quality standards for its products and the delivery time. The MNC pays the owner of the small-scale enterprise a certain amount which may not be sufficient for him to get a proper return on his capital. The entrepreneur hence pays low wages to his employees and makes them work for longer hours in order to cut costs and make a small profit. In such a case, one will find that both the employer as well as the employee is exploited by the MNC/ large industry. These examples in effect reinforce the structuralist view that the informal sector is indispensible to the formal sector.

The third theoretical approach is that of the legalists. This approach was developed by Hernando de Soto (1989), a Peruvian economist (b. 1941), who gained considerable fame because of his contribution to the understanding of the informal economy and urban poverty. The legalist theory states that the informal sector comprises small operatives who work outside the formal economy because they find the legal procedures too cumbersome to follow. These operators prefer to operate informally because the government procedures for giving them formal recognition are long-winded, complicated and difficult for them to understand. Hence these people, instead of being deliberate offenders, simply try to circumvent the rules because they find them too complex and time-consuming.

Micro-entrepreneurs such as those owning very small enterprises, street vendors, and home-based workers choose to operate informally in order to cut down their costs. This could be a result of the tax structure which may be a bit stiff for these tiny enterprises. Moreover, the process of registration is complicated involving both time and effort. The forms may be so complicated that the semi-literate micro entrepreneur may not be able to comprehend them. For example, a street vendor in Patna can get a daily licence to engage in his business only after he fills up a long and complicated application form, which asks for information such as the volume and cost of his goods, expected sales, place of operation, etc. In most cases, vendors are not able to provide such specific information. They, therefore, prefer to take the easier way of bribing the municipal authorities and the police so that they can operate on the streets.

According to de Soto, these people continue to manufacture/ sell informally because government procedures are time-consuming and costly. De Soto argues that in most countries, government bureaucracy evolves intricate rules that lead to either forcing the small entrepreneurs out or compelling them to adopt corrupt means. One can see this in a study of micro industries in Delhi (Bhowmik 2007). The rules for setting up such an industry (those that operate from one's home but employ fewer than five workers) are simple when it comes to registration which can be done by filling up a simple form. Once registered, the entrepreneur is entitled to certain concessions such as cheaper electricity, water, etc., and, most important to the entrepreneur, loans at subsidised rates of interest. This takes care of working capital and other investments. However, despite the simple registration process, once the entrepreneur starts manufacturing, they have to seek clearance from several departments from the government. In doing so, the entrepreneur has to fill in complicated forms for each of these departments. In most cases, the entrepreneur who may be barely semi-literate and not well-off, would need the help of a lawyer or someone similar for filling in these details and pay fees for these services. The entrepreneur therefore prefers to work without registration. They may be entitled to cheaper loans but there is a feeling that this is offset by the amount of time and money spent in the so-called legal activities. As a result, the entrepreneur works with low working capital. They hardly have any funds to improve or expand their business. At the same time, this should not be construed as the willingness of the small entrepreneur to function and operate without registration. In the same study which was done in Delhi on micro entrepreneurs, it was found that most of these enterprises are registered with the sales tax authority and they do pay tax on what they sell. Hence, it should be clear that these people are not habitual offenders, but had the bureaucratic procedures been simpler, they would have certainly been more prone to register.

De Soto himself had carried out an experiment (1989) through the institute that he founded, namely, Institute for Legality and Democracy, Lima, Peru. A fictitious clothing factory was set up in the small-scale sector by this institute. They decided that they would not pay any bribes for having this factory registered. While attempting to register this factory, they were asked to pay bribes at ten places. The application for registration had to go through several government departments and each of them demanded money for clearing it to the next office; with reluctance, they paid bribes at two places. The total time taken to register the factory was 289 days and the labour cost of the group was equivalent to 32 monthly wages. De Soto wanted to bring the fact to light that if these are the costs for registering a unit, it is hardly surprising that most such entrepreneurs would try to operate illegally. He notes, 'when legality is a privilege available only to those with political and economic power, those excluded—the poor—have no alternative but illegality.'

The other point that de Soto emphasised was that of property rights of the poor. He argues that the poor occupy property (slum dwellers' quarters and other forms of 'illegal' encroachments) but they do not have rights over this property, which they may have occupied for several years or decades. He feels that this is one of the major factors inhibiting the poor from pursuing their self-employed occupations. Had they possessed some legal entitlements, such as ownership of property, they could have mortgaged the same for getting institutional loans at lower rates of interest. In the present situation, the working poor have to depend on moneylenders and other usurers for funds at high rates of interest. As they borrow at high rates from informal sources, they have fewer surpluses from their business for reinvestment. This can be easily seen in the case of the street vendors. They are usually denied loans from institutional sources (banks and other financial institutions) because they cannot show any security. The high rate of interest at which they borrow money for running their business eats into their profits and leaves hardly anything for investment or expansion. In this manner, they continue to remain in the same profession and at the same low level of income.

In India, there have been several half-hearted attempts at legalising slums. For example, every plan from the Third Five Year Plan onwards has recommended that slum dwellers in urban areas should be given tenurial rights. The draft National Policy on Slums also stresses this aspect and notes that the urban poor make substantial contributions for the development and welfare of the city and their existence is needed if the city has to function properly. However, despite these recommendations, the urban poor remain where they were, i.e., as insecure residents who are considered as parasites to the system. More recently, the Rajeev Awas Yojana (RAY), announced in the 2009 Union Budget, was formed to provide permanent houses to slum dwellers in Indian cities in order to give them tenurial rights which was likely to improve their living conditions.

Though the three theories discussed above may appear to be

distinct and separate, in reality, we can find elements of each of them while analysing the informal economy. Hart's contention that as development takes place, the informal sector becomes a part of the formal sector, could be seen soon after Independence. Studies by Lambert (see Chapter 5) show that most workers engaged in these large factories had started their careers in small-scale industries. This perhaps reinforces Hart's stand. But more important would be the features that Hart has elaborated. The high rate of migration from rural to urban areas in the decades between the 1960s and the 1990s meant that a lot of the unskilled rural poor were forced to seek employment in urban areas. These people found gainful employment in the informal sector. Other scholars such as Sethuraman of ILO noted that the population growth rate in developing countries was higher than the economic growth rate, and so the formal sector was not able to absorb all the surplus labour which sought employment. Such an explanation may not be correct because mere economic development does not ensure labour absorption. We have seen that India, from the year 2000 onwards, has maintained a growth rate of GDP of around 8 per cent per annum, which is considered high compared to the growth rates of developing countries and also some developed ones. At the same time, it was found that as economic growth increased, labour absorption actually decreased. Hence, it is necessary to have economic growth followed by policies that are directed towards employment that will ensure equity in terms of jobs and employment.

Social and Legal Protection

The plight of the informal sector workers continues and their condition remains insecure and low-paid. The state has from time to time passed laws which benefit sections of the informal sector, for example the Beedi and Cigar Workers (Conditions of Employment) Act. The basic question which arises in the case of countries like India is: can the state afford to finance social protection? This issue was raised in the Mahatma Gandhi National Rural Employment Guarantee Scheme (MGNREGS, now MGNREGA) under the MGNREGS Act 2005 and the critics highlighted the costs of the scheme. It was said that initially the scheme would cost the government Rs 36,000 crores per annum. This is a huge amount, but it comes to a mere 2 per cent of the total expenditure of the country. It has to be admitted that all schemes of social protection cannot be funded totally by the state, and there has to be some form of people's participation. In the formal sector, social security schemes such as pension and provident fund are a result of the contribution of the employers and the employees. However, this is not possible in the case of the informal sector, because a large section is self-employed with no distinct employer. Other large sections such as construction workers, casual labourers and daily rated wage workers have employers, but they are not permanent. For example, a construction worker is a permanent worker because they work throughout the year on the construction site; however, this person is not treated as a permanent worker as in the formal sector because there is no permanent employer. In such cases, schemes for social protection through mutual contribution cannot take place.

At the same time, there are other ways and means of ensuring that social protection is granted to this section of the labour force. In the state of Kerala, there are welfare funds for different sections of informal workers, which include funds for construction workers, toddy-tappers, auto-rickshaw drivers, and so on. How are these schemes funded? In the case of construction workers, a small cess comprising 1 or 2 per cent of the total cost of construction is deposited with the construction workers' welfare fund. For toddy-tappers, a similar cess is imposed on the toddy sold. The fund for beedi workers under the Beedi and Cigar Workers (Conditions of Employment) Act comes from a cess imposed on each packet of beedis. Though the cess amount may be small, when added up, it comes to a considerable amount. For example, the toddy-tappers' welfare fund is so flush with money that it has even provided loans to the government. In the case of the beedi fund, it was found that several crores of rupees have been amassed, and in some states, this money has been used for providing housing and education of their children. The latter is especially important for beedi workers because it helps the next generation to move away from beedi rolling and find alternative careers. Similarly, the construction workers' board in Delhi has amassed several hundred crores of rupees through the cess it imposes on construction costs. These funds are used for sudden or large expenses such as deaths, marriages, and births. A member of the fund can avail loans at low rates of interest for these instances. Besides, these funds provide for education of the children, health insurance and housing. Hence, even though India is not a rich country, there are enough sources for raising funds for the informal sector workers. What is needed is a political will to implement such schemes, which is often lacking.

Unorganised Sector Workers' Social Security Bill, 2007

In 2007, the Government of India introduced a bill in Parliament called the Unorganised Sector Workers' Social Security Bill. This bill was passed in the winter session of Parliament, which was the last session before the five-year term of the UPA government ended, receiving the President's assent on 30 December 2008 (the UPA was subsequently re-elected for another five years). When the UPA came into power it had promised a comprehensive legislation on the working conditions of the informal/unorganised sector workers to cover, inter alia, working conditions that include hours of work (eight hours per day) and other amenities such as holidays and annual leave with pay; this part was unfortunately dropped. What we have now is a bill relating to social protection. In the following paragraphs, we shall summarise the main contents of the bill.

The bill defined an unorganised (informal) sector worker as a home-based worker, self-employed worker or a worker in the sector (section 2(l)). The unorganised sector (section 2(k)) refers to an enterprise, employing less than ten workers, owned by individuals or self-employed workers engaged in production or sale of goods or providing any kind of service. The bill (chapter II) mentioned that the central government may formulate suitable welfare schemes for different sections of these workers. Such schemes included insurance cover for life, and in case of disability, health and maternity benefits, old age protection or any other. In addition, the bill noted that the state governments could formulate and notify welfare schemes for different sections of these workers which could include: provident fund, employment injury benefit, housing, educational schemes for children, skill upgradation of workers, funeral assistance and old-age homes. It may be mentioned here that provident fund and employment injury benefit are available for workers in the formal sector who come under the Factories Act, Provident Fund and Family Pension Act, and the Workmen's Compensation Act, which are in operation in workplaces where the Factories Act has been enforced. Hence, workers in the small-scale sector (units employing less than ten workers) do not come under these Acts. The Unorganised Sector Workers' Bill noted that state governments could bring the informal sector workers under these Acts. Another important point was that (section IV (1)) schemes notified by the Central government might be wholly funded by it or jointly funded by the Central and state governments or it could be funded by both the governments along with other contributions collected from the beneficiaries or employers.

The operation of the Act would be through the National Security Advisory Board for workers in the unorganised sector. According to chapter III of the bill, the central government would form this board which would have 33 members including a chairperson appointed by the Central government and the director general-labour welfare as the ex-officio member secretary. The remaining 31 would include seven representatives each of following categories: unorganised sector workers, employers of unorganised sector, and eminent persons from the civil society. In addition, there would be five representatives of the state government and five of the Central government. At the state level, there would be a state social security advisory board for workers in the unorganised sector (chapter IV). The total membership would be 28, with a chairperson appointed by the state government and secretary-labour who would be the ex-officio member secretary. Of the remaining members, seven each would represent: unorganised sector workers, employers of unorganised sector, and state government departments concerned. In addition, there would be five members representing civil society. Chapter V of the bill detailed the registration process which is important because only after a worker is registered can they avail themselves of the benefits provided. There are two basic criteria for registration; firstly, the person must be fifteen years of age or more and secondly, he/she should declare that he/she is a worker in the unorganised sector. The application has to be made to the district administration and the worker, after registration, would be issued an identity card. In other words, such a process would make the unorganised sector workers more visible. At present the main problem lies in the fact that no organisation knows exactly how many workers there are in this sector and what types of work they perform. It is difficult to plan for the uplift of the unorganised sector if the planners are not aware of the numbers involved.

In conclusion, the bill in itself seemed attractive and could go a long way in improving the living conditions of the workers in the informal sector. Unfortunately, most of the schemes listed in the schedule of the bill related only to insurance-related activities. This was despite the fact that the bill aimed to upgrade the skills of these workers. The schedule did not contain a single scheme related to this aspect. The eleven schemes mentioned in the schedule included National Old-age Pension Scheme, National Family Benefit Scheme, National Maternity Benefit Scheme, Mahatma Gandhi *Bunkar* Bima Yojana (insurance scheme for weavers), Health Insurance for Handloom Weavers, Scheme for Pension to Master Craftspersons, Group Accident Insurance Scheme for Active Fishermen, Saving-cum-Relief for Fishermen, Janashree Bima Yojana, Aam Admi Bima Yojana and Swasthya Bima Yojana. Most of these schemes were in operation before the Act came into being. The schemes have been successfully implemented where there are trade unions for informal workers or NGOs working among them. For example, SEWA has been quite active in registering workers under these schemes. The National Association of Street Vendors of India (NASVI) has enrolled several thousand street vendors in the various schemes. Some NGOs like Centre for Civil Society and *Nidan* have also been active in enrolling members under the schemes.

Key Concepts/Definitions

Household Industries Small manufacturing units employing five workers or less.

Domestic workers Those who perform domestic chores in other people's houses for pay.

Home-based workers (ILO) Persons who work from their homes or in other premises of their choice, other than the employer's workplace for remuneration, which results in a product or service as specified by the employer. They are also known as industrial out-takers.

References and Readings

Bhowmik, Sharit K. 2007. 'Delhi'. In UNHABITAT, *Improving Regulatory Framework for Income Enhancement of the Urban Poor*. Nairobi: UNHABITAT.

Chen, Martha. 2007. 'Rethinking Informal Economy: Linkages with the Formal Economy and the Formal Regulatory Environment'. In UN/DESA Working Paper no. 6, July. http://www.un.org/esa/desa/papers/2007/wp46_2007.pdf. Accessed 29 May 2012.

Davala, Sarath. 1993. *Employment and Unionisation in Indian Industry*. Delhi: Friedrich Ebert Stiftung.

———. ed. 1995. *Unprotected Labour in India.* New Delhi: Friedrich Ebert Stiftung.

de Soto, Hernando. 1989. *The Other Path: The Economic Answer to Terrorism*. New York: HarpenCollins.

Dutt, Rudder. 1997. *Organising the Unorganised Workers*. Delhi: Vikas.

Government of India (GoI). 2005. Economic Survey 2005. Available on finmin.nic.in.

Hart, Keith. 1973. 'Informal Income Opportunities and Urban Employment in Ghana'. *Journal of Modern African Studies* 11 (1).

Ministry of Labour. 2002. 'Report of the National Commission on Labour' (Second Labour Commission), Volume I (Part I). Ministry of Labour, Government of India. Delhi: Akalank Publications.

Moser, Caroline O.N. 1978. 'Informal Sector or Petty Commodity Production: Dualism of Dependence in Urban Development'. World Development 6 (9–10).

National Commission for Enterprises in the Unorganised Sector (NCEUS). 2007. 'Report on Conditions of Work and Promotion of Livelihoods in the Unorganised Sector'. Academic Publishers.

Portes, A., M. Castells, and L. Benton, eds. 1989. *The Informal Economy: Studies in Advanced and Less Advanced/Developing Countries*. Baltimore: Johns Hopkins University Press.

Sethuraman, S. V. 1976. 'The Urban Informal Sector: Concept, Measurement, and Policy'. *International Labour Review* 114 (1).

7

Globalisation and Reorganisation of Work

Chapter Highlights

- The New Industrial policy of 1991
- Privatisation
- Small-scale industries
- Women workers
- Equal Remuneration Act
- Voluntary retirement
- Outsourcing
- Trade Union response

Globalisation, as we understand it in the present context, has resulted from the information and technology revolution. This started from 1985, with more efficient and economical communication systems. By the mid-1990s, the use of email as a tool for communication was becoming widespread. This was accompanied by introduction of systems of electronic transfer of funds. This facilitated and encouraged the mobility of capital between countries. It was possible to transfer millions of dollars from one country to another in a fraction of a second. In order that globalisation should succeed, it was necessary for all countries, especially the developing ones, to open or reduce trade barriers. Hence, institutional financial institutions like the International Monetary Fund (IMF) and GATT, replaced in 1995 by the WTO, were pressurising countries like India, China and others in South and South-East Asia with high economic growth to be more receptive to foreign direct investments. There was also a move to liberalise labour laws by arguing that laws that granted permanence of employment and social protection would be detrimental to industrial growth. Industrialists from outside would hesitate to invest because while it might be easy to start an industry it would be difficult to weed out labour if costs increased.

The World Bank (WB) which emerged as the main supplier of financial inputs to enable countries to cope with problems of globalisation laid emphasis on privatisation of assets and strongly recommended that the role of the public sector and of the government in economic activities in general should be reduced. It issued a slogan that governments should only govern and not get involved in productive activities. These should be left to the able hands of private enterprise, including international corporations.

Globalisation has other dimensions as well and several positive aspects. First of all, the information and technology revolution and the easy accessibility of the Internet have made transmission of information much faster. As the IT industry expanded, costs were reduced. We may recall that when mobile phones were introduced in India, they were costly and call charges were high, sometimes as much as Rs 12 per minute. At that time, only the financially better-off sections could afford mobile phones, which became a status symbol for them. However, within a few years, the rates were slashed, and today usage of mobile phones has expanded to remote villages, and even the poorer sections of the working class can afford them. Farmers in far-flung areas can get information about where to market their products through mobile connections. Some companies regularly supply information to farmers on prices, weather, costs of inputs, etc., by short message service, or SMS, if they become members at a nominal fee. The spread of satellite television too has enabled news and entertainment to be disseminated in all parts of the country.

Prices of consumer goods have fallen considerably, in addition to other goods such as cars, TV sets and so on. This has been a result of opening up of the markets which enabled imported, affordably-priced goods for the domestic market. This made Indian producers reduce the costs of their products in order to compete. Moreover, this form of competition provided alternative choices to the consumers. This in turn reduced costs while improving quality as consumers became more conscious and discerning.

On the employment front, globalisation has contributed to improving the situation. Opening up of the economy has led to the emergence of new types of enterprises. For example, the Internet and the media revolution have given rise to several opportunities in these sectors, right from low-paid jobs such as running and repairing cable TV connections, to technical jobs in television and computers. It has given rise to a host of actors, news readers, commentators and advertising professionals. The burgeoning courier services have enabled young people to get employed as courier agents. The multiplicity of organisations is mainly responsible for the availability of a large number and variety of jobs.

However, there are adverse aspects of globalisation that need to be considered. For globalisation to be effective, it was necessary to change the existing framework of laws and nature of production in developing countries, which had protected markets (e.g., India, China, the then Soviet Union, other socialist countries, etc.). It was necessary to structurally change the nature of employment and the key sections of the economy that were developed and maintained through a regime of protection. Thus, in India, there was strict control over import of goods, and imported luxury goods were either banned or taxed heavily. The developed countries realised that these protected economies had large markets which needed to be tapped. Hence, if globalisation was to be sustained, it was necessary for all countries to go in for structural adjustments. Thus, developing countries like Vietnam, Cambodia and the former socialist states which used to observe economic protectionism went in for restructuring and opening up of their markets to developed countries. These would include foreign direct investments as well as goods and services.

GLOBALISATION IN INDIA

Since 1985, India's economy was moving gradually away from planned development and towards market orientation. On 21 July 1991, Finance Minister, Manmohan Singh (who later became the prime minister), placed an Industrial Policy Statement before Parliament which was in tune with the approach of structural adjustment and globalisation of finance and investment. Other developing countries and the former socialist countries (Russia and the East European countries) too changed their policies in a similar manner around the same time.

The World Bank, as indicated earlier, had been propounding the idea that the only way countries of the South could promote growth was by encouraging private enterprise and reducing the protection for labour. The argument was that too much protection to labour in the formal sector had resulted in a small section of the working class being more privileged than the vast majority of ill-paid workers. The World Development Report of 1995 noted that, '[i]n many Latin American, South Asian and Middle Eastern countries, labour laws establish onerous job security regulations, rendering hiring decisions practically irreversible; and the system of worker representation and dispute resolution is often subject to unpredictable government decision-making, adding uncertainty to firms' estimate of future labour costs' (World Bank 1995: 34). In order to ease this process, many countries (especially those in Central and South America) relaxed or removed legal protection to workers in the formal sector. In India, too, there have been persistent pressures from industry to allow closure of industries and reduce the protection given to permanent workers.

Following Independence, India decided to adopt the path of planned development as implemented in socialist countries such as the then Soviet Union, and it was also decided that the country would have a mixed economy with both the state sector (public sector) and private enterprise, the latter to exist under regulations and controls. This included issuing of licences to start industry which would only be in areas that were not designated as core industries. We can briefly summarise the developments since 1950s till the era of liberalisation, which was ushered in by globalisation.

Planned Development

The First Five Year Plan (1951–56) stressed the role of agriculture. At that time, around 80 per cent of India's population was in the rural areas and agriculture was the mainstay of the economy. Hence, the planners felt that agricultural development would help in the uplift of the rural poor. Moreover, it did not seem feasible to go in for industrialisation of the newly independent country as it did not have much capital to invest. It was believed that the existing industries such as Tata Steel could be expanded to meet the growing needs of industrialisation. This turned out to be wrong because these industries refused to expand as the investment required to do so was high and they were not assured of a market for their expanded production.

It was necessary to develop industries as these help in increasing agricultural production. At that time, one line of thinking was that if the stress was on agriculture, the industrial aspect could be met through collaborations with developed capitalist countries. However, the latter were not interested in India's industrial development for they felt that newly independent nations such as India, Egypt and Indonesia should develop their agriculture and depend on them for supply of industrial goods. India then, turned to the socialist countries such as the Soviet Union and GDR for help. This shaped the Second Five Year Plan which was a marked departure from the first.

Before the second five-year plan was framed, the government passed the Industrial Policy Resolution of 1956, which is also referred to as India's 'economic constitution'. The Resolution focused on state intervention so as to enforce a certain pattern of industrial development and manner of utilisation of resources. This formed the basis of the second five-year plan, also known as the Nehru-Mahalanobis plan. India was politically independent, but this plan turned the spotlight on the country's economic independence, for which, the country had to be self-sufficient. Subsequently, this plan placed a lot of importance on promoting heavy, basic industries which included steel, coal and metals, power generation and infrastructure. It was during this period that units such as Bharat Heavy Electricals Ltd (BHEL), in Haridwar, Heavy Engineering Corporation (HEC), in Ranchi, and steel plants in Bokaro, Durgapur and Rourkela were set up, as also plants for manufacturing railway engines and coaches, among others.

These industries were established because power and steel were essential for the development of industry as well as agriculture. The hand pumps for irrigation or pipes for carrying drinking water and water for agricultural purposes needed steel. So also, the railways required steel for building lines as well as for their coaches and engines. It was felt that if we had to depend on developed countries for these goods, the nation would have to pay a heavy price in terms of foreign exchange. These large factories (which Prime Minister Jawaharlal Nehru described as the 'temples of modern India') were set up in collaboration with socialist countries. The terms were favourable because they accepted payment in Indian currency. Egypt and Indonesia also followed a similar trend in the initial stages, but later, their governments were overthrown by opponents who were supported by the developed capitalist countries and they started opening up their markets to foreign capital.

Owing to our focus on a socialistic pattern of society, core industries and a majority of the public utility services were concentrated in the public sector. The private sector was allowed to expand alongside, and the growth of the cooperative sector was encouraged. The Monopolies and Restrictive Trade Practices Act (MRTP), 1969, emerged as a regulatory mechanism that controlled business depending on their investment output, and the Industrial Licensing Policy of 1970 (and later in 1973) encouraged the growth of small, medium and ancillary sectors. The Industrial Policy Statement, 1977, had decentralisation at its core, while supporting the 1956 resolution which emphasised full utilisation of installed capacity, higher productivity, employment generation, correction of regional imbalances, strengthening of the agricultural base, promotion of export-oriented industries, economic federalism and consumer protection. From 1984 onwards, the policy focused on technological upgrading of industrialisation for promoting an increase in productivity and quality while trimming the costs. Modernisation at both technological and managerial levels was seen as the key for acquiring a competitive edge in the global market.

Move towards Liberalisation

In 1985, Prime Minister Rajiv Gandhi called for a review of these policies. He wanted the economy to open up to foreign competition and wished for a more proactive role for the private sector. He was not able to see his reforms through because of his assassination in 1991, when he was campaigning for the coming general elections. His Congress Party was critical of the public sector and recommended that its role should be restricted to only core or basic sectors. What was more important was that it scrapped the licensing system in almost all sectors and encouraged foreign investment. The New Industrial Policy of 1991 was a landmark because it laid the foundation for liberalisation of the economy.

This policy was a radical departure from the earlier industrial policies. Its focus was on opening up of Indian industry by allowing inflow of foreign capital and technology which meant relaxing controls on foreign investment. It also narrowed the role of the public sector to select areas such as infrastructure, while encouraging disinvestment in other areas such as power. The public sector came in for criticism in this policy statement, being denigrated as unproductive, corrupt, inefficient, and so on. The role of the government thereafter was reduced considerably, while the private sector was allowed to thrive.

The state had repeatedly asserted that the interest of labour would be protected in two ways: firstly, workers displaced from their jobs would be retained and deployed in alternative better jobs, and, secondly, those who cannot be retrained or redeployed would be provided a 'safety net' in the form of liberal compensation. This policy was admitting an exit policy through the back door. After the liberalisation policy came into effect, employers' organisations insisted that liberalisation could be effective only if government allowed industrial units to close down if deemed necessary, bypassing provisions of the ID Act (please see Chapter 5). The Ministry of Company Affairs appointed the Goswami Committee to examine this issue of closure, and it submitted its recommendations in two months. The report strongly recommended an exit policy. It reasoned that liberalisation had removed the licence regime and this would encourage foreign investment in industry as it was easier now to set up an industry. In the earlier dispensation, if a company wanted to shut down its operations it would have to undergo a lengthy process, which would deter foreign investors from investing in India. The committee recommended that both entry and exit should be made easier. The government was inclined to accept these recommendations but it hesitated because of strong opposition anticipated from the central trade union federations, including its own trade union wing, INTUC.

The 1991 policy seemed to be a refutation of the state-sponsored planned economy which had existed until then. On the other hand, one can argue that the policy was a continuation of the earlier policies. When India became independent, the capitalist class in India was at a nascent stage. There were a handful of capitalists such as the Tatas, Birlas and some others. Indian capitalism was not in a stage to take over the challenge of developing the country. The state, therefore, took on the role of the capitalist to develop the economy. This could be called state capitalism. Later, after the infrastructure had been set up through the heavy industries established by the state, the capitalist class started developing and expanding. When it had matured, the state handed over development work to the private sector through its liberalisation policies.

One can observe a similar trend in countries like the UK, whose economy had been shattered after WWII. The post-war period was a period of nationalisation. Core industries such as gas, coal, rail and road transport, and some heavy industries were run by the state. Later, in the 1980s, when Margaret Thatcher became the Prime Minister, the nationalised industries were thrown up for privatisation. In other words, after WWII, the capitalist class had weakened but in this intervening period, it was able to strengthen itself and, hence, industries were handed back to them. Thus it may be argued that the state has its own class character which does not favour the labouring classes.

An interesting feature is that the principle of privatisation has been accepted by major political parties and the past governments. Hence though there may be differences between the major political parties in the country, the policy of privatisation is not in dispute. For example, the National Democratic Alliance (NDA) government (headed by Atal Behari Vajpayee as prime minister) was at one time interested in privatising the petroleum companies. This was deferred because of sharp resistance from some of the alliance partners. The NDA government had appointed a minister, Arun Shourie, to speed up the process of privatisation, and under his aegis there was rapid sale of profit-making public sector enterprises. Many of them were sold at prices well below the value of their assets (Balco, Modern Bakery, Videsh Sanchar Nigam Limited (VSNL), Centaur Hotels in Mumbai, etc.). Centaur Hotels was sold to an industrialist for Rs 400 crores, and within six months that person sold the hotel to another party for Rs 1,200 crores. VSNL which had contributed Rs 1,200 crores to the government as its share in the capital was sold to an Indian MNC at Rs 1,250 crores. In most cases, sell-offs resulted in large-scale retrenchments and lay-offs due to mergers of the former public sector units (PSUs) with the buying company. The Economic Review for 2005 showed that the public sector's share in employment had reduced by 1 per cent, and around one million workers in the formal sector had lost their jobs. Representatives of industry were happy with these developments and one business magazine honoured Shourie with the title of 'Man of the Year'.[1]

A curious feature of industrialisation that was observed was the growth of informal employment within the formal sector. A study of eight large-scale industries in 1993 showed that between 30–50 per cent of the employment was through contract or casual labour. The study was initiated by a researcher, Sarath Davala (1993), and the

[1] This information was gathered by the author based on various newspaper reports published at the time.

industries that the study covered were tea, jute, coal, ports and docks, engineering, power, chemical and pharmaceutical industries. Other more recent studies have shown that many industries employ more contract workers than permanent workers, and in many factories, a large number of young workers are employed as apprentices. These people perform the work of a regular worker but are paid a stipend as remuneration. A study in the automobile industry showed that the large multinational companies operating from India routinely employed a large number of contract workers and apprentices. In one factory, the researchers (Gartenberg and Bandekar 2011) found that only 20 per cent of the workers were permanent. The other workers, especially the apprentices, had to perform the most hazardous tasks without adequate protective gear.

Growth of Employment in Small Industries

While the formal sector shows a negative growth in employment, the small-scale manufacturing sector shows a lot of buoyancy. The annual pre-budget Economic Surveys show that small industries have been growing steadily. The 2004–5 survey showed that this sector employed around 28 million workers and this was growing by over 4 per cent per annum. The number of workers in this sector is more than the employment provided by the entire formal sector. The remarkable growth of small-scale industries is an outcome of this sector's demarcation as a thrust area in the industrial policy of 1991. The policy had stated that the small-scale sector would be encouraged to play a dynamic role in growth and employment. The stipulation of initial capital investment for small-scale industries was raised from Rs 5 lacs in 1955 to Rs 1.5 crores in the Union Budget for 2007–8. This has made it possible to upgrade technology and include high-tech industries in this sector. In this case we find that the NDA government only extended what the Congress government had done. As a result, small-scale industries contribute in the region of thirty-five per cent to India's export earnings (GoI 2003). This is certainly a good sign, but it could have been appreciated even more if conditions of their labour component had not remained pathetic.

The rapid growth of small-scale industries is due to the above-mentioned policy measures and also the restructuring of large industries, especially in the consumer goods and pharmaceutical sectors. These industries were originally based in urban centres like Mumbai, Ahmedabad, Kolkata, etc. They started closing down their operations through downsizing the labour force and shifting their production to smaller towns where labour is cheap, there are fewer or no unions, and labour laws are not applied as stringently as in the urban-industrial sector. On the other hand, the government, in its bid to promote industrial development of these areas, demarcates special areas called 'industrial development zones' operated through the state's industrial development corporation. The state government concerned usually grants an array of incentives to induce industrialists to set up their units in industrial development areas. These include availability of land at low rent, industrial sheds, and exemption of local duties such as sales tax for a specific period of time (usually for the first five years). Several large companies take advantage of such offers and move production from the larger cities to these smaller centres to avail themselves of the benefits that lead to reduction in costs. This does not necessarily mean that the consumers will gain by getting goods at cheaper rates. This process is similar to the type of outsourcing in production witnessed between countries of the North and the South. Just as industrial production in the developed countries of Europe is outsourced to the less-developed countries, similarly, the large-scale sector in India outsources its production to the small-scale sector in non-urban areas, as costs are low. This is discussed in detail in the section on outsourcing below.

Small-Scale Industries and Flexible Specialisation

The issue of flexible specialisation was first raised by Holmstrom (1997). He argued that the Italian experience of small industries using microelectronic machinery could be the future for India's industries. He studied the electronics industry in Bangalore and found that it has the potential of emerging as the 'high road' to flexible specialisation. The small industries used Computerised Numerically Controlled (CNCs) machines and Computer Aided Designs (CADs) to manufacture high precision equipment, while the labour they employed was highly skilled, like those in the large industries. Another study of Holmstrom (ibid.) elaborated the concept further and worked out its implications. He noted that flexible specialisation happens when clusters of smaller firms cooperate in product development and marketing, which requires trust and collective provision of 'real services'. Holmstrom found that though engineers and workers are quality conscious and there is use of innovative techniques, the entrepreneurs are often too suspicious to co-operate or share information with other firms. Had there been greater trust, the system would have been much more profitable.

Other studies show that most small industries used the 'low road' of flexible specialisation which comprises low technology and low-skilled and low-paid labour. In labour-surplus countries like India, the choice is always of the low road. Production in the up-market fashion industry is mainly done in sweat shops, and garments are shaped by women workers who work for long hours on extremely low wages. Similarly, most of the cloth is produced in power looms situated in Bhiwandi in Maharashtra where workers earn around Rs 140 to Rs 160 a day, working for ten hours. Even the high-technology industry of Bangalore, which Holmstrom studied, could be taken as a form of low-road specialisation if we compare the wages and working conditions with those of the same industries in developed countries. These employees may be well-paid by Indian standards but they earn between one-fifth and one-eighth of what their counterparts in the advanced countries would earn for the same work.

Feminisation of Labour

Let us now examine the effects of liberalisation and globalisation on women workers. Women have been losing their jobs in the formal sector for a long time, much before the present policies were conceived. We saw in the previous section that employment in the formal sector has been sluggish, resulting in job losses. However, job losses among women workers in this sector took place at a time when this sector was expanding. In the 1920s, employment of women in the three traditional industries, namely, jute, cotton textile and mines, was over 20 per cent. By the 1970s, the number of women workers in the three industries had been reduced to less than 5 per cent. The only industry where women were employed in large numbers is the plantation industry where they form 50 per cent of the total permanent labour force, according to Tea Statistics 2006 published by the Tea Board of India, Kolkata. Their number continued to be high in plantations as women are more efficient in plucking of tea leaves.

The main observation we can make in this regard is that women faced job losses after certain laws were passed. The Factories Act not permitting women working in night shifts in factories and the Mines Act preventing women from working underground were ostensibly passed to protect women as it was believed that it would be unsafe for women to return home late at night after the shift ended and, in the case of mines, working underground was bad for their health. Moreover factory work was projected as masculine activity and thus unfit for women. A significant fact in this whole process was that women were never asked whether they wanted to work at night, or underground. It was presumed in a patriarchal society that women needed protection.

The 1991 census data showed that women workers formed one-seventh of the formal sector workforce while they constituted one-third of the workforce in the informal sector (Davala 1993). The female workforce in the formal sector owes its weightage to the large number of women employed in the plantation sector comprising tea, coffee and rubber as the main crops; it employs around 16 lakh permanent workers, of whom 8 lakh are women. It should be noted that the plantation sector offers the lowest wages in the formal sector. Elsewhere, women are mainly employed as nurses, airhostesses, school teachers, receptionists and secretarial staff. Salaries in each of these categories, with the possible exception of airhostess, are, or used to be, the lowest in the industry/profession concerned. We can thus see that women in the formal sector are mostly assigned to jobs that are identified and categorised as 'feminine'.

We have mentioned earlier that the argument for preventing women from working at night was mainly for their protection and safety. Even the ILO has a convention to this effect, and it also has a convention that states that women should not work underground. These are two of the few conventions that have been accepted by most countries. At the same time, when it becomes necessary for women to participate in the labour force, these conventions are overlooked. This happened during WWII. Men had to fight the war and women were recruited to work in factories and mines to keep production going. At that time, the 'safety norms' were conveniently ignored.

In the present phase, when there is a growth in call centres (discussed later) and production in the small-scale sector, the issue of women working at night has resurfaced. On 29 March 2005, the

Union Cabinet took a decision to amend the Factories Act 1948 so that women could work on night shifts. The main reason that guided the cabinet's decision was that after January 2005, the quota system for garments and textiles had been lifted by the WTO. Hence it was now possible for India to enter the international market in a big way provided the goods were cost-effective.

Though women occupy a better position in the informal sector in terms of numerical strength, their position in the work hierarchy and income is low. The better-paid jobs are taken by men and the lower-paying ones reserved for women. In fact, the types of work performed by them are those that can be replaced by technology. For example, in the construction industry, women are assigned tasks of carrying building materials to the work site and they carry bricks or crushed stones in baskets on their heads to these places. This task can be performed using conveyer belts, and when they are installed women lose their jobs. Bhagalpur in Bihar is regarded as the centre of the silk spinning industry where the entire task of spinning silk and twisting the yarn is done by women. This is a low-paid job that requires long hours of work. This industry is now facing a crisis because silk imports from China and Korea are fast replacing the domestic product. The obvious losers are the impoverished women spinners of Bhagalpur.

Technical changes, that are taking place at rapid rates at present, result in job losses if no new jobs are created. In agriculture, weeding used to be done by women. The use of pesticides has removed the need for manually removing weeds and hence this reduces the employment of women. In cotton cultivation, women were engaged to pick the cotton buds, but the use of combined harvesters has reduced employment of women.

In most of the cases mentioned above, women are paid wages that are lower than those of men, which is a violation of the law, but women are made to believe that the type of work they do is inferior and hence they are paid less. The Equal Remuneration Act passed in 1976 was meant primarily for workers in mines, plantations, construction industries, etc. Initially it was found that employers, especially in plantations, continued to pay less to women workers on the ground that the workload of men was higher and equal wages would discriminate against male workers. Under the Act, though they worked more than women, they would be paid the same wages. The government clarified in December 1976 that equal pay had to be given to male and female workers when the nature of work was similar irrespective of the volume of work. In other words, the nature of work in construction or in plantations is similar even though women may be assigned less workload than men. Tea plantations in West Bengal started paying equal wages soon after this clarification. However, in Assam, which employs half the plantation workers in the country, equal wages were first paid as late as 1990. In other industries and in agriculture, women continue to be paid lower wages than males.

We find that even in the informal sector, women are assigned the lowest paid jobs and even these are shrinking. At the same time, it would be incorrect to assume that after liberalisation and globalisation, jobs in the informal sector have decreased. In the construction industry, demand for women head loaders may have declined but there are higher demands for services such as carpentry, plumbing, electrical work, etc. Women workers are unable to access these jobs because, firstly, these are categorised as masculine jobs, and secondly, they are not trained, with the second point following from the first. In most cases, plumbers, carpenters and electricians learn their skills from their fathers. Boys are taught these skills when they accompany their fathers to their work but girls are never imparted such skills as these jobs are not meant for them. Hence, if women are to access these jobs they need training. If the state or NGOs provide such training to women construction workers, they could be more freedom of choice in their work. This would also help in eroding the gender-based barriers in work.

Voluntary Retirement Scheme

After the reforms of 1991, employers' organisations demanded that the government should frame an 'exit policy' that would enable any industry to close down. This was fiercely opposed by trade unions, and the government decided against such a policy. At the same time, it allowed companies to reduce their workforce through a process known as the Voluntary Retirement Scheme (VRS). The companies could offer voluntary retirement to their workers by giving them a better retirement package than what they would have got under the law. This would lure workers to accept these terms and quit. In reality what happened was that companies did offer the VRS but if the response was not as much as expected, they would use other tactics to 'convince' their workers. For example, one of the commonest ones was of spreading the rumour that the factory or office concerned would close down within a short while and workers would be transferred to another plant far away; hence, if workers did not accept the time-bound offer of VRS, they would have to either move to the other factory or, if they wanted to resign, they would get only the compensation provided by law and nothing more. It was found that the first offer of VRS had a lukewarm response from employees, but the second round (after these rumours were spread) fared much 'better'.

Myrtle Barse (2001) studied the impact of this scheme in some large companies in Mumbai. She found that it had a marked impact on the nature of employment and in changing the quality of life of the workers. Her paper has case studies of workers who have taken VRS and how their lives changed. Most could not find alternative work and their compensation evaporated within a few years. Their living standards fell drastically, and some could find only low-paid work in the informal sector. She suggests that the government or other organisations such as their trade unions or NGOs should help workers who accept VRS in investing their money properly and also provide for health insurance.

Ernesto Noronha (2001) studied the Bombay Dock Labour Board (BDLB) and how globalisation had changed its functioning. He noted that by setting up the BDLB, a modicum of social security was provided for a sudden economic crisis and at times of recession when work was not readily available. The advent of globalisation and containerisation had reduced the need for labour in the docks. The Board had to resort to VRS for the workers which turned out to be disastrous for them and for the Board too as it faced a fund-crunch after paying the large sums as compensation. This is one case when both employer and employee suffered because of VRS.

Ratan Khasnobis and Sudipti Banerjea (1996) came to similar conclusions while studying VRS in Durgapur in West Bengal. Their study explored the mechanisms behind the workers' acceptance of VRS in the Durgapur Industrial Area. Though there was willingness on the part of workers to accept compensation in some cases, there was a sizeable number of instances of coercion from the management. Moreover, the amount received was often used for unproductive purposes and the worker thus had little left to start self-employment ventures.

Outsourcing

A Case of Internal Outsourcing

We will briefly discuss the case of outsourcing by a unit we shall name Company1, an Anglo-Dutch MNC operating in India.[2] It has been operating since the days of colonial rule and is still the market leader in the detergent and toilet soap industry with market shares of 60 and 40 per cent respectively, having increased considerably over time. The company dominates the shampoo market with a 64.5 per cent share and has a 54 per cent market share in skin creams.

At the same time, the huge increase in production is not matched by an increase in the workforce employed by Company 1. In fact, there has been a sharp decline in the number of workers employed in the company's manufacturing units. In 1985, the company's largest manufacturing unit, namely, the factory in Bombay, employed around 4,000 workers but by 1996 the workforce had shrunk to 1,800. Even this, the company felt, was too high. In every shift a few workers were not given any work because the management stated that there was not enough work. By 2003, the workforce was reduced to around 1,200 workers. In other words, the workforce in this factory was downsized to a little over one-fourth of its size about twenty years back. Simultaneously, we find, the production of Company 1's products had increased substantially. This increase in production was mainly achieved by outsourcing production through other units.

The author had conducted a study on outsourcing at Company 1 in 2001–2. Outsourcing was done in several industrial units in the small-scale sector. There were some units that were promoted by Company1 as its subsidiary though a majority of them were owned by private companies or individuals that manufactured goods for Company 1. The units covered were located in the Industrial Development Zones set up by state governments in non-conventional industrial areas (as discussed in the previous section).

Units sponsored by Company1 had large numbers of workers but that most of them were engaged through labour contractors and not by the company. The number of permanent workers employed by Company1 in each of its units did not exceed 100, and this was done with a purpose. The Industrial Disputes Act states that any

[2] This information is based on a study done by the author in 2002.

manufacturing unit employing 100 or more permanent workers cannot close down without the permission of the state government. Thus by employing less than 100 workers, Company1 was able to close down any of its units with ease, and this happened quite often. In fact, Company1 had built up a dubious reputation of closing down its units when the period of subsidies expired. The company would set up its unit in the industrial development zone and avail itself of all the facilities given to a new unit, but as soon as the period of getting the facilities was over (usually it is for the first five years), it would close the unit and move to another industrial area where it can enjoy the same facilities.

Wages paid to Company1 workers at these industrial development zones were substantially lower than wages of workers in its factory at Mumbai. For example, the average wage of a worker in Daman was Rs 4,500 per month and in Khamgaon this was Rs 6,500 per month, while wages of workers in Company1's factories in Mumbai and Kolkata were between double and three times the wages of workers in those units. The outsourced industries paid wages that were even lower, ranging from Rs 1,500 to Rs 2,500 a month. Lower wages are paid mainly because workers in the industrial zones have low bargaining power. As these regions are less developed, there are few employment opportunities outside the industrial zones. Moreover workers in these units are not unionised, which reduces their bargaining power further.

Such large-scale outsourcing had two advantages for reducing costs, viz. firstly, exemption from Income Tax, and secondly, lower labour costs. Both factors should have helped in lowering prices of Company1 products, but this did not happen. Consumers paid higher prices mainly because of the brand name of Company1. The author found that in 2001, prices of Company1 brands in India (soaps, shampoos) were more than the prices of the same products in Germany, a rich, industrialised country! A small container of shampoo cost Rs 65 and the larger one Rs 130 in India, whereas in Germany, the same large container cost DM 2.50 (Rs 50); a cake of soap made by Company1 cost Rs 45 in India, while its price in Germany was DM 1.50 (Rs 30).

Internal Outsourcing in Other Industries

The above type of outsourcing is done not just by MNCs like Company 1 but by other large companies as well. For example, since the 1980s, quite a few large-scale textile mills have closed rendering hundreds of thousands of workers unemployed. The main textile centres were Mumbai and Ahmedabad (see Bhowmik and More 2001; Breman 2001). There were around eighty large-scale textile mills in these two cities in 1984. At present, these metropolises have not more than ten textile mills functioning between them. Production of textiles has not decreased due to these closures. Instead, production is now outsourced to the thriving power-loom sector. Power-looms are similar to hand-looms except that they are run by electricity and not by human energy. The technology used is backward, and much lower than that of large-scale textile factories. The power-loom sector becomes viable because, as discussed earlier, the wages paid to workers are low. In this sector too, low technology and low labour productivity are offset by low labour costs. The textile companies by and large get their products by outsourcing to the power-loom sector. The wages of a power-loom worker are between one-third and one-fourth of the wages in large-scale textile mills.

Products other than textiles are outsourced to the small-scale sector as protective legislation and regulations are lax or non-existent in this sector. Peter Knorringa (1996), a Dutch sociologist, studied the footwear industry in Agra. The shoe-makers belong to ex-'untouchable' communities and they have low social status. Knorringa found that the relations between the small self-employed shoemaker and the exporter's agent were based on the traditional relations in the caste hierarchy, the agent assuming the role of the upper-caste patron of the lower-caste shoemaker. In traditional caste relations, the lower or 'untouchable' castes comprised those who performed manual work and were usually associated with the so-called 'unclean' activities like working with hides, cleaning the village, providing labour for the upper-castes, etc. Their lower social status ensured that the remuneration they got, in an economy based on exchange, was much lower compared to the physical labour they were expected to perform. This formed the basis of the exploitation of the lower castes by the upper castes in the traditional system. Knorringa's findings show that by recreating traditional caste relations the agents revive the age-old forms of exploitation based on caste status, the relationship being not of worker and buyer but more of master and servant; the agent belongs to the upper caste and the worker is akin to the servant. In this feudal relationship, the workers are frequently short-changed for their work, and the agent is in a position to pay them less than they deserve.

Apart from Knorringa's study, there are other instances in different cities, viz. Kanpur, Kolkata and Mumbai, where low-caste leather workers are the main suppliers of good quality, high-priced leather products for the domestic and the export markets. Most of the branded shoes available in the domestic market are manufactured by such workers. As in the case of Company1, we see that large manufacturers of leather products have downsized their labour force drastically. The largest manufacturer in this field, which we shall name Company 2, had two large factories in India. At present, both factories have carried out drastic cuts in their permanent labour force and in production. Most of this company's products are now manufactured in the small-scale sector. In Dharavi, in Mumbai, reputed to be Asia's largest slum, there are clusters of sweat shops that employ workers to produce leather goods for the international market using assembly-line methods to ensure standardisation of the goods produced. The employees are largely Hindus belonging to the *charmakar* or *dhor* castes that were traditionally engaged in leather work while tanning was done by Muslims.

Outsourcing can be possible only if labour costs are low and so is the technology, production thus being labour-intensive. Low labour costs mean low costs of production. The combination of these factors has promoted outsourcing. This is what happens at the international level too. The less-developed countries have an edge over the developed countries mainly because labour costs are low. This has to be coupled with technology that is labour-intensive as only then can costs be reduced. Let us now look at outsourcing in the international sphere.

Outsourcing for the International Market

India is a land of contrasts. On one side there is high level of illiteracy (roughly 40 per cent) and on another side there is a highly qualified workforce that has spread all over the world due to its superior skills. Hence it is not surprising that India should be sought after by international companies for outsourcing work. These can be seen in diverse activities that are labour-intensive. Costs of labour, as mentioned earlier, are low as compared to international standards.

Outsourcing in India is prevalent at two extreme levels. At the bottom end, there are poorly-paid workers in 'sweat shops' who put together goods for the international market. At the opposite end, there is outsourcing in the microelectronic sector, involving large contracts for developing software, etc. The current trend is for Business Process Outsourcing (BPOs), involving operation of call centres on a wide scale and other forms of outsourcing such as back-office functioning. Legal companies, banks and other loan agencies outsource their office work to these Indian companies. Most of this work comes from the USA though the UK also has a fair share. The extent of outsourcing can be seen from the large number of call centres operating in various cities. Gurgaon, a city close to Delhi, has a large concentration of call centres, while Hyderabad is among the global centres of information technology for which it is known as 'Cyberabad' (Cyber City). In Mumbai, the suburb of Andheri has a large number of call centres and other BPOs. In Kolkata, the government has demarcated an area for software companies in Sector V of its suburb, Salt Lake. Bangalore is known as 'India's Silicon Valley' given the large concentration of software companies in the city.

Outsourcing in India started in the software industries over a decade ago. Bangalore was the city where this started. The microelectronic revolution of the 1980s brought about radical changes in production. The sudden improvement in communications led to rapid transfers of capital as well as trade between countries. The change in technology made it possible for countries like India that had a pool of technical personnel to take advantage of the changed scenario.

TABLE 7.1: Indian IT/BPO Industry Revenues, Software and Related Services, FY 1998–2009

USD Bn	FY 98	FY 99	FY 00	FY 01	FY 02	FY 03	FY 04	FY 05	FY 06	FY 07	FY 08	FY 09	CAGR
Exports	1.8	2.7	4.0	6.2	7.6	9.5	12.9	17.7	23.6	31.2	40.4	46.3	34.3%
Domestic	1.4	1.6	1.9	2.5	2.6	3.0	3.8	4.8	6.7	8.2	11.7	12.4	22%
Total	3.2	4.3	5.8	8.7	10.2	12.5	16.7	22.5	30.3	39.4	52.1	58.7	30.3%

Source: GoI 2009: 15.

Several leading MNCs and other international companies took advantage of the microelectronic revolution and decided to shift their activities involving communication and computer technology to countries like India. These countries had trained personnel who could be employed at low wages (compared to wages in developed countries). This led to the first forms of outsourcing. Holmstrom conducted a study of Bangalore as a techno-city where flexible specialisation was introduced (Holmstrom 1997). A more recent study on Bangalore details the problems of the software industry (Heitzman 2004). It traces the relationship between information technology and social organisation in the city.

Outsourcing in the software industry is done by large companies in the developed countries. For example, the entire accounting work of a German MNC is done in Bangalore and so is the ticketing for international airline companies. Similarly, the software upgrading of cell phones for US companies is also done in outsourced units. India has a comparative cost advantage as far as software is concerned. The level of living is lower and around US$ 1000 a month would be a fairly decent salary for a qualified software programmer. Similarly, the call centres have flourished because the operators know English and are available at cheaper rates than their counterparts in the USA and UK. The operators are paid around US$ 650–700 per month and supervisors/ group leaders earn around US$ 800–1000 per month. In the USA, they would be paid not less than US$ 3000 besides social security benefits. This is why companies in USA, Australia and the English-speaking parts of Europe have chosen India for outsourcing the call centres. The boom in call centres happened in the late 1990s with the sudden and rapid improvement in communication technology in India. It has provided employment to several thousand youths especially in the cities. A news report (*India Today* 2002: 36-49) noted that in late 2002 there were 336 centres employing 110,000 people.

The other form of outsourcing is the back office activities. These offices provide back-up services to companies in the developed countries, especially in the USA, providing information on various legal and other matters for the company that has hired them. The costs in this case too are low compared to those in developed countries for the same services. We have described the type of outsourcing that is done at the upper end of the market. Let us see what happens at the lower end.

Outsourcing in the developing countries is mainly prevalent in certain industries that involve low technology and low labour costs.

Thus in industries such as textiles and garments outsourcing is quite popular. Bangladesh is at present an important area for outsourcing in the garment industry. In India, outsourcing in garments is not very popular because there is a quota system for export of garments. Our textile industry is involved in export of better-quality fabrics. We have discussed in the section on outsourcing in the domestic market how the power-loom industry has replaced the large textile mills. In cities such as Surat, in Gujarat, the power-loom industry is engaged in outsourcing for markets abroad. Other industries that engage in outsourcing are the leather industry and the handicrafts industry. In these industries, the labourers have low literacy and are impoverished, the wages being low and working conditions extremely poor. In most cases, workers are paid at piece rates, i.e., according to the number of items they produce. The rates paid are usually low and the worker has to put in ten to twelve hours of work a day in order to produce enough for getting a minimum wage.

TRADE UNION RESPONSE

Trade unions have by and large opposed the liberalisation policies. They have organised nationwide strikes, *bandhs* (literally, stoppages) and rallies in different parts of the country. These have hardly had any effect in changing the policies. The only assurance given so far is that there will be no 'exit policy'. This is of little value, as we have seen earlier, as workers continue to lose their jobs through VRS and lay-offs caused by downsizing.

It is evident that all these forms of conventional protests may not be sufficient. There is need for undertaking a revaluation of the situation and developing new forms of opposition as well as alternatives to the present policies. While it cannot be denied that traditional means of protest including mass action play an important role in mobilisation of the working class and making them articulate their problems collectively, these methods may not achieve the purpose in the changing circumstances of globalisation and its onslaughts on workers' rights. Ever since the liberalisation policies were introduced, the government and the media have presented a positive and vibrant picture of a 'new' India. In such a situation, the role of organised labour through trade unions is not appreciated. It is projected that organised labour tries to raise unnecessary and unreasonable protests against the new policies. These views are widely accepted by the growing middle class which is the greatest supporter of liberalisation.

One of the weaknesses of the trade union movement during these critical times for labour was that it had by and large restricted itself to unionising labour in the formal sector ignoring the vast pool of labour in the informal sector. The verification of union membership by the Labour Department in 1987 showed that of the total membership of the seven recognised national federations, only one per cent of their membership lay in the informal sector. Even when the informal sector exists within the formal sector, trade unions have tended to overlook them. A study of contract and casual labour in eight industries showed that casual and contract labour formed between 30 and 50 per cent of the labour force (Davala 1993). Except in one industry, tea, these workers were not unionised. In some cases, unionised workers regarded them as rivals who would take away their jobs. Rare instances like SEWA apart, there are hardly any instances of trade unions in the informal sector. We shall return to this issue of unionising the informal sector later.

Fortunately, the national trade unions have tried to overcome this deficiency by enrolling informal sector workers in the unions. The membership verification of trade unions, as explained in Chapter 5, shows why membership increased five-fold. However, despite the increase in strength, trade unions are still ignored by government and the media whenever they stage protests. Protests in some industries though, depending on their strategic importance, can be more effective in highlighting the cause of the workers. For example, a strike in the banking industry for a single day can paralyse the economy; however, even if five times the number of agricultural workers strike, it might hardly be noticed. The unfortunate part of this process of change is that the authorities and a large section of the public have become insensitive to the problems of the working class.

At the same time, globalisation is something that cannot be wished away. It has led to a degree of pauperisation and insecurity of the working class all over the world. Labour in developed countries too has to face its consequences. For example, the outsourcing process reduces secure jobs in developed countries and it creates insecure jobs in the developing ones. But is this new for human society? Any sudden change results in situations that are not easily perceived. It therefore gets labelled as anti-people and there are moves to oppose it.

Globalisation has raised certain challenges for the working-class movement. The question now is: can the labour movement adapt itself to face these challenges? Or rather, the question can be reframed as: is the labour movement willing to adapt to the challenges thrown up by globalisation and develop new strategies to face these? Given the present orientation of the mainstream trade union movement in the country, this seems unlikely in the near future. Trade union strategies, as of now, revolve around two issues: firstly, use of traditional means of protest, such as strikes, rallies and bandhs, whenever the issue of closure or redundancy arises in the organised sector; And secondly, the issue of opposing globalisation itself. Both strategies have achieved limited success in their objectives. The question is therefore not of opposing globalisation per se, but rather, how best the interests of the working people can be safeguarded.

In other words, is mere opposition enough to combat the adverse effects of globalisation or should the labour movement promote some positive alternatives? A related, but more crucial, question is: can trade unions function merely as opposition bodies, or, should they offer alternatives? This is the crucial question facing the labour movement today.

Key Concepts/Definitions

State capitalism When the State takes on the role of the capitalist to develop the economy.

Outsourcing Movement of production from the main manufacturing/ services unit to ancillary units.

References and Readings

Barse, Myrtle. 2001. 'Voluntary Retirement Scheme: Problems'. *Economic and Political Weekly* 36 (52).

Bagchi, Amiya K., ed. 1994. *New Technology and the Workers' Response: Microelectronics, Labour and Society*. Delhi: Sage Publications.

Bhowmik, Sharit K., and Nitin More. 2001. 'Coping with Urban Poverty: Ex-textile Mill Workers of Mumbai'. *Economic and Political Weekly Review of Labour* 36 (52).

Breman, Jan. 2001. 'An Informal Labour System: End of Labour Market Dualism'. *Economic and Political Weekly* 36 (52).

Das, Subesh K., and P. Panayiotopoulis. 1996. 'Flexible Specialisation: New Paradigm for Industrialisation for Developing Countries?' *Economic and Political Weekly* (Review of Labour) 31 (52).

Gartenberg, I., and S. Bandekar. 2011. 'Challenges to Ensuring Core Labour Standards in Transnational Corporations: The Case of India'. *Indian Journal of Labour Economics*, 54 (2): 269–83.

Government of India (GoI). 2003. 'Economic Survey, 2002–2003'. Available on finmin.nic.in.

———. 2005. 'Economic Survey for the Year 2004–5'. Available on finmin.nic. in.

Heitzman, James, 2004. *Network City: Planning the Information Society in Bangalore*. New Delhi: Oxford University Press.

Holmstrom, Mark. 1997. 'A Cure for Loneliness? Networks, Trust and Shared Services in Bangalore'. *Economic and Political Weekly* 32 (35).

India Today. 2002. 'Housekeepers to the World'. Delhi 27 (46), 18 November.

Jhabvala, Renana, and Shalini Sinha. 2002. 'Liberalisation and the Woman Worker.' *Economic and Political Weekly* 37 (23): 2037–44.

Khasnobis, Ratan, and Sudipti Banerjea. 1996. 'Political Economy of Voluntary Retirement: Study of "Rationalised" Workers in Durgapur'. *Economic and Political Weekly* 31 (52).

Knorringa, Peter. 1996. *Economics of Collaboration: Indian Shoemakers Between Market and Hierarchy*. New Delhi: Sage Publications.

Ministry of Communications & IT, GoI. 2009. 'Report of Task Force to suggest measures to stimulate the growth of IT, ITES and Electronics Hardware manufacturing industry in India'. New Delhi 15 (http://www.mit.gov.in/sites/upload_files/dit/files/Task_Force_Report-new_21211%282%29.pdf)

Noronha, Ernesto. 2001. 'Dock Labour Board 1948–94: From Security to Insecurity?' *Economic and Political Weekly*, 36 (52).

Sawant, S. T., and Purnima Rao. 1993. *New Economic Policy: Problems and Alternatives.* New Delhi: Friedrich Ebert Stiftung.

World Bank. 1995. *World Development Report 1995: Workers in an Integrating World.* Delhi: Oxford University Press.

8

INTERNATIONAL LABOUR STANDARDS AND DECENT WORK

Chapter Highlights

» Categories of labour standards
» Implementation of workers' rights
» Child labour
» Decent work
» Need-based minimum wage
» Three issues concerning social protection
» Importance of discussions and negotiations

International Labour Standards deal with the rights of human beings at work. There are certain basic rights that workers all over the world are entitled to. These rights are an outcome of the workers' struggles over the ages. In the earlier chapters, we have discussed these initiatives in more detail. The ILO, which is a United Nations (UN) agency and has a membership of 174 countries, has been the upholder of labour standards. It is found that there are certain common labour standards that apply to workers all over the world. These basic rights are applicable to all the member countries of the ILO, irrespective of their levels of economic development. The general assembly of the ILO, which comprises representatives of all the member countries, the trade unions and the employers' organisations, has vowed to protect, promote and realise the fundamental rights of labour. These are known as the International Labour Standards (ILS).

The need for ILS springs from the fact that there are divergent conditions of employment in different parts of the world. The ILS attempt to improve conditions of workers with reference to their health, well-being and advancement at work. In many countries, workers have to fight for having the right to health care. In most of the developing countries, this right is denied to a large section of workers in the informal sector. International labour standards tend to convey the fact that, irrespective of the status, all workers deserve proper health care so that they can work better. This would help employers too, as labour productivity would increase.

Political motives played a part in the development of the ILO. This is the reason why issues such as ILS became crucial. Let us explain what this means. It was widely believed by most international agencies including the ILO that as the developing countries industrialised, most of the problems of the working class would be solved. We have seen earlier that till 1986, the ILO strongly believed that as development takes place, the informal sector would be absorbed into the formal sector. These hopes were belied because despite industrialisation there was an absence of similar improvement in the working conditions and rights of workers. In many countries, India included, certain rights were bestowed on the workers for their protection. Later, as these countries liberalised their economy, the authorities gradually usurped these rights. In other words, industrialisation had progressed, but the plight of the workers did not improve; in some cases, it showed signs of deterioration. Such a situation created a firm ground for social unrest. This had to be thwarted and the ILS became an important tool for doing so.

We can group labour standards into five categories. These are (i) freedom of association, (ii) effective recognition of the right to organise and participate in collective bargaining, (iii) elimination of all forms of forced and compulsory labour, (iv) effective elimination of child labour, and (v) elimination of discrimination in respect of employment and occupation. Let us examine each of these.

We had discussed in Chapter 3 how workers in England had to struggle to get the right to freedom of association. The bill granting this right was passed by the British Parliament in 1824. Earlier, any association formed by workers was deemed as illegal. The workers could be punished and even imprisoned for forming such associations, which was regarded as a conspiracy against the state. Engels had noted that after this right was granted, the trade union movement spread rapidly among workers across the country. The right to association is also a fundamental right granted by the Constitution of India. This implies that trade unions need to be recognised as the rightful representation of the working class. This is an important right for workers.

In India, better-paid skilled workers in some large companies have protested and even gone on strike because they were denied the right to form their trade union. For instance, in July 2011, a well-known automobile company based in North India had to face labour unrest because of a strike by its workers. This company was known for its non-hierarchical methods in the interactions between management and labour. The general manager would perform physical exercises with the workers before starting work; moreover, unlike most other large organisations, the company had a common dining hall for workers and managers. This company was praised for its unorthodox methods of interaction between labour and management. It would thus be expected that the company would be trouble-free and workers and managers would both be working towards the well-being of this company. In other words, this would be an ideal example for the Systems approach to industrial relations. Despite all these positive factors, the company had to face a strike which was later turned into a lockout by the management. The main bone of contention was the right of the workers to choose their own union. It was believed by a large section of the workers that the management was trying to influence them in selecting their representative union. The union which the workers had voted for did not find favour with the management; hence it did not get recognition as the official representative of the workers. The management tried to substitute the workers, which resulted in labour unrest. This occurrence came as a surprise to many analysts for it was believed that issues relating to wages and remuneration are the main causes for industrial unrest. The case of this automobile industry proved that this is not true. The workers did not put forth any demand concerning monetary gains and all they wanted was that the union that they had selected should be given the status of the representative union. This case is not an isolated one. During 2009–11, there were at least two cases involving better-paid, educated workers in technologically advanced industries who had struck work for similar reasons. In a multinational company manufacturing automobile parts for the international market, the workers went on strike for eighteen days as a protest against the sacking of sixteen employees who were trade union office bearers. The management finally had to relent and accede to the workers' demands. After the strike was called off, twelve of those workers were reinstated and assurance given that the remaining would be reinstated in a phased manner.

We can see that the right to form trade unions, also known as the right to freedom of association, is vital for the working class. However, forming unions alone is not enough for workers, if it is not recognised by the management. This would distinguish an official trade union from any other form of association by the workers such as a football club or a recreational club. The important aspect of a trade union is that it should be recognised as the representative of the workers. Hence, the second international labour standard becomes important, namely, effective recognition of the right to organise and participate in collective bargaining. The recognition of a trade union would imply that it becomes the representative of the employees in collective bargaining with the employers. We need to again clarify that collective bargaining is not restricted to only wage issues. It could include every aspect of the working life. The data on labour disputes in India indicate that only 40 per cent of the cases relate to wage issues, the remaining having to deal with working conditions and related issues. The workers would want their union to be involved in collective bargaining so that they can effectively intervene in managerial decisions. This aspect is important not only for getting them their rights but, more importantly, for their dignity.

The other labour standards will be discussed in the following section on Decent Work.

DECENT WORK

The 1990s ushered in the phase of globalisation and economic liberalisation. The socialist bloc, comprising USSR and Eastern Europe, had collapsed and with redrawn borders these countries later restructured their economies by opening up and decreasing protectionism. Other countries like India too went in for restructuring and liberalisation.

These policies may have helped in improving growth as far as India is concerned, but simultaneously they increased inequalities. One of the visible changes was in the nature of employment. It could be seen that formal-sector jobs had decreased and work in the informal sector had increased. This was due to a variety of reasons including outsourcing of production to less developed countries, such as ours, by the developed ones. Jobs in developed countries were shrinking or being replaced by low-income ones with minimal or no social security. International agencies such as World Bank (WB) and the International Monetary Fund (IMF) strongly backed such reforms. The *World Development Report* for 1995 (the annual report of the World Bank) titled 'Workers in a Globalizing World' noted that flexibility in the labour market and non-intervention of the state were absolutely necessary for achieving greater employment. The report stressed that countries like India and those in Latin America had put many restrictions regarding employment. What it meant was that the laws which granted protection to workers and permanence of tenure were inimical to growth of employment. The argument was that if there were too many laws protecting the workers' rights, employers would be wary of setting up industries and hiring workers.

The reality is that in most countries, a permanent job means a host of other facilities that include regulation of work and rest, leave, medical facilities and retirement benefits. These may be good for the workers but agencies like the World Bank pointed out that they were too costly. Cost of production increases because of the high cost of labour and, secondly, it is difficult, due to legal protection, to fire labour if found unsuitable. The World Bank argued that this prevents growth of employment. As a result, more and more countries have gone in for modifying their protective labour laws, thereby increasing reliance on insecure, unprotected labour.

What we see at present is that liberalisation may have increased employment in aggregate terms but the quality of jobs has declined. As mentioned earlier, the idea of a job for the worker implies a host of other facilities. However, the types of jobs that are generated now are often low-paid and insecure. If a job does not provide the basic requirements for the worker's family, it will be necessary for the other members of the family to look for employment in order to meet the deficit. For instance, in a city like Mumbai, the minimum income which would cover the basic family needs of food, clothing and shelter would be around Rs 5000 per month, even for a person living in a slum. If the main earning member in the family has a job which pays him Rs 3000 per month, there is a deficit of Rs 2000. His wife would perhaps work as a domestic worker or even a waste-picker in order to earn the extra income. If this is not possible, then even the children in the family would be made to work to make ends meet. This would mean that there is full employment in the family. On the other hand, a single member of the middle class may earn Rs 30,000 per month, and his wife and child do not work for wages. Hence, there is two-thirds unemployment in the family. Would this imply that the slum dweller whose entire family works is better off than this middle-class man?

This is where the situation becomes irrational if we restrict our arguments to merely increase in employment. The type of employment which is being generated after liberalisation would include courier services, cable TV, security services, etc. All these jobs involve long working hours (ten to twelve hours per day), and the remuneration is not at all commensurate to the work. Moreover, those workers can be hired and fired at will. But the pay offered would at most barely cover the minimum needs of a family. Hence, mere increase in employment without taking into account a living wage is of no consequence. One does not know whether this situation really helps the working poor in uplifting their economically weak position.

One is not questioning whether such jobs are necessary and should be abolished. On the contrary, for an impoverished worker even having a poorly-paid job with stiff working conditions is better than having no job at all. The issue is whether every worker has the right to live their life with dignity. This unfortunately is not often the case.

It has been argued that insecure workers make better workers because they work under pressure and they need to perform or else they will lose their jobs. Is this argument accurate? It can also be argued that improvement in the quality of work is good not just for the workers for employers too gain because healthy, secure workers would be more productive than half-starved workers. One can recall the situation in England in the 1840s. At that time, the industrial revolution was at its oppressive worst. Machine-made goods had replaced the products of craftspersons in the villages. These included ironsmiths, potters, weavers, etc., who had left their villages and flocked to the industrial areas in search of employment. Jobs were available but for too few compared to the number of job-seekers. At that time, if a factory owner needed 500 workers, he would select them and inform them about the working conditions and the pay. If, for example, 100 of them said that the pay was too low or the working conditions were bad, the employer would not bargain with them. He knew that if these 100 refused to work, there would be at least three times the number of job-seekers who would be willing to work for even less. This type of competition among the workers for getting a job started depressing the wages. For the individual employer/capitalists, this was encouraging because they were able to get cheaper labour. However in the long run, this would prove to be detrimental, because if wages kept falling to very low levels it would affect the health of the workers. They would eat less and work more and ultimately they would either fall ill or die. At that time, the trade associations of the factory owners realised that such a situation may be good for the individual owner but it was suicidal for the industry as a whole if productivity started falling due to low wages. It was then that the associations approached the government to enforce a floor wage. This was obviously not done because of concern for the impoverished worker but mainly because the worker must be paid enough so that he could work even harder. Unfortunately, even this modicum of sense does not seem to dawn on those engaging cheap labour in our society now.

In the midst of such a situation, the ILO thought of the idea of restoring dignity to workers by proposing the concept of Decent Work. In 1999, the Secretary General of the ILO, Juan Somavia, elaborated on this concept. In his address, in the background of decreasing quality of work worldwide, to the International Labour Conference, he spelt out the details. He presented an alternative to the prevailing situation. The basic concept of Decent Work presumed productive work under conditions of freedom, equity and dignity, where freedom would mean that the rights of the workers were protected, equity implied adequate remuneration for work, and dignity would include social coverage or protection. It also implied that all would have full access to income-earning opportunities.

Decent Work according to Somavia marks the high road to economic and social development where employment, income and social protection can be achieved without comprising workers' rights and social standards. Another aspect is the stress on tripartism and social dialogue. This would imply that all issues relating to work, employment and industrial relations should be sorted out through democratic processes that involved all three partners—the state, the workers and their union, and the employers and their associations. In brief, Decent Work is built on four pillars—rights at work, right to employment and work, social protection, and social dialogue. Let us elaborate on each of these essential aspects.

Rights at Work

This includes the ethical and legal framework for all elements of Decent Work. We could begin with the natural rights, more commonly known as human rights that are enshrined in the UN Declaration on Human Rights, 1948. The concept of rights at work is not merely having the right to permanent employment but it has a host of other implications. First of all, there should be no discrimination in employment. Quite often we find that discriminations are based on gender, race, religion and, in India, caste and language. The rights of women at the workplace are frequently absent or violated. For example, it took several years to establish separate toilets for women in factories. Though the Equal Remuneration Act, 1975, was enacted to ensure that there was no discrimination between the sexes in certain work areas such as construction, plantation, mining and agriculture, we still find that women are paid lower wages than men. The Equal Remuneration Act was earlier misinterpreted on the logic that since the workload of women was lower than that of men, this Act could not be implemented unless the workload was equalised. The government later, in December 1995, clarified that it was not equal *volume* of work but the *nature* of work which would determine equal wages. However, the differences in wages in all these industries, except plantations, continue unabated.

Violation of Other Rights

We have seen in Chapter 3 that joining a trade union or the right to form associations is one of the basic rights of a worker. Hence, it is an integral part of Decent Work. What we find in many cases is that forced labour is used for production. Forced labour can be seen in cases of bonded labour which exists in India and Pakistan. Here, the worker and his family are bound to serve under the landlord as payment for some help he had extended to them either in their lifetime or in the past generations. These are extreme forms of forced labour. However, we find that forced labour can also exist in other ways. When there is shortage of employment opportunities, workers may work at wages much below the sustenance level. This is a form of forced labour because the worker works at depressed wages due to economic hardship. One way of overcoming this type of forced labour is through provision of jobs by the state. The MGNREGS (now MGNREGA) ensures that one member of every rural household below the poverty line will get 100 days of employment in a year. The idea of such a programme is to ensure that rural workers have an alternative occupation which would boost the existing wages. If rural workers find that wages offered by land owners are low, they have the option to work under that scheme. The landlords then will be forced to increase the wage rate to draw the workers out of the public works scheme.

Implementation of Rights at Work

Having laws protecting workers at work is important, but more important is that these laws are implemented. Many countries including India have fairly extensive laws for protecting workers, but these are hardly ever implemented or implemented properly. A lot depends on the political environment and the attitude of the state. If the state believes in upholding human rights and rights at work, it will be proactive in implementing these rights. Normally, democratic countries show greater inclination in defending the rights of workers. However, there could be international pressures, as happened when the economy started liberalising and international agencies such as the World Bank, etc., insisted that our policies for protecting labour should be replaced by free market policies; having greater labour protection, they argued, would discourage international capital from investing in the country. The government did not amend the existing laws, but introduced riders which in effect weakened the laws. For instance, there has been considerable pressure for having an exit policy for industry. This means that the employer can close down a factory or a workplace if he finds that it is not profitable. The existing laws did not allow this to happen. The state then devised a plan for circumventing these laws and they allowed a policy of voluntary retirement from service, or VRS. This helped many companies to downsize and shed their permanent workers.

We find similar cases in countries ruled by dictators where labour may lose the rights they had secured through struggle in the past when there was democracy. Another example is provided by politically powerful countries such as the USA. Though it has been the strongest supporter of democratic rights, it has allowed the use of forced labour in manufacturing, as in the case of the popular brand of jeans called

'Prison Blues' which is also exported. USA would rather not disclose the fact that these jeans are made by prisoners in Pendleton (in the state of Oregon). Using prison labour for producing goods that are marketed is regarded as a form of forced labour. Besides, over 50 per cent of prisoners in the USA belong to the African-American community, which appears excessive, considering that black people constitute less than 13 per cent of the total US population. At the same time, USA has been highly vocal about the human rights of prisoners elsewhere in the world. It also initiated an economic boycott of Cuba (partial from 1960, and near-total from 1962 till date) because USA felt that Cuba had violated human rights, though there was little evidence to prove this. We can see this form of discriminatory action in the case of South Africa as well. That country had violated human rights by carrying out its apartheid policy (1948–90) that segregated whites from blacks, the latter being highly oppressed. Most Western countries criticised South Africa but did not take any concrete action in forcing the government to abandon its policy. The country now has a democracy, but that was mainly through the concerted struggles of the oppressed people.

Child labour has caused concern to many developed countries, especially when children are used for producing goods for exports. In the late 1980s, certain countries expressed concern over the fact that children were being used as cheap labour in the carpet industry in South Asia. The use of child labour was rampant because the value of a carpet depends on the number of knots that are tied; children have nimble fingers and can tie more knots than adults. Carpet weaving is hazardous to the health of the child as they inhale the lint or fluff resulting in respiratory diseases. Moreover, working in a constantly bent position can distort the shape of the spine. Germany led a movement of boycotting carpets that had used child labour in its manufacture. Strict checks were followed and child-labour-free carpets were given the label of 'Rugmark'. This helped in reducing the use of child labour in the carpet industry.

In India, the use of child labour is not totally banned, as in many other developing countries. The Child Labour (Prohibition and Regulation) Act, 1986 lays down the minimum age of employment as fourteen, and children are not permitted to work in hazardous industries. Initially, this was restricted to twelve hazardous industries or workplaces; at present, there are more than 86 of them. Some of the gravest violations of child rights can be seen in the planation industry. The Plantation Labour Act, 1951, permits the use of children in working in the plantations. This law has been amended in as late as 2010 mainly due to protests of international buyers of tea. The minimum age of employment is now 15 years.

TABLE 8.1: Percentage of Child Workers (5–14 years) across Industry Groups by Gender, 2004–5

Industry Group	Boys	Girls	Total
Agriculture	62.8	71.1	66.6
Mining	0.1	0.4	0.2
Manufacturing	14.4	20.5	17.2
Electricity	0.0	0.0	0.0
Construction	3.0	0.8	2.0
Trade	10.6	1.6	6.4
Hotels	4.4	0.4	2.5
Transport	1.2	0.1	0.7
Real estate	1.2	0.0	0.6
Education	0.0	0.0	0.0
Health	0.0	0.1	0.0
Community	1.8	1.6	1.7
Household	0.5	3.4	1.8
Total	100.0	100.0	100.0

Source: NCEUS 2007: 121.

Though there are laws preventing child labour, they are rendered ineffective when children continue to work in a clandestine manner. One of the arguments is that poverty drives children to work. Their families are unable to earn enough to make ends meet, hence children are sent out to fill the income gap; this view may or may not be true. A stronger view is that if there are no educational facilities in the vicinity, poorer families would prefer to send their children to work rather than sit at home doing nothing. In other words, providing accessible and free education facilities can be the most effective means of preventing child labour. Unfortunately in India, this does not usually happen, even after promulgation of the Right to Education Act in 2010, especially in the rural areas where children may have to walk for miles to reach the nearest school.

Employment and Work

Employment is a vital component of Decent Work. It does not merely cover wage-based jobs but includes all kinds of work such as wage-based jobs, self-employment, home-based work, etc., as well as full-time, part-time and casual work by men, women and children. Decent Work, according to the ILO, means that there should be adequate employment opportunities for all those who seek work. In addition, these types of employment should yield a remuneration (in cash or kind) that meets the essential needs of the worker and the members of their family. This aspect is extremely important. Employment is usually not a problem in developing countries. In India, less than 5 per cent of the population is unemployed, whereas, in several developing countries, the unemployment rate could be as high as 20–30 per cent. The basic difference is that in India the remuneration from employment is in most cases low, which means that if the main earning member does not earn enough to cover the basic needs of the family, the other members will have to work at odd jobs. In a poor family in a slum, besides the main earning member and his wife, the children may be pulled out of school and made to work at odd jobs. In this way, we will find that the whole family is employed. However, does this form of full employment mean that their standard of living has improved? We cannot properly discuss employment without taking into account the important issue of a need-based minimum wage.

A crucial aspect is how a need-based minimum wage is to be determined. In India, there are some measures through which one can determine the need-based minimum wage. This issue was raised in the 15th Indian Labour Conference (ILC) in 1957. The ILC is a tripartite body which includes employers' associations, trade unions and the state (labour department) and it meets every year to discuss labour policies. It is like a country-based ILO. There had been considerable debates in the past on the issue of wages. There were also laws that enforced payment of wages such as Payment of Wages Act, 1935, and Minimum Wages Act, 1948.

These acts laid down the guidelines for how wages should be paid, and if an organisation decides on a minimum wage, it has to pay it to all its employees. However, the basic issue of what constitutes the minimum wage was never resolved. The 15th ILC decided that a need-based minimum wage should consist of the daily minimum needs of three units of consumption. In other words, whatever was fixed as a minimum wage, it implied that that was the minimum need for reproducing labour for the next day. A sub-committee was set up to determine the various components of this wage. If a minimum wage was to cover the basic needs of food, clothing and shelter, it was necessary to decide what would be the inputs in terms of nutrition. These could be seen in the amount of cereals, vegetables, milk, egg, meat or fish and oil that would be consumed by a family for the daily nutritional requirements (set at 3000 calories, 15 gms of protein and carbohydrates, etc.). This could be converted into cash terms.

The other essential items were clothing, fuel and rent. The minimum needs of cloth for a family were fixed at 72 yards per annum for each family. It was decided that in the minimum wage, food and clothing comprised 80 per cent, and the remaining 20 per cent was for fuel and rent. In 1991, the Supreme Court ruled in a case (Unni vs Kerala Tiles) that schooling and sudden or unexpected expenditures due to death, marriage, or births should also be considered while determining the minimum wage, and that 25 per cent of the minimum wage should be set aside for these items. The minimum wage at present comprises food and clothing to cover 55 per cent of the total, fuel and rent to cover 20 per cent, and unexpected expenditures 25 per cent. A key aspect of the minimum wage is that it is non-negotiable. If an employer cannot pay the minimum wage, s/he should not employ labour. It was decided that the states would periodically notify the need-based minimum wage based on the above components and this would be mandatory for all employers within their jurisdiction.

If one takes each of these items at market value, the minimum wage would be fairly 'decent', enabling a family to live with dignity and possibly promoting the all-round welfare of the dependent members. In other words, children in the family would be able to have a decent schooling and women too would get some benefits. However, the actual minimum wage has never been decided. Right from the beginning, the states tried to cut corners by lowering some requirements. For example, they claimed that 3000 calories was too high for India, where the climatic conditions did not demand it (in cold countries, the calorie intake is higher). Hence, this was reduced to 2700 and subsequently to 2200 calories; in other words, the amount of cereals was slashed. The rent and other expenses were also lowered considerably. The resultant need-based minimum wage was not sufficient to fulfil the needs of the family. What was worse was that most employers, especially those in the informal sector, openly violated payment of even the revised and lowered stipulated minimum wages, and hardly any action was taken because in most cases the workers, to whom the minimum wages were paid were unorganised and helpless. Had they been unionised, they would have either collectively demanded proper wages or they could have complained of the violations to the authorities.

In addition to receiving a decent wage, employment would also include protection against accidents, unhealthy and dangerous working conditions and long hours of work. In other words, a minimum wage is given on the basis of the working day. In India, this is eight hours per day. One can see that there is another form of violation of minimum wages by extending the working day. For example, if an owner of a small industrial unit decides to pay the notified minimum wage, but makes a man work more than eight hours, he is effectively depriving him of his minimum wage; if that worker works for ten hours in a day, he is working for two hours without remuneration. Therefore, besides earning a wage that would take care of the minimum needs of the family, it is also essential to note that the working hours should be in congruence with the prescribed maximum hours of work, or else this would mean a cut in wages.

Along with the factors discussed above, namely, need-based minimum wage, protection against disease, unhealthy and dangerous working conditions, and fixed working hours, a worker also requires a degree of social security. This includes a savings fund which could be used for unforeseen expenses or which could be given after retirement, known as the provident fund. There could be other benefits such as health insurance and a pension after retirement. It is possible that all employers may not be in a position to bear the costs of all these facilities. Small industries operate on small profit margins, which do not leave much scope for pursuing welfare activities. It is necessary for the state to step in and ensure some form of social security for all workers. If this is done, work will become a source of dignity and satisfaction for the worker. We shall discuss social security/ protection in more detail in the next section.

Just as we raised the issue of employers and their inability to bear the above costs, the state too, may face similar problems. Developing countries do have financial crunches. However, it is not so much the funding but the way the policies are formulated that is the main issue. If policies are directed towards growth and employment rather than on growth alone, it would be possible to increase employment along with economic growth. In India, though we have achieved high growth rates of 8 to 10 per cent per annum, there is still a wide gap between the poor and the rich. Hence, it is clear that growth itself cannot solve the problems of the working poor. Policies directed towards the uplift of the working classes are more important, because only then can we hope to bridge this huge gap.

Skill formation is another aspect of employment. Merely ensuring that work is available is not sufficient. It is necessary that the working class not only works efficiently but is in a position to upgrade its skills to meet the changing technological needs of the day. Skill training for workers also promotes flexible labour. This means that workers develop multiple skills. Hence, if workers in a particular industry face imminent unemployment because the products manufactured in this industry have become outdated or the demand has fallen, they can be redeployed in other industries provided they have the minimum skills. It is seen that employment is better in countries where labour is flexible.

Another significant aspect involves gender and employment. The problems of women workers were overlooked in industrial employment. It was projected that industrial work was male-oriented, and unsuitable for women. This has been proved to be a myth because women have worked in industries when the level of technology was low and there was greater emphasis on physical labour. At that time, it was not deemed that factory work was a male bastion. Labour-intensive factories required the inputs of males, females and children. Later, as working conditions improved due to technological change and the need for labour decreased, women were excluded from the permanent labour force in factories . Matters became worsened when many countries, under the guidelines of an ILO convention, banned women from working at night in factories. It was felt that this would be unsafe for women though they were never consulted about this.

In developing countries like India, we find that women are largely concentrated in informal sector employment. It is estimated that only one of out every four working males and one out of every seven females are engaged in the formal sector. Women comprise roughly one third of the total employment in the informal sector. If any country is truly concerned with Decent Work, its priority should be on ensuring gender-friendly employment as opposed to open or disguised discrimination against employment of women.

Social Protection

Normally people, especially the vulnerable sections, have much insecurity in their daily lives. For the working class, the main insecurity results from work, and if one is not a permanent worker, it concerns whether work would be available the next day. In India, workers in the informal sector face this type of uncertainty and there is no security for them. On the other hand, workers in the formal sector are covered by a range of legislation that protects their employment and provides them benefits for unforeseen events such as illness, accident, death, and so on. These workers also have some financial benefits after they retire from work. This could be in the form of a lumpsum payment as provident fund or pension. Their wages are also protected through dearness allowance in the event of rise in prices.

Workers in the informal sector, who as mentioned earlier (see Chapter 6), form the overwhelming majority (93 per cent) of the working class, do not have most of these benefits. Hence, even if an informal sector worker is able to get a high wage because of his skills or any other reason, if he or a member of his family has a major illness or meets with an accident, the hospitalisation costs would push him below the poverty line. When this worker is old and unable to work, he gets no benefits. Therefore, he has to depend solely on his savings or on the income of his children.

Social protection for workers in informal employment has to be provided by the state or through other forms of mutual aid societies. Of late, the state has tried to provide some social security benefits to these workers such as an insurance scheme for illness or death. Before liberalisation, health facilities were available without cost to this section of the population from the government or municipal hospitals. However after liberalisation, government hospitals started charging fees, albeit moderate, for hospitalisation, operations and other major medical treatments.

Social protection is not restricted to health facilities. Its purpose is to provide security against a variety of contingencies and vulnerabilities, including ill health, maternity needs, accidents, unemployment, destitution, extreme economic fluctuations, natural disasters, and civil strife. In developed countries, the working population has some form of insurance against unemployment. In many cases, when jobs are lost or when one's business collapses because of extreme economic fluctuations, the state in the developed countries steps in to provide some relief. Most of the governments in Europe provide stipends to the newly unemployed for a specific period so that they are not left destitute; these stipends are expected to help provide a person with his basic needs till he finds a job. Most developing countries do not provide such benefits.

In the case of natural disasters, one finds that all governments provide some relief to their citizens after the event takes place. In most cases when these disasters take place in the developing countries, the international community too comes forward to help. We can see this in the case of major earthquakes which lead to mass destruction of life and property. The devastating tsunami of 2004 badly affected a number of less developed countries such as India, Indonesia and Sri Lanka. While India refused to take any aid from other countries, countries like Sri Lanka appealed to the international community for help.

In the case of civil conflicts like communal or caste riots in India, the government comes forward and tries to provide some relief to the affected people. In the case of civil war, the international community may step up to help one of the sides affected.

In most countries, orphaned and abandoned children are taken care of by the state in orphanages opened for the purpose. In some of the developed countries, single mothers are also provided support by the state. This could happen in the case of unmarried young women, especially teenagers. There could be female-headed households where the husband has either died or has abandoned his wife. Women by and large tend to earn less than men and hence a single-earning mother finds it difficult to run the household and provide proper facilities for her children. In some countries, such women are provided monetary assistance by the state. In India, they, as also destitute widows, are provided some assistance through the Sanjay Gandhi Niradhar Yojana.

In India, the government provides a meagre old-age pension for those in the rural areas so that they can tide over their financial disabilities. The disabled too, are given some form of protection though not as much as one sees in the developed countries. The government provides reservations for disabled people. However, in our country, public transport such as buses and trains are not disabled-friendly, and a woman who has lost her legs will find it difficult to board them. Providing assistance to the disabled requires some sensitivity in the government as seen in the developed countries. Such facilities could also be a result of a social movement of the disabled. This happened in some African countries that faced internal strife and as a result many people lost their limbs. In Uganda, for instance, there is a strong movement of the disabled which forced the state to provide facilities and also pecuniary benefits for the victims.

Social protection should not be restricted only to the employed but to all sections of the population. Only then can one talk about the feasibility of Decent Work. The ILO has laid stress on this. The ILO intends to focus on the issue of social protection in its policy debates in the near future, insisting on governments across the globe to design social protection systems to protect labour markets against external shocks. It is important to uncover the impediments to the provision of and access to social security for a bulk of the population. More importantly, it is also crucial to identify the role of trade unions and membership-based organisations in extending the scope and coverage of social security programmes in India today.

Strategic Elements in Social Protection

Traditionally, social protection was provided by the family, clan members, charitable institutions, employers and local authorities. In India, it has been common for the elders to expect that their children would look after them in old age. Even in the case of major illnesses, health, kinsfolk usually come forward to provide financial aid for treatment. This means that when a person is rendered destitute due to financial problems, ill health or any other reason for no fault of her/his own, the responsibility to help lay with the family and the kinsfolk. This is in fact a pre-industrial form of reasoning and it arises because the state does not provide support in such cases. Provision of support to parents by their children is a noble act but it cannot be a basis for social protection. In modern times, this gesture would be seen as a mark of affection rather than an obligation. The obligation to protect the vulnerable lies with the state and it cannot shy away from its duties by encouraging kinsfolk to take up its tasks. A controversial issue is that of the legal obligation of children to take care of their parents. In India, there is a law that allows destitute parents to appeal in the court of law in case their children do not take care of them; the law further states that if the earning sons refuse to allow their parents to live with them once they are old they have an obligation of providing them monetary help of at least Rs 5000 per month. This could, on the one hand, be taken as a positive aspect of the state to force erring sons to take up their responsibility of caring for their aged parents but on the other hand, it can be viewed as a means through which the state tries to shirk its own responsibilities. In this case, it may have social support because in traditional societies such as India, the young are expected to take care of the old.

There are three interrelated issues concerning social protection. *Firstly*, what should be the coverage of a social protection scheme? In other words, how much social protection should be granted by the state? We have seen above that in India, the state tries its best to reduce social security to cover the least ground. In more developed countries, social security generally has greater coverage that affects almost all aspects of a person's life. The *second* issue involves providing the organisational and institutional means of social protection. In many developing countries, there may be laws or even schemes to cover a large section of the population but they may fail because of a lack of institutional arrangements. For example, there is a scheme in India for pension for old peasants. How far has this been availed of by these people? The answer is, maybe not much. The failure lies in the fact that the institutions that are supposed to provide this support (offices of the district, sub-division and panchayat) have neither the requisite manpower nor the capacity to collect information on this section of the rural population. This is more acute in the case of the disabled in rural areas or in small towns. There is a measure of support given to these people, but it requires a live register of the disabled, or else, the concerned authorities have no means of knowing the amount of expenditure under this head. Such a system of registration is yet to take place in India. The *third* aspect is that of arrangements for financial support. We will discuss this in more detail in the following section.

The priorities for social protection may differ across countries. In the richer countries, social protection may centre on unemployment benefits, pension, compensation for accidents and problems caused by changes in work patterns. Some countries provide support to people who want to change their careers in the middle of their lives. For example, a person who is an economist may want to become a social worker because in a period of economic fluctuation, there are better jobs in the latter. In such cases, the state provides help and financial assistance for taking up a new career. However, in these countries too, with the intensification of globalisation, there is a tendency to cut down on social protection. The plea is that the state through public funding cannot provide for a wide range of social protection activities. There is also a tendency to encourage the private sector to start schemes for social protection, mainly in the insurance sector.

The issues before developing countries may be somewhat different. As mentioned earlier, many of these countries depend on family and kinship for the basic provisions of social protection. The state therefore tries to concentrate on how to provide some form of support to the poor and the destitute. The focus is on access to food and nutrition, drinking water, primary health, sanitation and shelter. Another important aspect is that of livelihood. We have seen that in India after liberalisation, the state has withdrawn from offering many of these benefits. These mainly concern health and hygiene. The issue of access to potable drinking water is directly related to health because 80 per cent of the common illnesses are water-borne.

The state has taken some important strides on the issue of livelihood and nutrition. The MGNREGS (now MGNREGA) is an example of the way in which the state is trying to help in the livelihood issue. Another scheme, which is hotly debated, is on providing 35 kgs of food grains to every family that lives below the poverty line. The debate mainly is on whether a poor country like India can afford to distribute food grains at subsidised rates to a large section of its population. The costs for this would be huge, some critics argue. This excess spending could lead to inflation and higher prices for other sections of the population. We will not debate on the merits of these views, but the basic fact is that if the working poor get proper nutrition, they will be able to work better, and labour productivity will increase. This will in turn boost the economy and offset the deficits faced by the scheme. A hungry population cannot be a productive population. Hence we can see that social protection should not be seen as a mere mark of charity offered by the state. Rather, it is an absolute necessity to ensure a healthy population which in turn would ensure a prosperous country.

Social Dialogue

An important component of Decent Work over and above productive work under conditions of freedom, equity and dignity is the right to negotiate. We have discussed in the chapter on labour movement how important this right is for workers. Hence, after workers' rights, employment and social protection, the fourth component of Decent Work is social dialogue. This deals with the importance of negotiations. Social dialogue stresses the need for both sides, employee and employer, to discuss problems that arise from work. They can find solutions to these problems together. Social dialogue, therefore, helps in avoiding confrontation and builds up means for peaceful solutions.

From the workers' point of view, social dialogue provides a voice and representation to the participants in the production process. It is the means to defend their interests and articulate their concerns and priorities and to engage in negotiations with other actors in the production/distribution system. The work situation is not easy to understand as it is highly diverse. The most commonly understood situation is of wage work in formal employment. But this is not all, for there are several other situations. Moreover, in India only about 8 per cent of the workforce is in formal employment, the rest being in informal employment. It is not merely in countries like India, but even in developed countries that we observe this trend of rise in informal employment. There are large sections of self-employed low-income earners in these countries, most of whom are migrants.

Informal employment includes part-time employment, casual labour, day-labourers (such as street corner workers) and the self-employed. Industrial relations is only one of the means for engaging in social dialogue and in most cases, it applies to formal employment. There are a large number of workers who do not have institutional representation, i.e., they do not have organisations to represent their cases. These include home-based workers, street vendors, domestic workers, casual labourers, etc. Some of these trades, such as street vending, may be considered illegal and the state does not bother to even listen to their problems. There are others such as domestic workers and home-based workers, who are large in number but are invisible and hence, the state may overlook their problems. It is in these cases that institutional representation is most needed.

The idea of social dialogue means that the state or the employers must enter into negotiations with these sections of the working class. They cannot be forced into doing so, but they can certainly be convinced that negotiations help in easing tensions. In the earlier sections, we have mentioned that social dialogue will differ in terms of institutional representation. There are sectors that have institutional representation but there are others who do not have such representation. Let us deal with each separately so that we can understand the problems of each.

The dominant mode of representation can be found in the formal sector. Trade unions are representative bodies of the workers and they can play a major role in social dialogue. At the same time, it is necessary to realise that negotiating through the union is not the only means of dialogue. A lot depends upon the framework of collective bargaining. There could be a works committee that decides on certain issues and it is a part of social dialogue. Similarly, joint management councils could be another version of social dialogue.

The most important mode of social dialogue is through the legal framework. This is where there could be some differences between countries. Their laws regarding industrial relations may differ. Most countries however frame their laws on the lines of the ILS which were discussed at the beginning of this chapter. In India, laws such as the ID Act of 1947, Factories Act of 1948, Shops and Establishments Act of various state governments, Provident Fund Act of 1952, Payment of Gratuity Act of 1972, Payment of Wages Act of 1936, Minimum Wages Act of 1948, and decisions of the Indian Labour Conference provide the framework for social dialogue.

There are different types of negotiations in the dominant model. These normally centre around how best the above-mentioned laws/ rights can be realised. For example, besides direct negotiations through representation or trade unions, there could be other bodies which help in this process. For example, the ID Act, 1947, provides for works committees in every factory having 100 or more workers. This committee has equal representation of management and workers, and it decides on issues relating to working conditions in the factory (lighting, safety, cleanliness, hygiene, etc.), functioning of the canteens, and declaration of holidays, among other issues. The Act also mentions that no issue relating to trade unions should be discussed by these committees. In other words, works committees cannot replace a trade union, though they can work alongside it. Other such models could be joint management councils which are a part of workers' participation in management. Most public sector factories have these bodies. Here again, there is equal representation from both sides. These bodies discuss issues relating to labour and management. It could deal with issues of productivity and how to raise it, and how to improve working conditions, among other issues.

Workers in the informal employment sector do not have the same type of legal protection as their formal sector counterparts. There are very few laws that protect these workers and there is no serious attempt by the state to promote institutional representation so that these workers can collectively articulate their problems.

Social dialogue must accommodate the different production systems and organisational arrangements. It cannot reflect the views of merely one section of the workforce. On looking at the diversities in the workforce, it is clear that it does not have a common objective. The priorities may differ for different sections. For example, if we take a work situation such as a factory or an office, which employs a large number of men and women, we can notice these differences. For men, better pay, better working conditions and perhaps more overtime payment which increases their total pay may be the priorities. For women, however, flexible working hours which give them time for household and childcare responsibilities, maternity leave, and childcare facilities and separate toilets at the workplace could be more important.

For women in informal employment, the priority may be remuneration as this is crucial to run their households. A domestic worker may be keen to have a law which protects her wages and allows her some leave to attend to her responsibilities at home. For home-based workers, remuneration would certainly be important, as also access to institutional credit, raw materials, marketing, training, etc. The self-employed, on the other hand, may have different problems which may be widely divergent. This section comprises a wide variety of trades/ professions. On the one hand, there are highly paid lawyers, doctors, consultants, etc., and on the other hand, there are small entrepreneurs owning small manufacturing units or street vendors. The needs may be different for these sections. For the former, issues of tax concessions or simplification of tax payments may have priority, whereas for the latter, access to public space, security of tenure, institutional credit facilities, skill development and training, and freedom from bribe-seeking officials may be more important. Social dialogue has to take into account all these situations.

There could be a diversity of organisations that could provide platforms for social dialogue. These could be cooperatives that are formed to provide uplift for marginalised workers, self-help groups, trade unions and other forms of associations like those of micro-entrepreneurs and other associations that may engage in mobilising people so that they can collectively articulate their interests through these institutions. The key to successful social dialogue is the state's encouragement to form associations of different types for negotiations. This would empower the marginal sections so as to give them a voice. Freedom of association, which is a fundamental right granted by the Constitution of India, does not merely mean allowing people to form associations. It also implies that the state must create conditions which would encourage their formation.

Key Concepts/Definitions

International Labour Standards (ILS) Labour standards set by the International Labour Organization to protect, promote and realise the fundamental rights of labour.

Rights at work Rights of workers at their workplace which promotes equality, non-discrimination, fair wages, right to collective bargaining and social protection.

Right to employment and work Adequate employment opportunities for all those who seek work under conditions of ILS.

Social protection (ILO) Inclusion and productivity by ensuring that women and men enjoy working conditions that are safe, allow adequate free time and rest, take into account family and social values, provide for adequate compensation in case of lost or reduced income and permit access to adequate health care.

Social dialogue (ILO) This involves strong and independent workers' and employers' organisations for increasing productivity, avoiding disputes at work, and building cohesive societies.

References and Readings

Ghai, Dharam. 2006. *Decent Work: Objectives and Strategies*. Geneva: International Labour Organisation.

ILO. 2002. 'Decent Work and the Informal Economy.' *Report of the 90th Session of ILC*. Geneva: International Labour Office.

———. 2000. 'Decent Work and Poverty Reduction in the Global Economy.' *Second Session of the General Assembly on the Implementation of the Outcome of the World Summit for Social Development and Future Initiatives*. Geneva: International Labour Office.

National Commission for Enterprises in the Unorganised Sector (NCEUS). 2007. 'Report on Conditions of Work and Promotion of Livelihoods in the Unorganised Sector'. New Delhi: Academic Publishers.

INDEX